Further praise for *Investing in Emerging Markets*

"Anyone who has money in emerging markets or is thinking about investing must read this book. Marr and Reynard gain access to some of the industry's best minds on emerging markets, but don't just get swept away with the euphoria and excitement – they have produced a measured and perfectly balanced guide. The issues are presented and explained in a clear and entertaining way; the conclusions are simple and unambiguous. They dare to ask whether this time 'it's different' – whether emerging markets will race ahead of Western markets. You will know the answer once you've read this book."
Andrew Oxlade, Editor, thisismoney.co.uk

"A lucid and balanced introduction to one of the key investment themes of our time – the spectacular rise of the emerging economies."
Daniel Ben-Ami, Editor, *Fund Strategy*

"The authors orchestrate a full and fair analysis of this century's hot investment topic, coaxing insights from a 'Who's Who' of emerging markets contacts."
Rob Burdett, co-founder of Thames River Multi-Capital LLP

"This is an enlightening and well-researched book that explains the history and various grades of developing economies, from the emerged BRIC economic powerhouses to the less well known emerging frontier markets. It examines their increasing importance in the global economic and investment landscape; shows why many reputations were enhanced during the recent financial crisis; and details the myriad ways in which investors can translate superior economic growth rates into superior investment returns – while being mindful of the higher risks attached to this asset class."
Andrew Pitts, Editor, Money Observer magazine

"We have here a lively and informed analysis of the prospects, challenges and opportunities offered by the seemingly irresistible transfer of economic growth and prosperity from the West to the emerging markets. The reader will be left in little doubt that we live in game-changing times and the evidence presented hints strongly at who might emerge victorious."
James Budden, Marketing Director, Baillie Gifford

"I believe that the development of emerging markets will be the biggest investment theme over the next decade. This is an insightful guide detailing the key issues for investors to consider."
Gavin Haynes, Managing Director, Whitechurch Securities Ltd

"Marr and Reynard are experienced financial journalists who have produced a very well balanced view of the opportunities and pitfalls of investing in emerging markets. The book benefits from the insights of investment practitioners who help the authors to move beyond the well discussed emerging market themes, allowing the reader to understand some of the more idiosyncratic dynamics these economies face."
Marcus Brookes, Head of Multi-Manager, Cazenove Capital Management

"For two decades emerging markets have had an exotic allure for investors, but like most things exotic are also fraught with dark dangers. Ignorance is the biggest danger of them all. This book will eliminate that. Before you reach for the cheque book I urge you to read it."
Stephen McDowell, Editor-in-Chief, Interactive Investor

The Chartered Institute for Securities & Investment

Mission Statement:

To set standards of professional excellence and integrity for the invest-ment and securities industry, providing qualifications and promoting the highest level of competence to our members, other individuals and firms.

Formerly the Securities & Investment Institute (SII), and originally founded by members of the London Stock Exchange in 1992, the Institute is the leading examining, membership and awarding body for the securities and investment industry. We were awarded a royal charter in October 2009, becoming the Chartered Institute for Securities & Investment. We currently have around 40,000 members who benefit from a programme of professional and social events, with continuing professional development (CPD) and the promotion of integrity, very much at the heart of everything we do. Additionally, more than 40,000 examinations are taken annually in more than 50 countries throughout the world.

The CISI also currently works with a number of academic institutions offering qualifications, membership and examptions as well as information of careers in financial services. We have over 40 schools and colleges offering our introductory qualifications and have 7 University Centers of Excellence recognised by the CISI as offering leadership in academic education on financial markets.

You can contact us through our website www.cisi.org.

Our membership believes that keeping up to date is central to profes-sional development. We are delighted to endorse the Wiley/CISI pub-lishing partnership and recommend this series of books to our members and all those who work in the industry.

As part of the CISI CPD Scheme, reading relevant financial publications earns members of the Chartered Institute for Securities & Investment the appropriate number of CPD hours under the Self-Directed learning category. For further information, please visit *www.cisi.org/cpdscheme*

Ruth Martin
Managing Director

Investing in Emerging Markets

The BRIC Economies and Beyond

Julian Marr and Cherry Reynard

A John Wiley and Sons, Ltd., Publication

Registered office
John Wiley & Sons Ltd, The Atrium, Southern Gate, Chichester, West Sussex, PO19 8SQ,
United Kingdom

For details of our global editorial offices, for customer services and for information about how to
apply for permission to reuse the copyright material in this book please see our website at
www.wiley.com.

Library of Congress Cataloging-in-Publication Data
Marr, Julian.
    Investing in emerging markets : the BRIC economies and beyond / Julian Marr and Cherry
Reynard.
        p. cm.
    Includes bibliographical references and index.
    ISBN 978-0-470-74825-1
    1. Investments, Foreign—Developing countries.   2. Developing countries—Economic
conditions—21st century.   I. Reynard, Cherry.   II. Title.
    HG5993.M357 2010
    332.67′3091724—dc22

                                                                            2010022094

A catalogue record for this book is available from the British Library.

ISBN 978-0-470-74825-1 (hardback), ISBN 978-0-470-71005-0 (ebk),
ISBN 978-0-470-71004-3 (ebk), ISBN 978-0-470-97739-2 (ebk)

Typeset in 11/13pt Times by Aptara Inc., New Delhi, India
Printed in Great Britain by TJ International Ltd, Padstow, Cornwall, UK

Contents

Acknowledgements

The authors acknowledge the investment professionals for whose guidance, time and help they are hugely grateful, including Jerome Booth, Marcus Brookes, Khiem Do, Peter Eerdmans, Philip Ehrmann, Slim Feriani, Alan Gibbs, Andrew Gillan, Robin Griffiths, Mike Kerley, Peter Kirkman, Michael Konstantinov, Urban Larson, Anup Maheshwari, Jing Ning, Chris Palmer, Stuart Parks, Michael Power, Richard Sennitt, Elena Shaftan, Claire Simmonds, James Syme, Ewan Thompson, Julian Thompson, Richard Titherington, Angus Tulloch, Bob Yerbury and Hugh Young.

The authors would also like to acknowledge the assistance of a number of investment houses in the writing of this book, including Aberdeen Asset Management, Advance Emerging Capital, Allianz Global Investors, Ashmore Investment Management, Baring Asset Management, BlackRock Investment Management, Cazenove Capital Management, Gartmore Fund Managers, F&C Investments, First State Investments, Henderson Global Investors, Invesco Perpetual, Investec Asset Management, JO Hambro Investment Management, J.P. Morgan Asset Management, Jupiter Asset Management, M&G Investments, Neptune Investment Management, RCM, Schroder Investment Management, Standard Bank and Threadneedle Investments.

1

An Introduction to Emerging Markets

1.1 INTRODUCTION

Two first-time authors would have to be very brave – or indeed very foolish – to challenge the wisdom of revered investor and mutual fund pioneer Sir John Templeton. The founder of the company that, incidentally, went on to employ legendary emerging markets investor Mark Mobius, famously said: "The four most expensive words in the English language are 'This time it's different'."

Thus, for example, investors who bought into the technology, media and telecoms boom of the late 1990s just before that particular bubble burst will be painfully aware that, that time, it certainly wasn't different. They probably won't be too impressed either with the two words "new paradigm" that were bandied around by technology champions as the argument that trumped all doubters.

But are not evolution and change – the possibility that, this time, it really is different – part and parcel of the whole business of investing in emerging markets? Surely investors buy into the emerging space to tap into the growth that, at least in part, accompanies a country's journey from nascent or frontier market to fully paid-up member of the global economy.

And if change is indeed an integral part of the emerging markets story, should we not at least consider the possibility – as this book intends to do – that the global financial crisis, which began in earnest when investment bank Lehman Brothers filed for bankruptcy on 15 September 2008 and very much had its roots in the Western financial system, may have closed the credibility gap between the emerging economies and those of the developed world?

That is just one thread – albeit a crucial one – of a book that will also look to identify what emerging markets actually are while weighing up their attractions as an investment. It will take a long hard look at the associated risks, before considering the pros and cons of different regions and individual economies around the globe. Along the way, it will also consider what part emerging markets can play in an investment portfolio and the various routes an investor can use to gain access to them.

1.2   WHAT ARE EMERGING MARKETS?

Whether they be professional or operating on their own time, investors have a tendency to see things as two sides of the same coin. So, for example, they may look to invest for income or growth, in large corporations or smaller companies, in equities or bonds, or with an active fund manager or through a passive, index-tracking investment. The way they see the globe is no exception and, in this regard, the most fundamental distinction made is between the developed world and the so-called emerging markets.

At their broadest – taking in Africa, Asia, Eastern Europe, Latin America and the Middle East and thus individual countries as diverse as, say, Nigeria, Singapore, Hungary, Venezuela and Jordan – the emerging and frontier markets do not really lend themselves to a nice and easy soundbite of a definition. Even listing them is not exactly straightforward with the major stock market index providers unable to agree exactly on which countries count as emerging markets.

At the start of 2010, FTSE, MSCI Barra and Standard & Poor's overlapped on 19 countries in their main Emerging Markets indices with China, India, Indonesia, Malaysia, the Philippines, Taiwan and Thailand representing Asia, Brazil, Chile, Mexico and Peru for Latin America, the Czech Republic, Hungary, Poland, Russia and Turkey for Europe and Egypt, Morocco and South Africa for Africa.

However, Argentina, Colombia and Pakistan are also included in the FTSE Emerging Markets index, Colombia, Israel and South Korea feature in the MSCI Emerging Markets index and Argentina, Israel and South Korea bolster the S&P/IFC Emerging Markets index.

Nevertheless, rather than giving up so easily and settling for defining emerging markets by what they are not – for example, the "advanced" or "developed" economies of the US, Western Europe and Japan – which is not very helpful, or by terms such as "Third World", which borders on the patronizing, a more useful approach might be to outline some benchmarks by which to judge a country's level of maturity.

These could include a country's growth rate – possibly the most attractive aspect of the emerging markets space over the years – in addition to the size and openness of its economy, the degree to which it is integrating within the global marketplace and the strength or otherwise of its political, legal and financial institutions.

The average level of income per citizen is another revealing factor as it is an indication of how far a country's standards of living are improving and whether the middle class, which is now seen by most commentators as a vital driver of any emerging market's internal economy, is growing.

Through its very make-up, therefore, an emerging market offers a mix of reward and risk and it is up to investors to judge how well these two elements are balanced. The rewards will stem from the potential for growth as the country develops as a nation and as an economy, both internally and in relation to the rest of the world. Meanwhile the risks will come as a result of a lack of political or economic stability or uncertainties stemming from a vulnerability to other internal and external forces.

"The risks are inherent in the question of what an emerging market is," says Richard Titherington, chief investment officer and head of the emerging markets equity team at J.P. Morgan Asset Management. "In my view, an emerging market is a country that has – and there are a lot of different reasons why this may be the case – a much higher degree of political and financial risk and instability than you get in the relatively small group of countries that we regard as developed."

The emerging markets can be split into four regions – Asia, Emerging Europe, Latin America and the so-called "frontier" markets, which are broadly to be found in Africa and the Middle East. All share certain general attractions for investors – and carry certain general risks. These are discussed in the next chapter but naturally they also have pros and cons that are more specific to a region or country and that is why we address the various emerging markets in six chapters grouped by geography.

Again, at their broadest, emerging markets represent some four-fifths of the world's population and almost three-quarters of its land mass. At the start of 2010, they accounted for roughly 70% of global foreign exchange reserves, more than half of global energy consumption and close to half of both the world's exports and, in purchasing power parity terms, its gross domestic product – the market value of all the goods and services produced by a country and known for short as "GDP".

Towering over everything else in the sector is the colossus of the emerging markets world known as "BRIC" – a term coined in 2001 by investment bank Goldman Sachs to cover the four biggest developing nations of Brazil, Russia, India and China.

According to the International Monetary Fund, China was the third largest economy in the world in 2008 with GDP of $4.3 tn – closing in on Japan on $4.9 tn but with still some way to go to catch up with the US at $14.4 tn. By the same measure, Brazil was the eighth largest economy in the world, Russia was 11th and India 12th. However, with the International Monetary Fund, as of October 2009, predicting China's GDP would grow by 9% in 2010 while that of the US would grow by 1.9%, the former looks set to be breathing down the US's neck within a decade or two.

For its part, Goldman Sachs is projecting that in 2050 the new world order will see China dwarfing every other economy in the world with GDP of $70 tn, with the US second on $40 tn and followed by India, Brazil, Russia, the UK and Japan – with China expected to surpass the US in 2027.

Together, the BRIC quartet are the flagships of the three main emerging market regions and, at the risk of oversimplification, encompass two of the globe's most powerful economic themes. China and India are two of the world's strongest domestic demand growth stories with a massive appetite for all kinds of natural resources. Neatly enough, Brazil and Russia are both leading exporters of natural resources.

Asia offers the broadest spread of emerging markets, both in terms of numbers and diversity. China's influence as a global economic superpower grows daily and the increasing spending power of India's burgeoning middle class offers great hope to investors. Meanwhile the positive example of more mature economies such as Hong Kong, Singapore and South Korea stands as a real incentive for neighbours who have not progressed as far along the development path, such as Indonesia, the Philippines and Vietnam.

Eastern Europe is dominated by Russia, whose fortunes are strongly dictated by the price of oil. The investment case for the rest of the region generally focuses on whether or not and to what extent individual countries would meet the necessary economic and financial criteria for membership of the European Union and, ultimately, the adoption of the euro – the so-called "convergence" play. Some, particularly the Baltic countries such as Latvia, have expanded too fast and consequently suffered as a result of excessive debt levels.

Latin America is also dominated by one country, in this instance Brazil, which arguably may be seen as offering the best of all BRIC worlds. Not only is it a leading exporter of commodities, such as oil and agricultural products, it is also an increasingly sophisticated economy that is expected to thrive on growing consumer demand.

Across the border, however, Argentina stands as a stark warning that not all emerging markets – no matter how large they may be, how sophisticated their population and infrastructure, how many advantages they may enjoy such as, for example, a rich supply of natural resources or how much foreign investment is ploughed in – necessarily live up to investor expectations.

The frontier markets are the latest wave of emerging economies to appear on investors' radars and are often plays on the ongoing global demand for commodities – for example, oil in Nigeria or mining in South Africa. Very much a case of achieving potentially high reward for assuming a commensurately high level of risk, frontier markets might usefully be viewed as a bull market phenomenon where people become less discerning as their appetite for risk grows. Often they can end up investing too late in an economic cycle.

Interestingly, although they suffered in terms of, for example, reduced exports, many emerging markets avoided becoming direct victims of the global financial crisis. This was partly because they were not so reliant on the Western banking system, which bore the full brunt of the crunch, and partly because, having suffered their own market meltdowns, such as the Asian crisis of 1997, governments and companies had learnt some valuable survival lessons.

1.3 A BRIEF HISTORY OF EMERGING MARKETS

For such a well-worn expression, the origins of "emerging markets" as a term are a little fuzzy although consensus now has it that it dates back to the 1980s and the International Finance Corporation. That was where Antoine van Agtmael, who is now chairman and chief investment officer of investment house Emerging Markets Management, was working as deputy director of the Capital Markets Department when his book *Emerging Securities Markets* was published in 1984.

Four years later, the International Finance Corporation became the first organization to launch a dedicated emerging markets index, which along with its entire Emerging Markets Database was acquired in 1999 by Standard & Poor's.

While we are on the subject of emerging markets terminology, the derivation of the other key grouping, the "BRIC" economies, is more certain. Credit for the acronym goes to investment bank Goldman Sachs, which published its paper "Building better global economic BRICs" in November 2001 and has remained at the forefront of thinking on the subject ever since.

The term "emerging markets" may date back only as far as the 1980s but the spirit of the concept can be traced back a good deal further. Arguably China and India, the two most populous countries on the planet, are merely in the process of returning to centre-stage, having dominated the global economy in terms of share of GDP for pretty much all of the last millennium bar the 20th century.

In a neat reversal therefore, that leaves the US as the archetypal emerging market – or, at the very least, an instructive parallel with the emerging markets of today. There is a line of thought that, if you really want to tap into the growth of an emerging or frontier market, then you shouldn't invest there. Rather you should go and live in one – if you're very optimistic about Cambodia, don't buy a Cambodia fund, go and open a restaurant or a hotel in Angkor Wat.

It is certainly a theory and one that – always assuming you are still reading and haven't dropped this book to pick up the phone to your travel agent – held true for the US in the 19th century, where one was generally better off going to live than investing through, say, a UK institution buying US assets. A catalogue of setbacks that will be familiar to any seasoned emerging markets investor – including civil war, currency crises, banking collapses, failures of infrastructure, scams and scandals – meant investors in the US endured a rough ride for a significant time.

For long periods, it was a very tough place to be a financial investor although, of course, ultimately, the country was fantastically successful and those who predicted the US would be the next big thing were utterly vindicated. As professional investor and financial commentator Jim Rogers once said: "If the 19th century belonged to Britain, and the 20th century to the United States, then the 21st century will surely belong to China."

1.4   A TALE OF TWO DECADES

Since their, well, emergence in the 1980s as an investment asset class in their own right, the emerging markets have experienced two distinct phases. The first was the boom and bust in the 1990s, when the loose monetary conditions of the first few years of the decade brought foreign investors flocking to the space before a number of spectacular crises sent them running for the exits just as quickly.

Ironically, it is partly because the first phase led to such pain that emerging markets could show such robust growth in the second phase, which really kicked in around 2004 and has been characterized by a period of extraordinary growth led by the industrialization of China.

The first phase followed the discovery of emerging markets by institutional and then private investors. In the mid-1980s, institutional investors, such as pension funds, began to search for investments that were less correlated – that is, moved less in line – with their existing assets at the same time as a number of developing markets began to hit their economic stride, including the four so-called "Asian tigers" of Hong Kong, Singapore, South Korea and Taiwan.

As equity values started to soar, investors' appetite for risk increased and a number of investment funds were launched that specialized in emerging markets. The early performance was strong, although trading volumes remained thin and, for the time being, private investors were largely uninterested.

Problems started to emerge as early as 1989 as interest rates rose and the global downturn began, but it was not until 1994 and the Mexican peso crisis – which also dented confidence across South American markets, including Brazil – that the economic travails of the emerging markets began in earnest.

In 1997, with the Mexican crisis – also more colourfully known as the Tequila Crisis – still fresh in investors' minds, Thailand was forced to devalue its currency, the baht, and over the course of the next year the "Asian contagion" spread across the continent as the tigers and their neighbours were well and truly tamed. The Asian financial crisis and ensuing slump in commodities prices, which hit countries reliant on exporting resources, then prompted the Russian debt crisis in 1998.

The central themes of these crises will not be unfamiliar to any experienced market watcher – the countries involved had borrowed heavily in foreign currency and, when economic problems forced them to devalue their own currencies, they were left with a huge overhang of foreign-denominated debt that it took many painful years of austerity to pay back.

Putting a more positive spin on this, however, one might also say that many emerging markets ended up learning to be very wary of excessive debt levels – a lesson that put them in a relatively strong position in the wake of the global financial crisis.

Around the same time, in Eastern Europe, the Berlin Wall fell and the Eastern bloc countries began to throw off the shackles of communism and embrace capitalism. The European Union immediately started to direct funds towards the area's major economies such as Poland and Hungary to help them to make the transition to market economies – with European Union membership the near-term goal. For investors, this marked the start of the "convergence" trade as countries in the region moved closer to Western European living standards and incomes.

For much of the late 1990s and the early part of the next decade, however, most emerging markets found themselves very short of friends. The domino effect of currency devaluations and economic crises had finally concluded with the Argentine peso devaluation in January 2002, but no one felt inclined to invest and most were directing any appetite for risk towards the burgeoning technology, media and telecommunications sector. After the resulting "tech bubble" burst in 2000, this appetite again disappeared.

Cometh the hour, cometh the Mandarin and it was about this time that investors began to pick up on the vast potential of China. In truth, China's modern growth story went back as far as 1978 when Deng Xiaoping set about instituting free market reforms and seeking to attract overseas investment. The brutal suppression of the student-led pro-democracy demonstrations in Tiananmen Square in 1989 led Western and Japanese companies to draw back from committing money to China but, soon enough, the trickle of capital turned into a flood.

The handover of Hong Kong in 1997 gave China convenient access to Western capital markets. According to the International Monetary Fund, China began to deliver consistent annual GDP growth of between 10% and 13%, thanks to a combination of its cheap labour force and the opportunity for low-cost manufacturing it offered.

The effects of this growth were felt around investment markets though nowhere more so than in commodities. The industrialization of China created an unprecedented boom in raw materials, particularly oil, which in turn provided a lucrative source of funds to other resource-rich emerging markets – most significantly Brazil and Russia.

This boom was not reflected in the stock markets of the emerging economies until 2004, but when the markets moved, they did so swiftly and decisively – many of them tripling in the period up to their peak in 2007. In the three years to October 2007, the overall MSCI Emerging Markets index rose 175% although this masked some even stronger growth among individual emerging markets – for example, the FTSE Xinhua B35 index of Chinese companies rose 282% over the same period.

The new-found wealth of many emerging markets was hived off into huge pools of money called sovereign wealth funds, which became a powerful new force in global financial markets but also helped to protect emerging markets when the credit crunch hit.

Although emerging markets largely avoided any problems with their banking systems, they were hurt by the slowdown in their major trading partners as export demand slumped as well as by investors seeking traditionally safer havens for their money. As such, the excess capital built up during the boom years helped them support their economies through infrastructure building, welfare packages and economic stimulus – a notable example being the $586 bn package of measures announced by the Chinese government in November 2008.

As a result – and with certain exceptions, primarily in Eastern Europe – the bounce-back for emerging markets was far quicker and far more robust than that of their developed market counterparts. Many of these economies did not even fall into recession and their stock markets reflected this – selling off heavily in the last few months of 2008 only to recover quickly the following year as the global economy appeared to get back on track.

The supportive monetary conditions the emerging markets had enjoyed back in the early 1990s returned once again – as did investors who could not resist the attractions of historically low company valuations. These investors would have been hoping the companies of Asia, Latin America and the rest were aware that, in order to avoid a repeat of the second part of the 1990s scenario, they would have to work to ensure earnings underpinned the valuations that naturally increased as a result of the large amounts of money flowing into those markets.

In return, emerging markets companies would be hoping that external money turns out to be a little "stickier" than in previous market cycles and that foreign investors prove less easily spooked than they have in the past. It is in the nature of investment that money is "rotated" from asset class to asset class and from sector to sector while cyclical flows back and forth between the developed and emerging markets will inevitably continue. Even so, are there more structural reasons for believing a smaller proportion of money will desert the emerging markets at the first sign of trouble than has traditionally proved the case? This time, could it really be different?

Some key dates for the emerging markets

1988: The International Finance Corporation launches the first emerging markets stock market index. At the time, six markets were open to investment – Hong Kong, Malaysia, Mexico, the Philippines, Singapore and Thailand.

1989: The Berlin Wall falls and Eastern bloc countries start the transition from communism to free markets.

1990: Deng Xiaoping reopens the Shanghai Stock Exchange, which had been closed since 1949.

1991: Collapse of the Soviet Union.

1991: Following a $1.8 bn bailout loan from the International Monetary Fund, the Indian government moves to liberalize the country's economy.

1993: Stock markets in Latin America and East Asia enjoy spectacular rallies.

1994: The Brazilian government introduces the Plano Real (Real Plan) in a bid to stabilize the country's economy.

1994: The Mexican peso crisis, also known as the Tequila Crisis, leads to the country's currency being devalued in December. Confidence in South American markets was also dented as a result.

1997: The sovereignty of Hong Kong transfers from Britain to China, giving the latter convenient access to Western capital markets.

1997: Thailand is forced to devalue its currency. After 10 years of strong growth, the economic downturn slows exports and growth. Following the devaluation, the economy goes into meltdown.

1998: Thailand's devaluation has a knock-on effect across Asia and the "East Asian economic miracle" unwinds.

1998: Asia's economic troubles and the ensuing slump in commodities prices, which hits countries reliant on exporting resources, prompts the Russian debt crisis.

1999: Start of the Argentine economic crisis, eventually leading to the devaluation of the peso in 2002.

2001: Goldman Sachs first uses the term "BRIC" to describe Brazil, Russia, India and China, which are seen as the next generation of economic superpowers.

2001: China joins the World Trade Organization.

2001: FTSE and Xinhua Financial Network announce the launch of the FTSE/Xinhua China 25 Index, a capped, tradable index featuring the largest, most liquid Chinese equities available to international investors.

2004: Historic expansion of the European Union as the Baltic states of Estonia, Latvia and Lithuania and the Central European countries of the Czech Republic, Hungary, Poland, Slovakia and Slovenia, as well as Malta and Cyprus, all join.

2007: China's stock market hits a peak, having seen a three-fold increase in just three years.

2008: The price of oil peaks at $147 a barrel on 11 July.

2008: Lehman Brothers files for bankruptcy on 15 September and there is a widespread sell-off in international stock markets.

2008: China reacts to the global slowdown by announcing a $586 bn stimulus package to support economic growth.

2008/09: Historically low valuations lead to strong flows of external investment into emerging markets.

1.5   DECOUPLING AND GLOBALIZATION

Speak to any emerging markets fund manager and you will face a barrage of reasons to be optimistic about the outlook for the emerging markets but, to the less involved eye, some would seem to carry more weight than others. Arguably some of these arguments – for example, supportive demographics or improving standards of living – seem so intuitive one accepts them almost without question. With others, on the other hand – for example, the theory of "decoupling" or the idea of a commodities "supercycle" – one can find oneself thinking: "Well, OK – but, even if that's true, there are other arguments that are just intrinsically more convincing."

That is the reason why Chapter 2 of this book weighs up the possible rewards – and associated risks – of potential growth drivers such as demographics, infrastructure and improving company processes under the heading of "The investment case for emerging markets" while decoupling and other less tried-and-tested ideas come under the microscope in Chapter 3, "New schools of thought – hype or reality?"

Decoupling really caught the imagination of professional investors in – note the timing – the first half of 2008. The theory ran that the emerging markets had evolved to such an extent they had "decoupled" from the rest of the world and thus the fate of their economies would no longer be determined by the fortunes of the US and Europe on the back of, among other things, a reliance on the West as export markets. This time it would be different and when the West sneezed, the emerging markets would no longer run the risk of catching a cold. Ah.

"Our view is that you cannot have decoupling in a globalized world because, very simply, the world is a more integrated and interlinked place," says Claire Simmonds, a portfolio manager for emerging markets at J.P. Morgan Asset Management. "A crisis that happens in the developed markets will impact emerging markets because of the linkages between capital flows, global trade and their greater integration with the world economy."

At the broadest level, that view looks difficult to argue against although, as ever in these areas that provoke the most debate, perhaps it comes down to a question of degree. In other words, while global markets may not have decoupled, some emerging markets' systems, institutions and structures have.

"In one sense decoupling is happening but in another sense not," says Hugh Young, managing director of Aberdeen Asset Management Asia. "It is not happening in the sense that all the countries we look at – most obviously China, India and Russia – are far more part of the world today than they were 20 years ago. Barriers have come down rather than gone up and trade has moved across borders so, in that sense, there will be knock-on effects.

"What's more, the global financial system will never decouple. The reason emerging markets went down in 2008 was because money was withdrawn by the West as they tried to de-risk their portfolios. On the other hand, for example, in terms of trade the US has become progressively less important.

"As for the nuts and bolts of the respective financial systems, the banks and regulators in the emerging markets were doing things very differently from the West and they generally didn't get things wrong. Luckily for them they kept a very 'plain vanilla' financial system, which the West did not.

"So I would say there are different layers of complexities of coupling and decoupling because, yes, the emerging markets are very different from the West. In one sense, that now comes down to a more traditional sense of values, hard work, a desire to make it – in fact, arguably all the things that made the US great all those years ago – that is now present in these developing markets."

For some commentators, decoupling is simply the wrong debate to be having. "The world is actually more complex than that," says Jerome

Booth, head of research at Ashmore Investment Management. "I hate the 'BRIC' phrase but the one I hate most of all is 'decoupling'. I find it ethnocentric and, fundamentally, a core-periphery concept.

"The base of the core-periphery concept is that the core affects the periphery but we ignore the effects vice versa – and that is a colonial attitude. It's not a question of whether decoupling is a myth or not – it's just the wrong model and you end up taking a very linear view of risk.

"The theory that all the countries are linked so that, if the US goes down, the emerging markets are worse off, is absolutely true but the conclusion you subconsciously draw from that is you therefore shouldn't invest in emerging markets because it's risky – and that is entirely the wrong conclusion."

Booth's thoughts about the relative prospects of developed and emerging markets in benign and worst-case economic scenarios are outlined in the next chapter, but he adds: "The right conclusion should be to accept that the relative performance of emerging markets will be substantially better in the worst-case scenario than even in the benign scenario.

"Therefore you should put money into emerging markets because it reduces risk in the worst-case scenario and yet the decoupling thesis precludes that thought process. It stops you thinking it because it is a core-periphery concept and, of its nature, one that prevents the impact of the periphery on the core being recognized."

That seems a good place to leave decoupling – at least until we reach Chapter 3 – so instead let us carry on with the other side of the coin, the continuing integration of emerging markets into an increasingly globalized world.

"Globalization is all about transfers – the flow of money and goods and services," says Chris Palmer, head of emerging markets at Gartmore. "How we react to globalization is where opportunities appear – just compare Argentina and Brazil.

"That comes down to each country's reaction to globalization. Both have roughly similar levels of education, social development, resources and history and yet they have reacted completely differently. The future is not just emerging market versus developed economy but also emerging market versus emerging market and developed economy versus developed economy."

In Titherington's view, as soon as you accept globalization, the growth of the emerging markets from every perspective is inevitable. "And the globalization of the world is a phenomenon that is frankly impossible to reverse," he says. "Once information has flowed, you can't take it away again and you shouldn't underestimate the importance of the Internet in that because one of the key elements of globalization is the flow of information.

"Globalization comes down to the basic opening of economies. Globalization doesn't happen in closed societies – North Korea, if you like, or Zimbabwe. Anywhere where a government can shut the society down, you won't see the impact of globalization but, over the last 10 years, the number of those societies has shrunk dramatically.

"I don't see that changing very much. You can make the comparison with history and, yes, there are people who argue globalization is just hype – that it was just part of the pre-credit crunch bubble – and that we've been through periods of globalization before that all ended in tears.

"But it usually ended with tears because there was a major war. Here the best comparison would be with the period before the First World War when people said Germany and Great Britain could never go to war because there was so much mutual trade and investment. But war is a very unusual event and, to say globalization is dead and consequently the emerging markets story is dead, you really do have to paint a pretty apocalyptic picture of war – a major war that shuts down trade and interaction between people and I don't see that on the horizon at all."

The rise of the G-20

The Group of Twenty (G-20) Finance Ministers and Central Bank Governors is an informal forum that was assembled to promote open and constructive discussion between industrial and emerging market countries on key issues related to global economic stability. The G-20 is made up of the finance ministers and central bank governors of the following 19 countries plus the European Union, which is represented by the rotating Council presidency and the European Central Bank. Members of the G-7 grouping of the world's richest nations are asterisked while the G-8 also includes Russia.

Argentina	Australia	Brazil	*Canada
China	*France	*Germany	India
Indonesia	*Italy	*Japan	Mexico
Russia	Saudi Arabia	South Africa	South Korea
Turkey	*UK	*US	EU

"The fact the reaction of the world's governments to the global credit crisis went from being a G-7 response to a G-20 response rather tells you all you need to know about where the world is going," says Titherington at J.P. Morgan Asset Management. "No fewer than 11 of the G-20 are emerging markets countries and it's very important that, at a time of such crisis, nobody was talking about having a G-7 meeting. Even at a time when China is so obviously important, nobody was talking about a G-2 meeting either. It wasn't Beijing and Washington sitting down to try and sort out the world – that wasn't even on anybody's agenda."

1.6   AFTER THE STORM

As 2007 and 2008 brought the global credit crisis, mayhem in the financial sector and indiscriminate devaluations of stocks regardless of their actual strength or otherwise, emerging markets companies could have been forgiven for thinking they had travelled back in time to the previous decade.

Yet this time around, it was not Asian tigers, Latin American monetary policy or Russian borrowing that was at the heart of the problem. Instead, Western governments, companies and consumers had become overburdened with debt while the Western banking system was now paying the price for being all too complicit in allowing that situation to come about.

On the other hand, emerging markets governments, central banks and companies now appear to be substantially better equipped to ride out periods of economic and financial volatility precisely because of their chastening experiences in the 1990s.

The Asian financial crisis, to take one example, was caused, as the International Monetary Fund later put it, by "a combination of inadequate financial sector supervision, poor assessment and management of financial risk, and the maintenance of relatively fixed exchange rates". More than a little of that sounds distinctly familiar.

As tends to happen, this encouraged banks and companies around the region to borrow large amounts of international capital but catastrophic devaluations followed when questions arose as to whether such debts could be repaid.

However, over the first decade of the new millennium and across the emerging markets, governments and central banks pursued more responsible and credible economic, monetary and regulatory policies while those companies that weathered the various storms moved to restructure their balance sheets, pay back debt, improve their corporate governance and so emerged stronger.

All in good time, of course, to see the Western financial system go into meltdown itself although, from an emerging markets perspective, this was perhaps a case of it being an ill wind that blows no good – or at least further proof that what doesn't kill you makes you stronger.

"From a selfish point of view, it is good that the financial crisis happened because it is a test we needed the emerging space to pass," says Slim Feriani, chief executive officer of Advance Emerging Capital. "All the cynics were saying emerging markets were a basket case and that, come the next crisis, they would all crumble.

"They argued they would be on their knees because they had seen that with the Tequila Crisis and the Asian Crisis and the Russian Crisis and so on. But the contagion effect stopped. We did have a contagion problem in the 1990s but what has happened since is the emerging market economies decided to clean up their acts and we can see the difference. So we had the Turkish Crisis at the start of the new millennium but that didn't really affect the rest of the emerging market space – and that's a big change."

According to Urban Larson, director of emerging equities at F&C Investments, the experience of their various crises has also served to stand emerging markets investors in good stead. "It was interesting to watch the developed market investors panic as volatility hit the markets and how much calmer most of the emerging markets investors were," he says.

"We're a lot more used to volatility. We've seen a lot of crises originating in emerging markets over the last 30 years although this is the first time we've seen a major crisis originate in the developed world – and it's been very satisfying that it's not our fault.

"What became clear from the crisis was that large parts of the imbalances were in developed rather than emerging markets and that, in general, emerging markets – with some key exceptions in Central and Eastern Europe – had underleveraged private sectors, underleveraged public sectors, solid fiscal positions, credible monetary policies and strong balance sheets.

"In other words, this was not the same kind of crisis for the emerging markets as it was for the developed world. It was a cyclical downturn and the advantage the emerging markets have in the recovery phase is they don't have to work off any excesses in order to resume growth. Yes, in some cases they need strong demand from developed markets but in other cases it's a little simpler and really more a matter of getting the animal spirits moving again."

One crucial element in the post-financial crisis phase of the emerging markets story comes down to how their continued growth is to be funded. Not every emerging market is going to be playing on a level playing field, whether they would be hoping this funding is derived internally – for example, through consumer demand or reserves held in central banks – or externally from foreign investors. According to Khiem Do, head of Asian multi-asset at Baring Asset Management, the differences can be seen most starkly within the BRIC grouping.

"Their growth development paths haven't changed," he says. "All four economies still have a formidable growth path ahead of them in terms of industrialization, modernization and so forth. However, in the wake of the financial crisis, the obvious question is – if you all want to develop this and modernize that, how are you going to fund it? That's the key differential between the four BRIC countries.

"The shape of BRIC is now very different from a funding viewpoint and that obviously has been reflected in the currency, bond and stock market performance. These days a 10-year view gets reflected very quickly – and then it will change again – so you might say that these views only hold true in the short term. Maybe next year it will all be different.

"Even so, for now, the world has judged that Russia, despite its foreign exchange reserves, has over-evolved and overspent and overcommitted. So the question is whether the banking system around the world is going to be generous again to Russia – and to India – and just pour money in. Money will definitely come back but will it pour in? I doubt it."

Do argues it will take years for the big global banks to fix the damage done by the credit crisis and, while they do so, they are likely to become more domestically focused. "So, for example, the US banks will now say their main focus has to be on the US and anything outside is less important," he says. "This means, if they can obtain a good price for foreign investments, they may be more likely to sell up and concentrate on the US."

"If that theory is correct then, unfortunately, it won't be very encouraging for the potential borrowing trends of those countries and governments that need the money to fund their massive infrastructure and modernization programmes. Banks will not be thinking of profits but of how to safeguard the banking system in their own nation first, which is why it will be important to differentiate between those growth economies that are in a position to fund themselves internally and those that are not."

Do suggests the market will already have formed a view on which countries can and cannot do this and, while such a view may change in, say, the next five years or so, it is less likely to do so over the next one or two. "From our own analysis of the assets and liabilities of the four BRIC countries then, over the next two years, we believe China ranks number one by a long distance with Brazil in second place," he says.

"India ranks number three and Russia number four. What's more, Russia needs the oil price to stay solid but that introduces another factor into the equation. If you are reliant on something that is volatile, it becomes more complicated because there are many more potential outcomes."

1.7   SO FAR, SO GOOD

In effect, the global financial crisis can be viewed as something of a "stress test" for the emerging markets and even some fund managers find themselves surprised how well they have acquitted themselves – thus far. "Yes, 2008 was the worst-ever year on an absolute basis for the emerging markets – down 54% in US dollar terms," says Claire Simmonds.

"But if you put that on a relative basis, the emerging markets only underperformed by 12% to global equities over the year. That's a much better outcome than if we look back to 1997 and 1998, where the asset class produced double-digit negative returns versus global equities that were up in the positive double-digits.

"So emerging markets have had their new combination of better macroeconomic fundamentals and improved micro-level performance stress-tested during this crisis – which, importantly, was a developed market crisis that originated in the US but impacted the emerging markets because we live in a globalized world. In our view, the sharp rally in 2009 was very much a reflection of the improved macroeconomics and also an acknowledgement that the financial system in the emerging markets is not broken."

Going a step further, one might even argue the credit crunch was fundamentally good for the emerging markets because it forced the world's central banks and policymakers to confront the issue of global monetary reform. Has the so-called Bretton Woods international financial system, which was agreed towards the end of the Second World War and established, among other things, the International Monetary Fund and the World Bank, had its day?

"It is absolutely clear there has to be a move away from the defunct Bretton Woods system and that will involve a change in the reserve currency status of the dollar and the inclusion of emerging currencies in the basket of currencies deemed appropriate as reserves," argues Booth. "We're going to see an end to the recycling of capital and that inevitably will lead to much more retention of savings by emerging markets and the bulk of that is obviously going to go into real assets.

"Really there are two important adjustments countries will have to make. First, they have to absorb more capital – and that's going to involve putting in place the right institutional and regulatory structures so they can have billions and billions going into infrastructure and real capital expenditure – and, second, they need to get the financial markets to help do that, which means building local bond markets.

"What the credit crunch has done is speed up the development of this process. The credit crunch is a very positive force because it has changed more rapidly the need for people to rethink what the global economy looks like, how to invest in terms of asset allocation and what risk is."

What the credit crunch has already done, says Booth, is to show the emerging markets' system worked – at least with regard to the reserves of currency held by central banks and monetary authorities to back their liabilities. "The emerging markets now know the right levels of reserves they need and that they now have enough," he says.

"They're probably not going to reduce them that much but they don't have to have more either. That naturally means that when the dollars start coming in they won't immediately build up reserves. They will move towards some kind of current account deficit – or current account balance certainly – and they won't allow further big surpluses. They will allow their currencies to appreciate and focus on domestic demand. Ultimately, emerging markets are going to invest across each other rather than in the dollar."

1.8 INTERACTION BETWEEN EMERGING MARKETS

The fact that emerging markets have been seeing a change in the make-up of who they do business with is another important development. While they have undoubtedly been shaken by the recessions in the US and Western Europe, many emerging markets are losing their traditional reliance on developed economies. This growth in trade between fellow emerging markets has helped them weather the economic storm that followed the credit crisis.

Leaving aside any arguments on the existence or otherwise of decoupling, what this really boils down to is the degree to which the emerging markets can insulate themselves from any slowdown in the US economy. Two elements that suggest they can are favourable demographics – for example, young and increasingly wealthy populations generating a boom in domestic consumption – while, crucially, export destinations have greatly diversified so there is no longer such a reliance on the West.

Instead, there has been a dramatic jump in trade between emerging markets so that, to focus on just one example, in May 2009, Brazil's Ministry of Development, Industry and Exterior Trade published statistics that showed China had replaced the US as the country's biggest trading partner, thereby interrupting a relationship that dated as far back as the 1930s.

Indeed, in one sense, the future of emerging markets is all going to come down to relationships – how the developed world interacts with emerging markets, how emerging markets interact with each other and how the smaller economies interact with the giant BRIC economies in each region.

"All the smaller countries in the emerging markets have got to define their relationships with the big four – and out of that you're seeing some pretty clear winners and losers," says Titherington. "For example, Argentina is a loser because it is becoming irrelevant as Brazil is increasingly dominating the whole of South America. Argentina is just flapping in the wind now, wondering what to do. In fact, everybody else is really struggling to have any relevance there – it's why Hugo Chavez is making such a fuss in Venezuela, because he wants to be relevant in some way.

"By the same token – and principally because of the impacts of the Asian crisis on the world – Asia is increasingly dominated by China. All the other countries – South Korea, Taiwan, the Philippines, Thailand and so on – are going to have to work out what they do about that.

"The whole point about the next five years is it is going to be a harder environment with less access to capital and less natural investor enthusiasm and so people, countries and companies are all going to have to work harder to attract attention – and the risk is that the BRIC countries will dominate all the attention."

Perhaps the relationship that is causing the most global interest – although in some quarters "concern" might be a better word – is that between the BRIC economies, most particularly China, and the continent of Africa. "China is building up control of the natural resources," says Bob Yerbury, chief investment officer of Invesco Perpetual. "There are the obvious natural resources but there are also the more obscure metals that the Chinese will control production of. There is a great danger of Western economies waking up in 10 years' time and it being too late."

More fool them, the Africans, the Chinese and their other BRIC counterparts would presumably reply. Be that as it may, it is the BRIC countries and not the developed economies that are redefining Africa's role in the global economy, driven by a clear-eyed combination of "solid commercial needs and common interest," according to Simon Freemantle and Jeremy Stevens, economists at Standard Bank and co-authors of the paper *BRIC and Africa: tectonic shifts tie BRIC and Africa's economic destinies*.

Having worked out more than a decade ago that Africa would play a crucial role in its own development, China has led the continent's economic transformation and the relationship has grown to such a degree that, by 2008, Africa was receiving 30% of China's entire bilateral aid budget.

China's President Hu Jintao has made official visits to Africa every year since 2003 while, in November 2009, premier Wen Jiabao pledged $10 bn in new low-cost loans to Africa over the following three years – in passing taking the opportunity to reject accusations the country was "plundering" the continent's oil and minerals.

"The main reason Africa has not participated on the global economic stage until recently is an almost complete lack of infrastructure," says Titherington. "At the most basic level, the crops rot in the field if you can't transport them to a port and onto a boat.

"The lack of infrastructure might be down to corruption or political instability or plenty of other reasons but, without it, no country is going to progress. It is interesting therefore that the biggest investor in Africa is China and what they are concentrating on is building infrastructure. In the near term, if the Chinese decide to stop building infrastructure in Africa because they need to concentrate on building it at home, then that would be a big negative."

Perhaps the biggest obstacle to China quitting Africa is that the commercial and diplomatic benefits are increasingly mutual. "China's interest in Africa is far from cyclical," say Freemantle and Stevens. "If anything, the speed of China's engagement with Africa since the turn of the century underlines that China relies on Africa as much as Africa relies on China."

Turning to the other BRIC countries, Freemantle and Stevens say Russia's involvement in Africa appears to be geopolitically motivated and, as a result, its activity has been focused on the energy sector – specifically oil, gas and uranium. "By 2009, Russia was supplying 20% of Europe's natural gas and moves to secure additional supplies destined for Europe in Libya, Algeria and Nigeria suggest its ultimate intention may well be to increase its bargaining power with the West," they explain. "In an interesting extension of this theme, Russia was reported to have been showing interest in securing uranium supplies from Namibia, now the world's fourth largest producer."

India's interest in Africa is more blatantly commercial. "While total BRIC-Africa trade in 2008 amounted to $157 bn, India has set an objective to bring its own individual trade with Africa up to $70 bn by 2013," say Freemantle and Stevens. "Although one of India's key priorities has been to diversify its oil supplies away from the Middle East, Africa-India trade covers a broad range of technological and manufactured products, facilitated by Africa's sizeable population of Indian origin."

Of the BRIC quartet, Brazil's involvement in Africa is perhaps the least well recognized but it has been growing steadily – partly down to strong linguistic and cultural links with Angola and Mozambique, courtesy of their earlier joint ties with Portugal, and the fact that more than 45% of Brazilians claim direct African descent.

"Brazil's activity in Africa has been highly focused on the energy sector, in particular bio-fuels, in which it has particular expertise," say Freemantle and Stevens. "More than 75% of all new Brazilian cars run on a mixture of petrol and bio-fuels." Brazil's other energy-oriented interests on the continent include offshore oil-drilling projects in Angola and Nigeria and mining operations in Mozambique.

According to research from Standard Bank, Africa is both a large and fast-growing consumer market and a vital source of growth and this has enabled BRIC-African trade to increase from $16 bn in 2000 to $157 bn in 2008 – a compound annual growth rate of 33%. "This is no mere 'flash in the pan'," say Freemantle and Stevens. "Given the BRIC economies are the fastest growing in the world and, on a medium-term view, are likely to equal the importance of the world's developed economies, Africa is positioned to play a pivotal role in that development for the foreseeable future."

1.9   THE ETHICAL DIMENSION

Since we have just raised a metaphorical eyebrow concerning the motives behind China and Russia investing so heavily in Africa, this would seem as good a point as any to flag up an issue that tends not to receive a huge amount of coverage – the ethics or morality of investing in emerging markets.

Ethics and investing in general have always had a strange relationship – hence the growth of a whole subsector of socially responsible investment, which at one end of the spectrum avoids investing in companies linked to, for example, arms manufacturing, gambling, pornography and alcohol and tobacco products and at the other seeks to encourage better corporate behaviour, particularly with regard to the environment and employee welfare.

A survey of financial services consumers carried out by the UK-based Ethical Investment Research Service towards the end of 2009 identified a shift away from worrying about what might be termed "sin issues" – alcohol, gambling and so forth – towards a greater focus on more contemporary ethical concerns, such as the environment, human rights and fair trade.

Indeed, in terms of the issues consumers wanted banks and other financial institutions to prioritize, the one considered the most pressing of all was protecting human rights, which arguably also has the most resonance in the context of the emerging markets.

Certainly, one of the dangers in writing this book has been typing an idea that, while perfectly sound from an investment perspective, does not read back so easily in more human terms. By the same token, some of our experts have occasionally tied themselves in knots in an attempt not to sound too callous – and it is not entirely coincidental that it tended to be on the subject of China and democracy.

"Obviously China is not democratic but, because it is not democratic, it can push through unpopular structural reforms much more quickly than in other systems," began one. "So that's an advantage and a disadvantage. There are a lot of cases where you would wish to have more transparency and a fairer treatment of people in general – there's no doubt about that – but in terms of speed and execution of restructuring the economy, the existing system is the one that can enable it the fastest."

Even more bluntly, on the difference in the development paths between China and India, another expert said: "So far, most rational analyses would say that the relative lack of democracy in China has been to its benefit. In other words, it's growing faster because it hasn't had, dare I say, the 'impediment' of elections and democracy and it's been able to build out its infrastructure very much faster and at a more efficient rate because people just do things – however distasteful that may be to Western ears."

In both instances – as with the observation of yet another of our experts that "No country ever got wealthy through free trade" – it is hard to argue with the theory although such statements do lack a little in the compassion department. On the other hand, as already suggested – much as one may wish it otherwise and the socially responsible aspect apart – investment and compassion don't always make for easy bedfellows.

Perhaps this is most starkly illustrated by the actions of foreign investors in China after the brutal suppression of the student-led pro-democracy demonstrations in Tiananmen Square in 1989. Levels of foreign direct investment into China may have stuttered for a while but by 1992 it was up to $11 bn and in the latter half of the 1990s stayed consistently between $40 bn and $45 bn a year. In the world of investment, to misquote the old saying, you makes your choice and you pays your money.

As a final note on this subject, we acknowledge that increased consumption – one of the pivotal arguments in favour of investing in emerging markets on the back of continually improving living standards and the development of aspirational middle classes running into the hundreds of millions – does not sit too easily with the prevailing mood of austerity, environmentalism and sustainability in parts of the developed world.

We offer no view on this beyond saying it will be an interesting match-up between the environmental lobby and the millions of newly middle-class consumers in, for example, China and India being told they should not enjoy the white goods, the air travel and the all-round standard of living the developed nations have taken for granted for decades.

1.10 CONCLUSION

So will it be different this time for the emerging markets? To avoid having to dare to contradict one of the greats of investment, perhaps we might simply say emerging markets have the opportunity for that to be the case. That opportunity has come about partly thanks to the emerging markets' own positive actions in the wake of the catalogue of economic crises suffered in the past and partly from the damage done to the Western financial system – both reputationally and arithmetically – by a crisis that was very much of the West's own making.

The credibility gap has narrowed and the playing field has been levelled and that is before we even come onto all the reasons for considering investing in emerging markets that are outlined in the next chapter alongside, yes, the reasons why one should also tread carefully.

"There are always going to be concerns with rapid growth," says Yerbury. "Go back to October 2007 when the Western banking system started falling apart and at no point did we feel we should be cutting our emerging market exposure. There was no argument about it being risky or speculative – we saw it as a genuine long-term opportunity and believed we should stick with it."

2

The Investment Case for Emerging Markets – A Balanced View

2.1 INTRODUCTION

When we began researching this book in the spring of 2009, this might have been the shortest chapter in publishing history. The latest forecasts from the International Monetary Fund (IMF) had the emerging markets accounting for all of the growth in world output in the coming two years – up 1.6% compared to their developed counterparts' drop of 3.6% in 2009 and up 4% the next year compared to a flat zero on the part of the developed world. So why would you invest anywhere else but the emerging markets?

Of course the forecasts changed – as forecasts tend to do – and when the IMF published its *World Economic Outlook* in October 2009, output from the emerging markets was expected to grow 1.7% in 2009 and 5.1% in 2010 while the corresponding figures for the developed economies were a 3.4% fall followed by a marginally less anaemic 1.3% rise.

For the sake of completeness, looking out as far as 2014, the IMF expected year-on-year output growth of 6.6% for the emerging markets compared with 2.4% for the developed economies. Fortunately for the authors – if not for publishing history – the investment case for emerging markets is more than just a matter of numbers.

2.2 WHY INVEST IN EMERGING MARKETS?

That said, some of the numbers associated with the emerging markets are certainly eye-catching. As we saw in the previous chapter, emerging markets represent some four-fifths of the world's population and almost three-quarters of its land mass. At the end of 2009, they accounted for roughly 70% of global foreign exchange reserves, more than half of global energy consumption and close to half of both the world's exports and its GDP, in purchasing power parity terms.

Yet, at the end of 2009, emerging markets represented just 12% of world equity markets, as measured by market capitalization. "Clearly there is a significant disparity between developed economies and the emerging markets, which are the coming economic force globally," says Claire Simmonds, a portfolio manager for emerging markets at J.P. Morgan Asset Management. "We believe that by 2020 these markets could be up to anything just below 30% of world equity markets, based on their higher trend growth rates and the demographic support.

"This is a fact not lost on global political leaders with the growing significance of a G-20 grouping of countries – ahead of a G-7 or a G-8 – testament to the increased importance of emerging markets in the global economy. With that increased importance, our view is that it will lead to a greater representation within global capital markets."

Historically, emerging markets have tended to offer a growth premium of 4% to 5% above the developed world – the only period since 1987 when this was not the case being over 1997 and 1998, when the space was suffering first the Asian financial crisis and then the Russian debt crisis. "It would be naïve to think the emerging markets would not suffer from a global financial crisis and clearly the more open, smaller economies – those which are more heavily reliant on trade – would suffer more," says Simmonds.

Even so, taking into account GDP and industrial production numbers as well as the IMF forecasts, emerging market champions argue that the traditional growth premium for the asset class should remain in place, with the emerging economies ultimately proving to have fared better during the global financial crisis and exiting it ahead of the developed markets.

A key argument in support of such a view runs that this is because of the development model driving the emerging markets – what emerging markets commentators like to call the "structural tailwinds" that are driving their growth. The argument focuses on an idea that is far more independent and self-sufficient – a virtuous circle of urbanization, industrialization and infrastructure spending – than the more traditional perception that the emerging markets are essentially reliant on the health or otherwise of the US consumer.

This virtuous circle involves greater industrialization and manufacturing growth leading to more people heading to the cities and thus greater urbanization, and then to an increased demand for infrastructure that leads to yet more industrialization and so on. What is more, these developments have been helped along by the better macroeconomic policies being employed by emerging markets and also by the ongoing globalization of the world.

As the global financial crisis illustrated all too well, globalization can have negative consequences for the emerging markets in that they move more in line with the developed world and, by extension, the problems that affect them and which are not necessarily down to their own economies. However, it also brings tremendous benefits in the form of greater integration in the world economy, outsourcing, trade, the passing on of technological know-how and improved living standards.

Simultaneously, and nicely in time to deal with the global economic slowdown, the governments and central bankers at the helm of the emerging markets have become far more adept at handling macroeconomic policy – for example, moving from fixed currencies (usually "pegged" to the US dollar) to floating currencies; from hyperinflation to inflation targeting; and generally to more prudent fiscal and monetary policies.

"This is a continuous process and it is a process that is particularly powerful because it is happening to some of the largest populations in the world," says Simmonds. "It is also happening at a time when these two enablers are not only in sync but are also happening on a historic scale. As such, we're very comfortable with the long-term structural case for the emerging markets."

2.3   CAPTURING THE OPPORTUNITY

Arguably the greatest issue for emerging markets investors – and often their greatest frustration too – is how to turn the obvious potential into hard cash. The top-line numbers – whether they are coming from individual governments or more independent bodies such as the IMF – are often mouth-watering but are of little use to investors unless they can somehow be translated into corporate profits and earnings growth and thus shareholder returns.

China would – as is so often the case with emerging markets – be the biggest example. "Over the last decade or more, investors have watched China grow a lot and yet, for very long periods of time, the Chinese equity markets didn't do very much," says Slim Feriani, chief executive officer of Advance Emerging Capital. "So that could very easily be used as a counter-argument and as a sign that you don't get to benefit from that growth as an equity investor.

"However, if an economy isn't really going anywhere, then you won't easily see very much earnings growth. So the reality is that you need that top-line growth, which comes on the back of GDP growth, trickling down to earnings growth in a company's accounts."

Part of the link between a country's growth potential and shareholder returns will come down to the way an individual company operates and we will consider that further when we address the thorny question of risk later on in this chapter. The other part of the link, however, revolves around whether or not so-called investable themes exist and, crucially, that they be long-term.

Indeed, investors will ideally be looking for themes that are structural – that is, built into the fabric and fortunes of developing economies – in the hope that the emerging markets can put behind them their reputation as a more cyclical asset class.

Here their champions believe emerging markets do not disappoint, highlighting themes such as demographics, consumption, infrastructure, financial services and even a structural case for commodities as countries such as China and India demand more and more resources to sustain their growth (more on which is covered in the next chapter).

"While the overarching themes may be dissimilar, there are many ways to play them," says Simmonds. "Whether it be an Indian microfinance company, a Chinese beer company, a Russian steel company or a South African mining company, there are multiple ways to play these themes that will dominate emerging markets over the next 10 or 20 years."

2.4 DEMOGRAPHICS AND CONSUMPTION

Demographics – essentially the characteristics of any given population – remains one of the most important drivers for the emerging markets although investors should keep in mind that it will play into different economies in different ways.

One aspect of demographics, population growth, is perhaps the biggest factor influencing GDP growth over the longer term, not least because it implies the existence of household formation. So, for example, while spending on children has a way of taking the place of savings or long-term investment in the developed economies, in many emerging markets having children and then ensuring they are healthy and educated equates to investing in one's own future.

So companies will be looking toward areas where populations are still growing – such as Latin America, South East Asia and the Middle East – with a view not only to introducing their products into those markets but also to tapping into potential new workforces for outsourcing, say, or employing in a factory.

Between 1980 and 2010, the working-age population – that is, those aged 15 to 64 – has doubled in the emerging markets from 1.6 bn to 3.2 bn while in the developed world it has only risen from 713 m to 836 m. "It is very difficult to generate growth without hundreds of millions of extra people in the workforce and being part of the global village," says Feriani.

"All of a sudden we have this new engine that was in standby mode but has now reached critical mass. China is neck-and-neck with Japan as the second largest economy in the world with $5 tn in GDP but in the 1990s you couldn't have predicted that. You wouldn't have been talking about critical mass with emerging markets because the trillion-dollar economy was non-existent.

"Today you have trillion-dollar economies such as Brazil and Russia but then you have China at $5 tn and growing. The demographics are right there and helping it – along with productivity. So you not only have the people – and more people coming into the workplace on a daily basis – but also better productivity and those together are bound to lead to faster growth rates."

A second demographic consideration is that emerging market populations are generally becoming wealthier so they are changing their buying habits. At the most basic level, for example, this means people are switching from staples to the sorts of consumer products that have brands and packaging and are sold in supermarkets rather than in village markets.

However, the part of this that is perhaps most exciting to professional investors relates to the creation of a so-called middle class throughout the emerging markets, the more geographically-specific elements of which are examined in later chapters. "This is a domestic engine that was literally non-existent 20 years ago," says Feriani. "There were very, very few people you would define as middle-class."

Opinion is divided among commentators as to whether GDP per capita of $1500 is a good indication of whether a country has a growing middle class or whether it is nearer $3000 or $3500 but, either way, there are more countries now boasting that sort of range of per capita wealth than two decades ago. Taking the global auto industry as one example, rising sales of cars in the BRIC economies crossed over with declining sales in the US in the autumn of 2008 and the two look unlikely to cross back again.

"These trends are irreversible, structural and backed by favourable demographics," says Feriani. "This is very exciting for all of us as global citizens because it is not a zero sum game. That is something a number of people tend to ignore or forget – it is all about growing the global wealth pie to the benefit of as many people as possible. Yes, there will be some losers but, on the whole, the global wealth pie keeps on growing."

The increasing demand for mobile phone handsets in the emerging markets is another interesting case because of the lack of penetration there compared with the developed economies. According to the World Bank, in 2009, the US boasted 89 mobile phone subscriptions per 100 people, the UK 123 and Germany 131. In the emerging world, the corresponding figure was 48 for China, 42 for Nigeria and 30 for India.

When one starts from a low base such as this, the upside potential is huge and, regardless of the areas in which they may specialize, global companies are waking up to the opportunities presented by populations of 1.3 bn in China, 1.1 bn in India and almost 1 bn across the African continent.

"There are 350 million middle-class people in China," says Graham French, manager of M&G's Global Basics fund. "Latin America's the same and, in five years' time, India will have the same dynamic. So the whole modus operandi of a company should be how do we get into China? What do these people want? How do we get into India? How do we get into Latin America? That's the fundamental question."

Furthermore such a desire to supply looks set to meet a similar level of demand. "Middle-class people in Brazil or China or India know what's going on around the world," says Richard Titherington, chief investment officer and head of the emerging markets equity team at J.P. Morgan Asset Management. "They watch TV, surf the internet and, following the global slowdown, that immediately affected their consumer confidence.

"That's a negative aspect of globalization but it also works the other way around because they have the same aspirations as people every-where else. One of the things we continue to like as an investment theme is mobile telephony. Why? Because people's aspirations are the same. A kid in Nigeria is no different from a kid in London – as soon as they have got any money at all, they want a mobile phone. That's the fundamental force that's driving what's going on – the fact that everybody in the world has the same basic aspirations."

Eventually, of course, the momentum offered by the emerging markets in general will slow – just as it is already slowing in some of the more advanced parts of the developing world. "It would be hard to see GDP per capita increasing in South Korea or Taiwan at the same rate it previously did so you're going to see incrementally smaller gains from wealth creation and household income growth in those markets," says Chris Palmer, head of emerging markets at Gartmore.

"The bottom line is you want to see growth of those two factors. You can have low population growth if you have extremely high wealth creation, like in Singapore, but a blend of the two makes a good environment for an investor to go and hunt for reasonable opportunities."

Turn all these arguments on their head by looking at the US, Western Europe and Japan and one can see where the growth argument becomes more difficult. These populations are not growing – except through immigration – and in some cases they are shrinking, which means they need more wealth at the household level or increased spending at a corporate or government level and this is growing harder to find.

"On this very simplistic demographic argument, their ageing populations make the US, Western Europe and Japan look very unattractive from an investment point of view," says Palmer. "We can talk about which countries have good or bad policies – and that really does make a difference – but the reason you should probably be enthusiastic about emerging markets for the next 10 or 20 years is that they are creating the people who are going to create the opportunities."

Emerging consumption, developed opportunity

A good example of how companies in the developed world can tap into the growth potential and consumer demand of the emerging markets is Louisville, Kentucky-based Yum! Brands, the largest restaurant company in the world. Owner of the Kentucky Fried Chicken, Pizza Hut and Taco Bell brands, it operates more than 36 000 restaurants in more than 110 countries and territories.

"This is a classic example of what is happening in the emerging markets," says French at M&G. "Fifteen years ago the company was predominantly in the UK and the US but then it went to China and set up KFC. Today it probably sells more KFC and pizzas in China than it does in the US. If you had said that 15 years ago, no one would have believed you.

"So why has Yum! been successful? Well, it got very lucky because the KFC brand is red and red in China is lucky. So it's a good colour and it's also why Manchester United are so well supported. It's simple, but no maths will tell you that. No computer will tell you that. Manchester United got very, very lucky.

"On top of that, the Chinese have an absolute passion for food. They like to touch their food, have it in their hands before they put it in their mouth – and so that big KFC bucket is heaven. Now imagine how this single company is transformed when that happens. KFC in the US is static, but in China, there are 1.3 billion people and if they develop a taste for it – which they are doing – the company is transformed.

"That's the problem for investors now because 10 years ago you knew the Chinese, the Indians, the Brazilians and so on wanted electricity cables, clean water and housing. That was a no-brainer. But over the next 10 years, working out which companies will win out is going to be harder.

"So there's a fundamental question you have to ask. It's the only thing you really need to understand. The whole modus operandi of a company should be how do we get into China? What do these people want? How do we get into India? How do we get into Latin America?

"Right now there are 350 million middle-class people in China. Latin America's the same and India will have the same dynamic soon enough. And what is it the Indians want? If Indians get a taste for KFC, that's another 700 million people. So that would be another ten United Kingdoms eating KFC. It's the only question there is."

2.5 INFRASTRUCTURE

In the context of individual countries, infrastructure essentially takes in the structures and systems needed for it to function properly, including roads and other transport networks such as airports, railways and ports as well as utilities, such as water supply, power grids, telecommunications and sewers. Sometimes a distinction is made between these "harder" elements of infrastructure and "softer" ones such as education and hospitals.

As an investment theme, it most obviously benefits housebuilders and other areas of the construction industry but will also have a trickle-down effect into many others sectors. It gained extra momentum in the wake of the global financial crisis as many governments looked to shore up their internal economies through stimulus packages that often included significant infrastructure spending plans.

"One of the keys to unlocking emerging markets' economic potential is infrastructure," says Titherington. "You saw this in the pre-credit crunch period when there was a lot of finance available to build infrastructure and that was a big positive. So, looking ahead, those people who are still able to access finance and build infrastructure will do relatively well and those who are locked out of that cycle will struggle.

"It's important to identify the winners and losers on that side of things, which is why people are still pretty optimistic about China – and I think rightly because they still do have access to finance and can continue to build infrastructure – and why one can still be pretty optimistic about the emerging world."

Leading the way in the emerging markets space – and also grabbing the headlines – in November 2008 China announced a 4 tn yuan ($586 bn) stimulus package in a bid to pull the country through the global recession. This was to be spent over the following two years on a range of "hard" and "soft" projects that are summarized in the box overleaf as an example of how far-reaching infrastructure can be as an investment theme.

"While the spending on rail, housing, roads and other 'hard' infrastructure was well publicized, the 'soft' elements attracted fewer headlines," says Jing Ning, portfolio manager on the BlackRock Global Funds China fund.

"These elements, such as investment in medicine, education, ecology, technical innovation and regulation, yield less, but are arguably more important to sustainable growth in the long run. Their inclusion in the package demonstrates that, even as China's government was scrambling to avert a short-term crisis, it still had one eye fixed on the new path for China's growth."

Investors – be they government, corporate or private – should not, however, make the mistake of believing infrastructure is always a positive and instead need to ask what any piece of infrastructure is, what it is going to be used for and whether the money could be better spent elsewhere.

"What we don't want to see are roads to nowhere, paper mills in the wrong place or tall buildings in cities that don't need tall buildings," says Palmer. "Infrastructure is usually a social positive but it can also be quite wasteful. It does offer the prospect of immediate gratification but you certainly wouldn't want a country to undermine its long-term financial strength by overinvesting in infrastructure.

"It needs to be carefully weighed against what other forms of spending might be appropriate to that country. Weighing infrastructure versus education, for example, with education you don't get the instant gratification and there are fewer areas to invest in, in any asset class, but it's clear the pay-off is incredibly high. We all know education needs to be included in infrastructure but, unfortunately, the benefit only really comes out over time and a lot of investors don't want to spend time observing where the correct infrastructure has been built."

Summary of China's 4 tn yuan stimulus package from 2008

"Hard" infrastructure spending:

To speed up the construction of affordable housing for the low-income population and boost low-rent housing construction.

To increase spending on rural infrastructure facilities, especially on rural roads, power grid construction and the water supply system.

To expedite investment in the transportation network, especially fast-track investment in the railroad network for passenger transportation, coal transportation and the western rail system, and to upgrade the national highway system, build more airports in central and western China and secondary cities and fast-track the urban power grid system.

To speed up post-earthquake construction in Sichuan Province.

"Soft" infrastructure spending:

To increase investment on medical services, culture and education.

To increase spending on ecology protection, especially fast-track investment on tainted water and garbage recycling, water anti-pollution projects and energy-saving projects.

To expedite technical innovation and economic restructuring and boost hi-tech sector technical innovation and service sectors upgrading.

To boost disposable income for urban and rural households, raise the minimum purchasing price for wheat and rice in 2009 and increase subsidies to rural areas.

To implement reform in the value-added tax system, which would reduce the annual VAT paid by all enterprises by 120 bn yuan ($17.6 bn).

To boost the role of financial markets in supporting overall economic growth. This includes removing all lending ceilings on commercial banks in order to encourage more lending to priority projects, rural China and small and medium-sized enterprises as well as technical innovation and mergers and acquisitions.

2.6 FINANCIAL SERVICES

Financial services – taking in areas such as personal loans, mortgages and corporate lending, which have great potential for expansion – is interesting in this context because it is not only an investment theme through which to tap into emerging markets growth, it is also an argument for why that growth looks so attractive in the first place.

One reason why the case for emerging markets looks so strong is because they are so underleveraged – that is to say, compared to the economies of the US, Japan and Western Europe, they have much lower levels of government, corporate and personal debt.

If, for example, you took the ratio of mortgage loans as a percentage of GDP as at 2009, the UK stood at 82% and the US at 73% and yet many significant emerging markets were in low single digits. For example, India had a mortgage penetration rate of 8%, Indonesia, which has the fourth largest population in the world, was on 4%, as was Turkey, while Brazil had a rate of just 2%.

"This is a reflection of the fact we've barely started," says Feriani. "As important as they have become, the emerging markets consumer still has a long way to go. You can only imagine the next two, three or four decades as they converge towards developed world levels – although hopefully not to the same extent. We don't want them up at those levels but they will certainly have greater access to credit going forward.

"Look at the loan-to-value rates of the emerging markets countries and you don't see the 100% mortgages you had in the UK. Really, loan-to-value rates of around 50% are what emerging markets banks do and that is one of the reasons why the banking systems in a lot of emerging markets are much healthier than has been witnessed in the US and the UK."

On a different level, emerging markets governments look to have been every bit as prudent as their banks and citizens. According to emerging market specialist Silk Invest, in 2009 global debt as a percentage of GDP was 146% while global reserves as a percentage of GDP were

12%. In the European Union, those figures were respectively 180% and 2% while in the US they were 216% and zero.

In the emerging markets, however, a much healthier picture emerges with Asia at 60% and 40% respectively and Latin America at 58% and 12%. Meanwhile, the Middle East and Africa were the only regions of the world with more reserves than debt, which offers them more flexibility to deal with financial and economic setbacks.

"Unfortunately the developed markets crisis led to a problem in the emerging market countries," says Feriani. "But it was a problem of the West and of the developed markets, which is a big change from what we've seen in the past. Historically, emerging markets crises have led to a bit of a hiccup in the developed market world but it's the other way around now and emerging markets are working from a much stronger base than they ever have before."

2.7 VALUATIONS, EARNINGS AND RETURN ON EQUITY

Regardless of any long-term structural arguments involved, investment tends to be cyclical in nature and emerging markets are no exception. Within that cycle, therefore, there will be better times to invest and times when your money will not go as far. Of course, there will be times when you lose money.

With the benefit of hindsight, that most useless of investment tools, late 2008 and the beginning of 2009 – just when people were predicting the collapse of the global financial system – would have been a spectacular time to invest in emerging markets.

"At the start of the 2009, we saw valuations touch briefly below 1× price-to-book," says Simmonds. "A simple rule of thumb, historically, has been that when emerging markets are below 1.4× or 1.5× price-to-book, it has been a very attractive entry point into the asset class, providing investors with positive double-digit returns over the next one-, three- and five-year periods.

"By September 2009, valuations were around two times price-to-book and, while that made them slightly elevated against their developed market peers, it's worth recognizing this was not so much a reflection of emerging markets looking expensive but more developed markets still looking very cheap."

At such levels, valuations were still fairly low compared with where they had been back in 2006 and 2007, so professional investors remained unconcerned but emerging markets were no longer the significant investment opportunity they had been at the start of 2009. What needed to happen next was for company earnings to start coming through in order to support the new valuation levels.

According to J.P. Morgan, of the four sources that contribute to emerging markets investment returns – valuations, foreign exchange, earnings per share and dividends – by far the biggest contributor in the period from 2002 to 2008 was earnings and the company expects that trend to continue all the way to 2014.

"Foreign exchange and valuation will become a much smaller part of what you're playing and what you're achieving when you invest in the emerging markets than perhaps historically," says Simmonds. "Differential earnings are particularly attractive within infrastructure, consumption and financial services."

By autumn 2009, Gartmore's analysis was also indicating that the growth outlook for emerging markets had begun to normalize, favouring a return to earnings-oriented investing. "The market rally over 2009 was characterized by an initial rebound from depressed levels of valuation," says Palmer. "However, the next phase is driven by growing corporate profits. Companies that can finance their growth through their own cashflows have a key advantage."

For Palmer, the really positive news at the time was that a recovery and rebounding cash generation was happening across a broad range of sectors and industries. This meant investors could have a healthy exposure to energy and other cyclical industries that, in some developed markets, were still constrained by relatively tight credit conditions.

Domestic consumer trends in emerging markets also remain strong, noted Palmer at the time, adding: "The global economic recovery does nothing to discourage investing in a broad range of domestic consumer discretionary companies, from automakers to manufacturers of branded consumer durables."

If the first positive stage of the emerging markets investment cycle is a liquidity-led reflation rally – when investors' appetite for risk comes back and money flows towards emerging markets simply because they are emerging markets – then the second stage revolves around company earnings as investors look to judge the quality and sustainability of a company's income stream.

Put another way, that first stage can lead to a lack of discrimination – or, as the old investment adage has it, "A rising tide floats all boats" –

so, during the second stage, investors have to show more restraint and be choosier about where they put their money.

At this point a final company-specific consideration for investors comes more sharply into focus in the shape of return on equity – a measure of a company's profitability, expressed as a percentage, that shows how much profit it generates with the cash shareholders have invested. "It is refreshing to note the emerging markets have systematically seen an improvement in the return on equity from back in the 1980s and early 1990s," says Simmonds.

"Even in this environment, we believe return on equity will bottom at 12.9%, which is still a very comfortable level, and we can see 15% as a sustainable level for the emerging markets asset class over the long term. This has been a reflection of the improved policies at the corporate level – return on equity has been improving as borrowings have come down and asset turnover has gone up and so it is a very sustainable level.

"Anecdotally, when we meet companies, we emphasize the importance of their capital discipline and in those conversations we have with them they have significantly changed their tune. We therefore believe this is entrenched in their business policies and in their mindset and therefore is sustainable over the long term."

2.8   SOME TECHNICAL CONSIDERATIONS

So far, we have only concentrated on the positive case for investing in emerging markets – a not inconsiderable parade of risks follows very shortly – and you may or may not be convinced. However, to a certain extent, the success of emerging markets becomes something of a self-fulfilling prophecy because, as the asset class attracts more money, so still more investors have to consider directing yet more money that way.

As recently as December 2002, investors who used the MSCI All Country World index as a benchmark needed only to allocate 4% of their portfolio to emerging markets whereas, just seven years later, they would have had to allocate three times that amount. "As a global asset allocator, when it was 4%, you could ignore such a small asset class," says Feriani. "But it could cost somebody's job if they ignored something that accounts for 12% – particularly if it were to outperform by 40% or 50%.

"So, all of a sudden, there is a technical factor where global asset allocators – particularly in the US, where there is most of the money, but also around the world – cannot ignore emerging markets. You could be underweight and maybe go to 5% versus 12% of the global benchmark but going to zero could be extremely risky.

"However, we are seeing more and more people going neutral or overweight because they have taken the view that, over the next 10 or 20 years, this is an asset class that is bound to outperform. What we're seeing now is a bit of a wake-up call for the rest of the world. They're taking emerging markets more seriously."

Even if investors were to direct a fraction more of their overall portfolios towards the emerging markets space, that in itself would be likely to prove a powerful driver. Flows of money can take on a disproportionate significance in what are still small markets.

"If you have an increasing number of people recognizing the structural shift that is happening in this world and investing more money, then the impact could be powerful," says Feriani. "We're seeing signs of that as more people realize the case for emerging markets. However, we don't want to see it all happen at the same time so we'd still like to have a lot of sceptical people coming to this camp over the years.

"Otherwise we could even have a bubble, which is not something we would like to see. We'd much prefer a nice sustainable trend in the emerging markets space but a bubble is quite possible because, with excess liquidity, a lot of things can happen." That leads us neatly enough into the potential downsides of investing in emerging markets.

2.9   RISK

Risk is a little word but it looms large over the emerging markets space. Investors must go in with their eyes open and there are certain actions they can take to mitigate risk, which we shall discuss shortly, but there is no getting away from the fact that investing in emerging markets inherently involves a number of potential downsides.

Of course, to a large extent that is rather the point. Investors are rewarded for taking risk – for contributing some capital to, say, a company that will hopefully, for any of the reasons above, be creative and profitable but equally, for any of the reasons below, could see that capital halved or destroyed completely.

Investing in anything involves a constant trade-off between risk and reward and your own exposure will depend on your personal circumstances. It is why some people will never invest in emerging markets at all and, at the other end of the spectrum, why one fund manager we spoke to was very comfortable having half a percentage point of a portfolio in Zimbabwe – "as a warrant on the margin of improvement".

Continuing one of our running themes, risk might be split into two areas – the possibility that what we believe or hope will happen to boost our investment does not materialize, although nobody is to blame, and the possibility that hoped-for boost never materializes, only this time it is because of the action or inaction of a state, government, company or even an individual.

Beginning with that first set of risks, it may be instructive to refer back to our reasons for investing in emerging markets. What risks do the demographics, consumption and infrastructure arguments carry? What risks, that is, beyond the obvious and simplistic answer that one or more or all of them just do not work out?

Well, demographics is a two-way street so that, when a baby boom reaches working age, that could offer a boost to a country's GDP or else it could lead to more unemployment and the negative consequences that spring from that. Equally, when a baby boom reaches retirement age – a prospect China is at least beginning to have to recognize – it can place a greater burden on a shrinking workforce.

The risk to the consumption argument introduces an interesting ethical or moral dimension. It is human nature to aspire to a better standard of living, which as we have seen naturally leads to greater consumption of goods and resources. But as the world focuses more on environmental issues and the sustainability of resources, could this impact on corporate ambitions across the emerging markets?

Or, to turn that argument on its head, how will millions of the new middle classes in China, India, Brazil and so on react to being told that they should not have the consumer goods, the cars, the air travel and the all-round standards of living the developed nations have taken for granted for decades?

As for infrastructure, we have already discussed how it should be a social positive if it is of the right kind and the best use of money but, in the wrong hands, risks being a considerable waste of resources. The wrong hands? Now we are onto matters of trust, which takes us to the second set of risks.

2.10 MATTERS OF TRUST

At one press briefing we attended, when the two speakers had finished their presentations on the attractions of emerging markets, they politely waited for questions, but what they received was closer to a rant. Why, demanded one journalist, who seemed affronted there might be anything positive to say about the asset class, had they omitted to focus on the political realities of some emerging markets? Why had they omitted to mention "failed states", the journalist asked, before reeling off a long list of countries, most of whom we should say now we have no intention of touching on ourselves, even in the chapter on frontier markets?

This may or may not be an extreme example – but, once bitten, twice shy, and emerging markets provoke a number of fears among potential investors that are more than justified by the asset class's history. Can we trust the country? Can we trust its president? Can we trust its government? Can we trust its institutions? Can we trust the corporate culture? Can we trust the particular company we want to invest in? Can we trust our fellow investors? Hang on – can we even trust our own judgement?

These questions carry more or less weight depending on the country or area concerned – for example, a North Korea boasting nuclear weapons certainly adds an extra dimension to the emerging Asia story – and, as such, will be considered to a greater or lesser extent in this book's six geographical chapters. This section will concern itself more with some more general issues.

"With emerging markets, you are looking at higher returns but with that comes higher risk and risk can be measured in many different ways," says Simmonds. "In terms of political risk, for example, there are those events such as 9/11 that you simply cannot predict – although, as an investor, you can benefit afterwards through the uncertainty it brings and therefore the valuation opportunity it creates."

Then there is the kind of risk you stand a better chance of predicting, which would include immature political systems, corrupt governments and weaknesses in regulation. "Here you have a much higher chance of forming a view on how they will impact economic policy, which ultimately will impact the companies you're investing in much more," Simmonds explains. "Where the risk is so extreme you are not being adequately paid to take it, then that is not an attractive investment opportunity."

At this point, Simmonds suggests the only way truly to understand risk and evaluate it properly in a portfolio is to have local analysts on the ground, who understand the local, cultural and political aspects of investing in those markets and those companies and who can assess whether you are being suitably paid to take on that risk. It is a view to be expected from a professional fund manager but, even so, not one to be lightly dismissed.

Has the global financial crisis had any effect on investor perceptions of risk, particularly with regard to the respective merits of emerging markets and the developed world? "If you look at the difference between the pre- and the post-credit crunch world, people probably think there is a lot more risk in the developed world today than they did before," says Titherington.

"Is a bank in China more or less risky than a bank in the UK? People's perceptions on that have probably changed a lot in recent years but it is still in general true that political, legal and financial institutions are much stronger in the developed world – and that is why they are developed – than they are in the emerging world.

"The UK could argue, and probably fairly, that a depositor in, say, Royal Bank of Scotland did not lose any money as a result of the credit crunch and it was only the shareholders who suffered – and they take that entrepreneurial risk. On the other hand, when there are banking crises and so forth in emerging markets, there is a much higher degree of risk.

"So the fundamental risk of emerging markets is always your vulnerability to at least one, if not all three, of political, legal and financial instability. There are many different reasons why countries are like that – whether it is revolution, extreme poverty or extreme income distribution differences or others that are frankly harder to explain. Why, for example, is Argentina not like New Zealand? You could probably write a whole book just on that."

Perceptions do change – one professional investor tells the story of attending a conference in 2009 where one of the largest Western private equity firms argued the political risk involved in an infrastructure project in the UK had grown significantly larger than for a similar one in Brazil, in the sense that the chances were much higher that the then Labour administration would arbitrarily change the economics of the deal before it had been completed.

However, emerging markets in every part of the world have traditionally been associated with political, institutional and financial risk – the nagging doubt among some investors that their governments, other organizations and companies cannot always be trusted to do what they say they will – and the asset class is not going to shake off that reputation overnight.

Even so, while investors should always bear such risks in mind, they should not be overstated. Many emerging markets are run as dictatorships and others only pay lip service to democracy but the Heritage Index of Economic Freedom, which compares the relative economic freedom of different economies based on trade freedom, business freedom, investment freedom and property rights, throws up some surprises. For example, the 2009 global table was topped by Hong Kong and Singapore while other emerging markets such as Chile, Botswana, South Korea, Hungary, Mexico and South Africa all scored higher than, for example, France and Italy.

Still, as another set of country rankings proves, there is no room for complacency anywhere. Transparency International's 2009 Corruption Perceptions Index, a measure of domestic, public sector corruption, had the likes of Singapore (ranked 3rd out of 180 countries), Hong Kong (12th), Chile (25th) and Estonia (27th) straddling Germany (14th), Japan (17th) and the US (20th) as the least corrupt countries in the world.

All scored more than 6.5 out of 10 in the composite index that draws on 13 different expert and business surveys. However, the great majority of countries scored less than 5.0, with Brazil (75th), China (79th) and India (84th) all scoring less than 4.0 and Indonesia (111th), Nigeria (130th) and Russia (146th) less than 3.0.

"At a time when massive stimulus packages, fast-track disbursements of public funds and attempts to secure peace are being implemented around the world, it is essential to identify where corruption blocks good governance and accountability, in order to break its corrosive cycle," said Huguette Labelle, the chairperson of Transparency International.

"Stemming corruption requires strong oversight by parliaments, a well-performing judiciary, independent and properly resourced audit and anti-corruption agencies, vigorous law enforcement and transparency in public budgets, revenue and aid flows, as well as space for independent media and a vibrant civil society."

Sometimes trust simply comes down to whether one believes the numbers – whether they are published by an arm of government or by a company. Hugh Young, managing director of Aberdeen Asset Management Asia, takes a pragmatic approach to this question. "We accept all the statistics and then go for the most boring, stable companies within that," he says. "Other people buy far higher-risk companies in what are already high-risk areas. We want people who are as careful as us with our investors' money and how they look after it."

A cautionary tale

Standing tall as a warning to any investor who may still believe that every emerging markets story has a happy ending is Argentina. One of the earliest economies to attract external investor interest and cash, the country has been completely eclipsed by its neighbour Brazil.

"Argentina thinks wealth already exists and just consumes it whereas Brazil is more interested in creating wealth," says one fund manager. "Argentina is a sad story of wasted potential and it's not the first time it has done this. Historically the wealth has been generated in the countryside and consumed in Buenos Aires, which is essentially a giant parasite."

Marginally less bluntly, Urban Larson, director of emerging equities at F&C Investments, says: "Argentina isn't even officially an emerging market any more – it is a frontier market – and it is its own fault. People used to get very excited about investing in the Argentinean agricultural sector but Brazil has a lot of the same climate and land availability and the same advantages as Argentina.

"The difference is that Brazilians understand that in order for people to invest, they need to be treated reasonably. The Brazilian government has been a lot more investor-friendly and the country has been a lot more predictable place in which to invest. Argentina has lost a lot of its competitive advantages with respect to Brazil because Brazil is just a much more welcoming place."

2.11   CORPORATE GOVERNANCE

We have already touched on the link between broader macroeconomic growth in emerging markets and shareholders actually receiving some sort of return and obviously a hugely important part of the chain is corporate governance – the policies and processes that dictate how a company operates.

"Where we've seen problems in the past is between sales growth and a company's bottom line because the ultimate shareholders don't benefit from that top-line growth," says Feriani. "But, as we see better accounting systems and better corporate governance, then that growth on the top line does trickle down to the bottom line – with a growing proportion distributed in the form of dividends – and therefore we benefit from it as investors.

"Sure enough, if somewhere in the middle the money goes somewhere else – to buy the CEO a yacht or second home or whatever – then you don't end up with your return on equity or any profits, let alone any dividends. Of course there are some exceptions out there but, on aggregate, we are in a much better situation today, where emerging markets countries and companies are very aware of the potential benefits to them. So, for example, lots of families are giving up 100% control of their businesses because they do see the benefits of a re-rating as they improve their corporate governance and grow more transparent."

When you invest in emerging markets companies, you are not investing in GDP growth but in the companies' profitability, their cash flows and their return on equity. It is why Latin America has tended to outperform emerging Asia despite having significantly lower GDP growth rates.

The link comes from structural themes – from, as we have discussed earlier, industrialization, urbanization and infrastructure spending sustaining higher trend growth rates within the emerging markets companies that are the market leaders in those structurally underpenetrated areas where there's a secular catch-up story.

"This is where you can achieve differential growth," says Simmonds. "The break with the past comes from a change in corporate discipline and capital discipline and the ability for companies to translate that growth into shareholder and company returns.

"If you break it down in terms of return on equity, you're seeing all the aspects of that formula starting to appear. There is a sustainable trend of return on equity improving as companies combine better capital discipline with better corporate governance practices – as they start to put into place developed-world business practices in an emerging markets context.

"Clearly many companies are not doing this and that's where the opportunity exists for fund managers – to identify companies that are able to build up what we call 'franchise-quality' businesses, which can achieve a sustainable return on equity and maintain a competitive advantage over time. Ultimately, compounding superior growth rates over long periods of time is, on a mathematical basis, going to give you a much higher return than short-term changes in valuation or currency."

Furthermore, just as perceptions of the reliability of developed world governments can change, so it is with corporate reliability. It cannot be ignored that many recent corporate scandals have involved Western companies – for example, Enron, Madoff and WorldCom in the

US and Northern Rock, Parmalat and SocGen in the UK and Western Europe.

"I'm often asked about general transparency of information on listed companies and I would say it has significantly improved in Brazil, Russia, India and China," says BRIC expert Michael Konstantinov, head of global emerging markets equities at Allianz Global Investors' RCM. "Of course, there can always be improvements but many companies are now reporting quarterly and according to international accounting standards – some of them both locally and internationally.

"They are quite open with investors, who typically have very good access to the managements as well, so all of these things have significantly improved. Clearly there are always companies that can cheat but we have also seen many scandals in the US and Europe – it's not exclusive to emerging markets."

In this respect, the 2009 collapse of Satyam Computers, India's then fourth-largest software firm, is instructive – not so much that a billion-dollar fraud should have happened in India but that the international reaction was so muted compared to what it would undoubtedly have been even a decade earlier.

2.12   HELL IS OTHER PEOPLE

Just as the "For" column for investing in emerging markets includes an increasing flow of money away from their more developed counterparts, the "Against" column must logically acknowledge that this will never be a smooth upward line or one-way street. For one thing, investors of all types get spooked; for another, investors of all types change their minds.

"From a stock market point of view as opposed to an economic one, emerging markets are still very dependent on developed-world investors," says Titherington. "So the events in the developed world – financial events that affect the risk appetite of developed-world investors – have a very direct and sometimes almost instantaneous impact on emerging market stock markets.

"If you are a US pension fund and you cut your allocation to the emerging markets, the stock market in Egypt or wherever is going to react to that pretty quickly, regardless of the economic fundamentals. It is in my view impossible and wrong-headed to believe in both globalization and decoupling – you can have one or the other but you can't have both."

In the same way – and, while this may only be a short-term risk, it is all but inevitable – there will come a point in the investment cycle when emerging markets look less attractive than developed ones. We have already identified the first positive stage of the emerging markets investment cycle as a liquidity-led reflation rally and a second stage as when investors become more discriminating in their search for more sustainable earnings.

Eventually, however, investors cannot help themselves and the sheer weight of money means company valuations grow overcooked. Investors move from realizing there is a recovery to realizing that with a recovery come higher interest rates and then markets tend to pause for breath. At best, investors start noticing more attractive opportunities elsewhere and "rotate" in those directions; at worst, as Feriani said earlier, emerging markets potentially enter bubble territory.

This tendency can be seen in the obsession some investors have with finding the next frontier market – neatly illustrated by one leading emerging markets investment house launching a Vietnam fund some six years before the country even had a stock market and closing it two years before the market's performance eventually quadrupled.

"The problem with frontier markets is they are a bull-market phenomenon," says Titherington. "People get more and more enthusiastic and they want to take on more risk but the danger is that they invest when markets are expensive. The idea of investing in frontiers is not a bad one – it's just that people typically do it at the wrong time."

Bob Yerbury, chief investment officer at Invesco Perpetual, is even more pragmatic on the subject, asking: "Why limit yourself to the frontier markets? As an investor, you don't have to be the pioneer. You can wait until things have developed a little more in terms of accounting and governance. Some investors have a compulsion to find 'the latest market' but you are always better off operating where you have more confidence."

A good point – so what about trusting one's own judgement? After all, we began this book by recalling Sir John Templeton's maxim about how "This time it's different" are the four most expensive words in the English language. What if the upturn in emerging market fortunes in the wake of the global credit crisis is really just a cyclical upturn like the start of the 1990s that, just as in the 1990s, will only end in tears?

Certainly, by the end of 2009, there were clear parallels to be drawn with that period in the shape of very loose monetary conditions and a liquidity-driven market rally. Accommodative monetary conditions have historically been very supportive for the emerging markets as an asset class and, as in the early 1990s it could be that markets continue to extend their gains even as earnings drift along the bottom.

Could it be déjà vu all over again? "It's too early to say but it's worth remembering that liquidity-driven rallies can extend for long periods of time," says Simmonds. "As we saw back in the 1990s, it really only ended with the tightening-back of monetary policy in 1994 so while we have seen a very sharp reflation rally from the emerging markets, we wouldn't rule out that these things can be extended, given the very supportive conditions in the global economy."

Ultimately, risk and emerging markets are part of the same game – you do not have to play if you do not want to but if you do play you need to know the rules. That said, while an awareness of the risks is critical, one should try not to be overwhelmed by them as you would end up never going outside your front door.

Take global risk specialist Maplecroft, which rates individual companies both in terms of "dynamic" and "structural" risk. Obviously it is the company's job to dissect risk but the end result can be a little unnerving – for example, dynamic risk is broken down into Governance Framework (made up of regime stability, rule of law, business integrity and corruption and rule of law), Political Violence (conflict and political violence, terrorism risk and human security) and Business and Macroeconomics (regulatory framework, business environment, macroeconomic environment, economic diversification and emerging powers).

It makes one nervous just reading that paragraph but, really, as Justin Urquhart Stewart, investment commentator and co-founder of Seven Investment Management, said when the global financial crisis looked most bleak: "You have to take a view. Do you think things are going to be better or worse in 10 years' time? If you think worse, then buy a case of scotch and a shotgun and go pick out your cave in Wales. If you think better, then you should be investing now."

An alternative view of risk

"My definition of an emerging market is that all countries are risky but the emerging markets are the ones where the risk is priced in," says Jerome Booth, head of research at Ashmore Investment Management. "A developed country, on the other hand, is a country where a domestic investor does not price in their own sovereign risk.

"The idea that emerging markets are riskier than the developed world is just plain incorrect. You don't go to emerging markets because they are risky and you might obtain a higher return, you go to emerging markets because it's safer because there is less leverage. That's a fundamental thing most investors haven't worked out yet.

"In particular you go to the emerging markets because it's a massive hedge against the very worst-case scenarios. Say you have a scenario where the US and Europe grow at minus 5% for each of the next three years. In that scenario, emerging markets grow at 'only' plus 4%, say, so that's 9% difference in growth.

"On the other hand, say we have the very best and most benign scenario we can think of and the US and Europe grow at plus 1.5%, then the emerging markets grow at plus 7%. That's much better but actually the gap is bigger in the worst-case scenario.

"The theory is that these countries are linked so, if the US goes down, the emerging markets are worse off. That's absolutely true but the conclusion one subconsciously draws from that is one shouldn't invest because it's risky – and that is entirely the wrong conclusion.

"The right conclusion should be to acknowledge that, in that scenario, the relative performance of emerging markets is substantially better than even in the benign scenario. So therefore you should put money into emerging markets because it reduces risk in the worst-case scenario."

2.13 BUILDING EMERGING MARKETS INTO A BALANCED PORTFOLIO

Investment has always been and always will be an area where risk and reward go hand in hand and, as we have seen, the world's emerging markets are no exception. We trust the preceding pages have shown that the asset class is one that needs to be approached with, if not caution, then certainly due care and consideration.

Risk is a double-edged sword, however, and just as there could be a danger from too much exposure to emerging markets so there could be a danger in not having enough. While it may once have been tempting and even understandable to see emerging markets as peripheral to the global economy, there are few people now who would try to argue that is still the case.

Regardless of the precise percentages in benchmarks such as the MSCI All Country World index, with China now challenging Japan for the title of second largest economy in the world and India, Russia and Brazil all within the top dozen, to leave these countries out of an investment portfolio would mean excluding a huge proportion of global trade and wealth – and the fastest growing areas to boot.

As such, an investment in emerging markets should ideally reflect their growing significance in the global economy – although the precise level must depend on an individual's age, investment time horizon and attitude to risk. Certainly there seems little point looking to the professionals for guidance in this regard as there is a worrying divergence of opinion.

Taking the US as an example, as of 2009, the country's public pensions system had somewhere in the region of 3% of assets allocated to the emerging markets and yet some of the big university endowments funds had allocated 10 times that amount. Then there are those professional investors who argue allocations should be based on GDP – which would lead to a portfolio that was almost half invested in emerging markets.

The time for such an approach may well come but at present that would seem a shade bullish and we would reiterate the need to think carefully about one's own individual circumstances, possibly in consultation with a financial adviser, before taking any action.

Try, however, to avoid the temptation to look in the rear-view mirror when deciding the composition or "asset allocation" of an investment portfolio. Investors can make the mistake of basing decisions on the size and importance of countries over, say, the past decade rather than on a more thorough examination of who are likely to be the economic superpowers of the future. Anyone with a time horizon of 20 years or more – for example, those investing towards their retirement – would be advised to try to identify the growth areas of tomorrow.

Despite all the strong arguments for investing in emerging markets, this remains a volatile asset class that is subject to huge price fluctuations in the short term and you should think very carefully about investing for anything less than a 10-year time horizon.

"This is an asset class where the volatility is not going to go away any time soon – certainly not in the next 10 or 20 years – so investors do need to take a long-term approach," says Simmonds at J.P. Morgan Asset Management. "They need to be aware of the risks associated with the emerging markets and, even more so, with some of the frontier markets where the risks are even more accentuated because they are at even earlier stages of development."

A time-honoured way of reducing risk, although never eradicating it completely, is through diversification – that is, spreading your money across a range of different investments. In the same way that it would be dangerous to put all your money into bonds or commodities or Japanese smaller companies, so it is important not to have all your emerging market exposure invested in one country.

The diverse nature of emerging markets means different countries will perform better at different times and in different types of environment. For example, as we will see in Chapter 4, the fortunes of Russia are heavily tied in with the price of oil, while India is a more inward-looking economy and therefore less linked to global growth. A blend of emerging markets within a portfolio should create a more balanced return.

"The beauty of emerging markets is that, while the various indices define the space as between 20 and 25 countries, actually there are more than 50 to pick from and there really is a time for everything," says Feriani at Advance Emerging Capital. "You might meet people who are hugely bullish about Iran, say, and then, at the other end of the spectrum, you have Brazil, which is enjoying the sort of stability it hasn't seen for a long time.

"When you have a government being re-elected democratically, that's quite a big change and stability breeds more stability, which breeds confidence – investor confidence and consumer confidence – and you see what happens afterwards. Places such as Brazil have seen phenomenal change and this has led to more stability, less volatility and therefore steadier growth, better earnings and better returns."

2.14 HOW TO INVEST

As we have seen, the emerging markets encompass a wide-ranging number of regions and countries and the asset classes to which it is possible to gain exposure are no less diverse. One way of breaking those asset classes down would be as listed equities, government debt, corporate debt, property, commodities, private equity, hedge funds, currencies and frontier markets although no doubt some professional investors may view such a list as still missing a few niche categories.

Furthermore, to return to investment's rather binary worldview, do you invest in individual securities or through a collective fund? And, if you choose the latter route, should you choose an open-ended investment company or a closed-ended fund? And would you prefer your investment to be actively managed or to track a market index?

To be honest, the practicalities involved in investing directly in individual emerging market securities is likely to make them off-limits for all but the most single-minded private investor. For example, the degree of research necessary in building your portfolio and the constant monitoring of it afterwards are demanding while cost and liquidity considerations – the ease of buying and selling stocks – constitute two more considerable hurdles.

That said, if you are set on undertaking this risky approach to an already risky area, one solution would be to focus on your home market as, regardless of where they are based, many listed companies in the developed world now generate a significant proportion of their earnings from emerging markets, while usually being subject to more stringent requirements on disclosure and transparency.

"Any company is likely to be thinking about making its next investment in an emerging market country and every company executive will have an emerging markets strategy," says Palmer at Gartmore. "By the same token, remember that risks are not eliminated by buying a developed market fund – for example, these days a Japan fund manager will be seeking out Japanese companies that are looking for emerging markets-generated performance."

Even so, investing in a collective fund is likely to be the more practical and indeed preferred route for most private investors. After all, the more generalist emerging markets funds are able to provide straightforward and cost-effective "one-stop" access to a diversified range of countries, sectors and companies.

Furthermore, in common with any other collective investment, emerging markets funds allow you to tap into the expertise of specialist managers who will look to construct balanced portfolios that should serve to spread risk across a range of different assets. Managers of more generalist funds in particular will have the ability to increase their exposure to areas that are doing well and cut back on those that are struggling.

While these generalist portfolios – often known as "global emerging markets" funds – offer the most flexibility, there are also a number of specialist funds investing in just one country, such as China or Vietnam, a region, such as Latin America, or indeed just the BRIC quartet. Obviously the more focused a fund's investment objective is, the riskier it will be although it should also have the potential to produce very strong returns at certain times.

Active funds do depend on the skill of an individual fund manager or team and the resources of the investment house that employs them and, as such, should be carefully vetted. When choosing between individual funds, factors to be borne in mind include the manager's experience, their investment process, how they research potential investments and the level of support they receive from their team and the company they work for. One further consideration would be a demonstrable ability to produce consistent and solid returns over a number of different time-frames.

A good actively managed emerging markets fund should be able to identify future sources of growth, such as infrastructure or the developing consumer economy – after all, its manager should be continually looking out for new opportunities as emerging markets are constantly evolving. Such funds also have the flexibility to move out of companies or regions where the risk has grown too great, which can be important in protecting capital in difficult times.

Depending on their fund's investment remit, the manager may also be able to access some of the other asset classes listed at the start of this section, such as hedge funds, commodities – the fortunes of which are so interwoven with the emerging markets story – and private equity.

"Private equity is where we gain access to the 'hidden gems'," says Feriani. "Emerging markets are still not as deep or as mature as we would like and therefore we have to go to family-owned or privately-owned stock in order to gain access to some of the most exciting opportunities."

Whatever the asset class, they will still be governed by the outlook both for emerging markets as a whole and for the different regions and countries considered in more detail in the six geographical chapters of this book. If you detect in these chapters a bias towards company shares at the expense of other asset classes, that is because all the main emerging economies have thriving equity markets while bonds – issued by governments and, to a lesser extent, companies – have far more significance in countries such as Brazil and South Africa than in India and China.

2.15 BONDS

A separate section on bonds is unlikely to appease the asset class's more passionate champions, such as Booth at Ashmore Investment

Management. "It really is about the bond market more than the equity market," he says. "Frankly, the equity market should always be the last thing you build even though investors tend principally to think of equities. But why go for the riskiest asset class first? It's just not rational.

"It's because people are faced with an industry where, because equities are more granular, there are many more people trying to sell them equities than there are bonds but the emerging bond markets in local currency are already massive compared to equity markets – much broader and much bigger than the dollar debt market – and they are only going to grow much, much more."

A bond is a debt instrument issued by a government, other institution or company, which then agrees to pay the principal amount of the loan at a specific time and may also agree to pay interest periodically. Emerging market bonds are generally seen as carrying less risk than emerging market shares but should still be treated with care.

"Emerging market debt is a sort of 'in-between' asset class," says Peter Eerdmans, head of Investec Asset Management's local currency emerging market debt team. "The volatility is around 10% or 11% whereas global equities are more like 16% or 17% and global bonds are more like 6% or 7%. Historically, the rewards from the yields have been more than enough compensation for the risk taken."

Historically emerging market bonds have paid a premium on the assumption that the issuers were more likely to struggle to pay back the loans or interest than their counterparts in developed markets although such logic now looks a little flawed in the face of increasingly over-indebted governments in the developed world. For income-seeking investors who can tolerate the additional risk, the higher income on offer from the asset class is an attractive feature.

The most important development for emerging markets debt over the course of the first decade of this century has been the shift away from governments issuing bonds in US dollars, which used to be the easiest way for them to gain access to capital markets.

But as emerging markets have developed more of a local financial industry – more banks, a pension fund sector, a mutual fund sector and so forth – so they have also been able to develop a local bond market. "This is very beneficial because once there is a government bond curve in local currency, there is a benchmark for mortgage rates, there is a benchmark for corporate bonds, you can get the credit markets working and people can borrow to invest and so on," says Eerdmans.

"A country needs to be a bit more advanced to have a local bond market but then that helps the country to advance more so it's kind of a virtuous circle."

There is still plenty of dollar-denominated debt in the emerging markets space, particularly issued by economies with less advanced bond markets. The sector saw something of a resurgence in the wake of the global credit crisis as dollar debt became a lot cheaper but bond experts were confident local currency debt would regain its place in the spotlight once the crisis passed.

According to Eerdmans, local currency emerging markets debt is preferable to the dollar-denominated variety for a number of reasons, starting with the prospect of higher returns. Local currency debt offers two bites of the cherry with returns potentially generated from the currency element as well as from yield compression – a fall in yields means the capital value of the bond has risen.

"If you buy dollar bonds you're tied into the dollar so you just get the yield compression part of the equation," Eerdmans explains. "Secondly, you can buy a better quality of bond as the average rating of the local debt market is around BBB whereas the average rating of the dollar debt market is BB. So you buy into the higher-quality markets but you still receive broadly a similar yield, which compensates you for the currency risk."

Other factors in favour of local currency debt, he adds, are better diversity of returns; better long-term risk-return characteristics; the fact that liquidity is generally better in local debt; the fact that the US dollar is not quite as safe a bet as it once was; and the better opportunities for generating outperformance. More generally, bonds can help reduce the volatility of a portfolio because bond markets react differently to a slower growth environment. "That is particularly the case with local debt because you get returns from those two sides," says Eerdmans.

"Bonds behave a little differently from currencies in different economic cycles with currencies benefiting a lot from high growth and money flows while the bonds themselves react more to inflation. What we saw in 2008 was that, on average, the bond market still posted a return of 5% whereas the currency markets on average were down about 10%. Overall, therefore, the asset class was down 5% but of course that was a lot better than most other markets. That balance between bonds and currencies also provides some stability in debt markets and helps keep volatility a bit lower."

2.16   DECISIONS, DECISIONS

Another choice facing investors is between actively-managed funds and so-called "passive" investments. These passive investments, such as exchange-trade funds or "ETFs", will track indices for a single market such as Brazil's Bovespa index, or a broader index such as the MSCI Emerging Markets index.

Offering generalized exposure to the largest and most liquid stocks in each country, ETFs have the advantage of being readily tradable and cheap to buy. However, with this sort of approach, investors rather by definition only gain exposure to the larger stocks that have performed very well up to that point and so may only be accessing companies that have already enjoyed their best growth rather than those whose glory days have yet to come.

Furthermore, the largest emerging markets companies, which will dominate their local markets, can be very international in scope as opposed to domestically focused. As a result, there is a growing body of opinion that their investors are taking on all the risk of an emerging markets company – for example, political or corporate governance risk – but missing out on potential growth drivers such as increasing consumer demand in their home economy.

One final consideration when putting money into a collective investment is whether to do so through a single lump sum or to "drip-feed" a series of smaller payments – usually on a monthly basis. Due to their potential for extreme movements in both directions, emerging markets funds do lend themselves to this sort of regular saving as it allows you gradually to build up a level of exposure while at the same time helping to bypass any concerns about trying to enter the market at the "right" time – something that, in any event, most professional investors would privately concede involves far more luck than judgement.

2.17   CONCLUSION

The world's emerging markets represent an exciting investment opportunity but since their many attractions are balanced by just as many reasons for care, this opportunity is not one to be taken lightly. Be aware that there are times when the value of your investment will fluctuate dramatically and so, ideally, try to take a long-term view of at least 10 years.

Do look to invest in emerging markets as part of a balanced portfolio and, within that allocation, consider a range of different regions and asset classes in order to spread risk. Collective investments can be a practical way of achieving this goal and also introduce the option to "drip-feed" money through regular savings. Finally, never lose sight of the fact that emerging markets are a higher-risk investment, so do not invest money you cannot afford to lose.

3

New Schools of Thought – Hype or Reality?

3.1 INTRODUCTION

The last chapter sought to draw a distinction between two types of arguments that are put forward as part of the case for investing in emerging markets. The first type involves ideas that feel almost so intuitive one is tempted to accept them without question, while the second type can seem at best less intuitive and at worst contrived.

You may find some of the following arguments for investing in emerging markets – and one against – more persuasive than others but generally one can find oneself thinking: "Well, OK – but, even if that's true, there are other arguments that are intrinsically more convincing."

3.2 ARGUMENT 1: DECOUPLING

In the pre-crunch enthusiasm for emerging markets, the now-familiar concept of decoupling emerged. This idea suggested emerging markets could forge their own growth path, separate from that of the developed markets on the back of intra-emerging market trade. The concept lost a good deal of credibility in the credit crunch when global equity, bond and commodity markets sold off simultaneously but the rapid bounce-back and economic resilience of emerging markets once again brought it to the fore. Does decoupling have real relevance for emerging markets investors?

The problem with the concept is that the world is increasingly interconnected – globalization and the free movement of capital mean few countries can exist in an economic vacuum. There is also the issue of the inherent weakness of any export-led economy.

After the Asian financial crisis of 1997, Asian nations realized they had to build up foreign exchange reserves to decrease the vulnerability of their economies to exchange rate shocks and the vagaries of capital market sentiment. As such, they put incentives in place to ensure their countries built a strong export base. In the same way, many of the Eastern European countries built their economies on the back of being a cheap manufacturing base for the rest of Europe, particularly in the car industry.

Of course, the problem with an export-led economy is that it is only as good as the countries to which it is exporting. For many, their biggest export partners were the US, Western Europe and Japan, which – after all – remain the largest economies in the world but the credit crunch put this dependency into sharp relief.

Exports slumped, particularly in those countries that specialized in vulnerable sectors such as car parts, including Thailand, the Czech Republic and Hungary, or sophisticated electronics, such as Taiwan and South Korea. Following on from this slump in exports came a similar drop in GDP, with many export-dependent countries seeing a double-digit annualized drop in GDP in the first quarter of 2008.

Asset prices slumped, as did global stock markets, and the anti-decoupling camp was in the ascendancy. It was ridiculous, they said, to think you could decouple from the world's largest economies. The US, Europe and Japan still provided the largest markets for almost all goods – from oil to clothing to cars – and it was naïve to imagine emerging markets growth could transcend their weakness.

However, the recovery has reignited the debate. Economists – in particularly Jim O'Neill, chief economist at Goldman Sachs – have argued that the swift bounce-back for many emerging markets in the face of ongoing weakness in the US shows they have in fact decoupled.

Although globalization means there can never be such a thing as full decoupling, China has proved it has the capacity for independent growth and therefore can provide a new export destination for many countries. Indeed, it has been powerful enough to pick up the slack left by developed nations. The bounce-back in Thai and Taiwanese growth has been led by exports to China, for example. There is also increasing evidence of the growth of intra-emerging market trade, with Latin America's Mercosur, the so-called "common market of the South", having as its ultimate aim a continent-wide free-trade area.

The strength provided by their reserves has also been part of the decoupling process for the emerging markets. China and many other emerging market countries were not forced to borrow to generate their various stimulus packages as has been the case in the UK or the US.

In fact, many could afford their stimulus packages a number of times over. The decline in exports didn't matter because they could spend on infrastructure to bridge the gap. This helped their economies continue to grow as Western markets weakened, providing at least a temporary element of decoupling.

There are also some emerging market countries that are not dependent on exports and can therefore generate their own internal economic momentum, with India and, to a certain extent, Brazil, falling into this camp. "Even though stock markets behaved badly, there was evidence of decoupling through the financial crisis," says Chris Palmer, head of emerging markets at Gartmore.

"In general, emerging economies didn't need to bail out their banks. The only places where that happened were those that were trying to emulate Western banking systems – such as Eastern Europe, which was trying to converge with Western banking standards.

"But there are countries with different regulatory regimes, different saving systems and different types of pension funds where there has been a degree of decoupling. For example, in China, the stock market fell a long way, but after that drop, it still had a banking system that could begin lending again."

In presenting some of the evidence in favour of decoupling, it is worth sounding a note of caution. Yes, China, India, Brazil and other emerging markets have shown they can forge their own economic path, but much of this has come from stimulus packages, which in turn have come from reserves. They have the economic firepower to do this for a while but cannot do so indefinitely. At some point, domestic demand will have to emerge in these countries to pick up the slack.

The emergence of a domestic demand story is discussed widely elsewhere in this book and ultimately seems to be on track – for example, China and India's retail sales are rising fast and indeed, according to the National Bureau of Statistics, China's retail sales grew 16.9% in 2009. But it remains far from assured and only when strong evidence of domestic demand emerges can it truly be said that emerging markets can grow irrespective of the situation in the developed world. At that point, it becomes less about whether emerging markets have decoupled and to what extent, and more about whether they can remain so.

At first glance, world stock markets are not an obvious place to look for evidence of decoupling and certainly correlation was much in evidence during the sell-off in late 2008. Emerging market indices tracked and, in many cases, exceeded the falls in developed markets, suggesting that whether decoupling existed in the wider economy or not, it would make no difference for investors.

But is this really true? In the sell-off, global investors were faced with a liquidity crunch. They had to sell something and so they sold where there was liquidity and where they had made money. "When you go into a sudden bear market, everything correlates," says Robin Griffiths, technical strategist at Cazenove Capital Management. "Investors only have to need cash and even previously non-correlated assets suddenly correlate. It is on the rebound that the non-correlation creeps back in."

Palmer agrees there may be a breakdown in correlation between emerging and developed markets over the longer term, adding true decoupling comes through "alpha" – the performance of stocks over and above the market – rather than "beta" – the performance of the market. This has been evident in the significant outperformance of emerging markets over developed markets since the turn of the century.

Taking the UK and China as an illustration, by the end of 2009, the FTSE 100 index still stood some 25% below its level on 1 January 2000 and, while this picture is slightly distorted by the bursting of the tech bubble, over the same period the Hang Seng rose 44%, and the Shanghai 180 A Shares market rose 140%. This looks suspiciously like decoupling.

Brazil versus Argentina

In the debate over whether decoupling is theoretically possible, the examples of Brazil and Argentina show how policy decisions can bring about the success of one country and the failure of another from a similar starting point.

Brazil risked domestic food shortages and potential inflation in becoming a major commodities supplier to China, but its government decided that was a risk worth taking. Argentina, on the other hand, did not want to risk its domestic consumers paying more for locally produced commodities or the inflation generated by high demand from Asia and closed its markets. The long-term outcome is not yet clear, but the relative economic performance and market reaction have spoken volumes in the shorter term about the success of the Brazilian approach.

3.3   ARGUMENT 2: THE COMMODITIES SUPERCYCLE

The idea of a commodities "supercycle" has plenty of noteworthy champions. Jim Rogers, co-founder of the Quantum fund with George Soros, is such a bull on China that his two small daughters have a Chinese governess and speak fluent Mandarin. He believes the strength of China will create a multi-year bull market for commodities. Meanwhile Graham Birch, BlackRock's commodities guru, believes the supercycle has at least another decade left to run.

Why is this important? At a very simplistic level, emerging markets may be divided into commodity consumers, such as China and India, and commodity producers, such as Brazil and Russia. If China, in particular, continues its buoyant demand for commodities, that pushes up prices, which spells good news for Brazil, Russia and the other commodity-producing countries. As their citizens grow wealthier, they demand more goods and a virtuous circle begins. The problem for the likes of China, however, is that the commodities needed to industrialize become more expensive – everyone knows they are needed.

The Birch/Rogers argument is a straightforward one of supply and demand. Rogers says that in the 1980s and 1990s mining and resources companies invested little in uncovering new sources of supply. He points out there has been no giant oilfield discovery for 40 years and only one lead mine found in 25 years. Inventories are the lowest they have been in a decade and he believes it will be at least 10 years before new production comes online. Until it does, supply and demand remain out of kilter and the supercycle in commodities continues.

There is also the question of the long-term weakness of the dollar. As the global financial crisis receded, the US government was left over-indebted and facing the prospect of having to raise taxes and cut spending. Bradley George, head of the global commodities and resources team at Investec, says this is likely to lead people to "real" assets that are not dependent on the strength of developed market governments. This is partly the reason behind the relative strength of gold, with the gold price continuing to hit new peaks as investors see it as the "ultimate currency".

Nevertheless, the supercycle argument was derailed – at least temporarily – by the global downturn. Oil slid from a high of $147 a barrel in July 2008 to just $38 in January 2009 while the Comex High Grade Copper futures index fell two-thirds from 395 in June 2008 to 130 in

December 2008. These sorts of falls were seen across a wide variety of commodities and, to date, few have recovered their previous highs. Mining equities led global stock markets up in 2009 but remained well off their peak prices.

Before the credit crisis, agricultural commodities had become the latest "can't fail" investment trend. The confluence of a growing global population, rising wealth in emerging markets and a decreased supply of agricultural land through erratic weather patterns and the preponderance of biofuels was set to push prices sky high. This did happen – briefly – but agricultural commodities were sold off during the crisis and remained sold off. Wheat, for example, peaked at 1191 in March 2008 and continued to fall, only bottoming out in September 2009 at 441.

So has the credit crunch exposed the idea of a commodities supercycle as flawed? On the demand side, according to Investec, China was responsible for just over 40% of global commodities consumption in 2009. What is more, its share of this consumption has increased as developed market consumption has fallen – for example, in 2008 China accounted for 28% of copper demand and 52% of iron ore demand; in 2009 those figures were 40% and 75% respectively.

The trouble is, the US and Europe are also extremely important buyers of commodities. In the credit crisis, they ran inventories down, which created enormous selling pressure. Given the amount of "hot" money in the sector, it only needs a small change in sentiment to create a relatively large fall in prices. In the longer term, of course, developed market demand should normalize, but this is by no means assured and remains a risk to the commodities supercycle argument.

Equally, the supercycle argument relies on the ongoing strength of China, which is likely but not certain. It also depends on China industrializing in the way people expect – in other words, in a resource-intensive way, rather than finding alternative technologies. Coal is a good example of this latter point. The popular theory has been that coal prices would rise and rise because supply is contracting, but – as Credit Agricole argues in its *End of the Commodities Supercycle* research – climate change concerns and technical progress may reduce the use of fossil fuels for electricity. Coal consumption may decline while resources are still plentiful.

The demand picture in China is also not entirely clear and it may not be the case that it is buying commodities, using them and then buying more. There is evidence, according to BlackRock, that Chinese companies may be buying copper and iron and stockpiling. Perverse though it sounds, the communist Chinese government has proved itself a canny capitalist and it would be surprising if it did not do something to insulate itself against rising prices. Stockpiling would be a logical solution to reduce its vulnerability. If so, this also undermines the demand side of the supercycle argument.

On the supply side, it all depends on individual countries being able to meet demand. In Mexico, for example, with its oilfields nearing maturity and no new sources of supply in the offing, oil may cease to be a revenue generator. Yet, for all that there are relatively few new sources of supply, there is some evidence the supply side is not as anaemic as the supercycle supporters suggest. For example, according to Investec, in 2009 Saudi Arabia was holding 4 million barrels a day off the market, at a cost of some $100 bn a year – 25% of its GDP.

The supply side for oil and, to a lesser extent, other commodities looks to be reinforcing. In many cases extra supply has not come on line because it hasn't needed to. There are oilfields to tap, but they are more expensive and therefore companies want to see higher oil prices before they make a financial commitment.

There is also the ongoing problem that commodities markets attract a lot of speculators. Investors will trade on margin in the futures market, which naturally drives up the price. This may continue to happen, but not if the future looks less assured. Up to the crash in 2008, the commodities boom was a "fact" and therefore self-perpetuating.

The speculators will have to be as convinced as those who buy into the fundamentals but commodities seldom trade at what would be deemed "fair value", leaving the price more difficult to predict. "Although we believe the outlook for commodities remains good, credit constraints mean we are not likely to see a return of the profligate speculation we saw in commodity markets in 2007 and 2008," says Palmer at Gartmore.

Finally there is the issue of inflation versus deflation. Commodities help create inflation and therefore also protect against it. Many expect that inflation is the logical outcome to the amount of money that has been pumped into the global economy – in which case commodities are likely to attract more international capital.

"The demand is there but the demand will be reduced," says Khiem Do, head of Asia multi-asset at Baring Asset Management. "Russia is slowing down, the Middle East is slowing down, Latin America is slowing down somewhat, India is slowing down. Obviously the supercycle concept has to be reduced because the momentum is slowing.

"Supply is the key and it's very difficult to find new supply examples of these hard commodities. As for soft commodities, industrialization means there is less land available for agricultural purposes. So I'm not going to mock people who talk about supercycles – what they say is fundamentally correct but within that there are cycles, like everything else."

Ultimately, the long-term demand for commodities looks relatively secure, though there are short-term issues. Whether that will translate into prices reaching the highs they achieved in 2008 is a different matter – the speculators will have to remain convinced that this is the trade to be in.

The outlook for the supply side is less straightforward. There has certainly been underinvestment in new supply but higher prices may spur that investment because it then becomes economically viable. There may well be a commodities supercycle, but it is by no means clear-cut.

3.4   ARGUMENT 3: SOVEREIGN WEALTH FUNDS WILL TAKE OVER THE WORLD

State-owned investment funds – better known as "sovereign wealth funds" – have attracted plenty of comment since they first appeared on the world stage. They are the behemoths of global markets, using their financial clout to alter the direction of stocks, gobble up companies and gain political traction beyond their home territories.

As the majority of these funds are controlled by emerging market governments, this has reinforced the idea that power is shifting in that direction. But how influential are sovereign wealth funds really and do they exert as much control as some politicians and financial commentators have argued?

It is easy to see why sovereign wealth funds make people uneasy. Their size alone ensures them influence on the global economic stage. Some such funds have existed since the 1950s, but much of the cash generated as a result of the growth of China and resulting commodities boom has found its way into these funds, giving them far greater economic firepower and thus much higher profiles.

Estimates from State Street Global Advisers at the end of 2009 put the amount invested in sovereign wealth funds at more than $3 tn, with the biggest funds tending to be fed by oil wealth, including the largest of them all – the $625 bn Abu Dhabi Investment Authority.

They have also been involved in some high-profile deals – for example, the Qatar Investment Authority bid for Sainsbury's in the UK in 2007, though ultimately withdrew – and have provided "white knight" cash to many failing Western institutions, including Barclays, Credit Suisse and Porsche. They are also significant holders of US Treasuries and oil investments.

Partly, this is by necessity. There are a limited number of places with sufficient liquidity for this type of cash to be invested. Initially it aroused the protectionist heckles of Western governments, who feared sovereign wealth funds could abuse companies and markets while having little accountability to regulators, shareholders or voters. But their contribution to the bailout of Western institutions was much appreciated and governments were forced to curb their initial reservations.

Part of the power of sovereign wealth funds stems from the length of their investment time horizon. Many have no agenda beyond long-term cash generation – in contrast with other institutional investors such as pension funds, which have to meet income requirements at a set point in the future – and this gives them useful flexibility when investing.

To date there has been little mischief-making by sovereign wealth funds. Generally, they have recognized they need full and unrestricted access to capital markets and, as such, are not keen to rock the boat too much. However, many have come under domestic pressure after the credit crunch left them nursing significant losses. In some cases this has led to a new resolve to increase activism to generate better returns.

Clearly this influence could work for good or for bad. After all, emerging market sovereign wealth funds may choose to follow the lead of Norges Bank Investment Management, the $47 bn fund set up to manage Norway's oil wealth, which believes sustainability issues represent some of the greatest long-term threats to the companies in which it invests. As such, it has an extensive programme of engagement with its underlying companies, examining their strategy on water, child labour and other sustainability issues.

But what if the opposite were true? Could sovereign wealth funds use their influence for less altruistic goals after all? It is understandable these funds want to ensure their investments are better protected after the recent failure of financial regulation although it would be surprising if countries as disparate as Russia, the United Arab Emirates and Norway teamed up to overthrow the capital markets' status quo.

Still, Western economies have left themselves vulnerable by over-borrowing – relying on Asian governments to back their sovereign bond issuance, for example – and can hardly blame sovereign wealth funds if they no longer want to invest or want more say in how their assets are run.

In general sovereign wealth funds have used their clout to protect internal interests rather than exert dominance globally although it became increasingly clear throughout the credit crunch that their funds and other government reserves have been vital for the governments that control them.

They have allowed such governments flexibility in terms of monetary and fiscal policy and they have allowed them to stimulate their economies without imposing a vast debt burden on future generations. They were, in short, crucial in protecting emerging market economies against the global slowdown. Indeed, some countries have had sufficiently strong reserves not to have had to call upon their sovereign wealth fund at all – an unimaginable luxury to many developed economies.

There are clear signs sovereign wealth funds are working together, but this is apparently being done in a rational and ethical way. The Santiago Principles, the generally accepted principles and practices for sovereign wealth funds, cover three main strands – the legal structure of the fund and its relationship with the sponsoring state; institutional structure and governance mechanisms; and investment and risk management frameworks. While the principles are a voluntary code, they propose greater transparency in terms of the purposes of a fund, its sources of funding and investment activities.

State Street has suggested sovereign wealth funds may also forge alliances with other institutional investors to ensure their interests are fully met. The group also suggests that some sovereign wealth funds are backing certain companies in order to gain access to proprietary information and technology that can be used in their home countries to boost economic development. This "reward for investment" is seen as helping to justify the investment to stakeholders.

None of this is to suggest that sovereign wealth funds are without problems of their own. A lot of their wealth was built up on the back of high oil prices and with oil prices well off their peak, their income has been eroded and with it their investment flexibility. Furthermore, some are facing a considerable domestic backlash about their actions during the credit crunch.

Although there is increased recognition between international capital markets and sovereign wealth funds that the two sides need each other, the funds are likely to become more assertive in future, which could cause friction down the line. At the very least, the credit crunch has demonstrated the power of sovereign wealth funds and they will want to ensure they are able to take better care of their investments in future.

3.5   ARGUMENT 4: THE EAST IS IN THE ASCENDANCY WHILE THE WEST IS IN DECLINE

Received wisdom now suggests the West is in permanent decline, while the East – particularly China – will be the future engine of world growth. The argument goes that Western economies have been left vulnerable by the freewheeling capitalism that once made them powerful. Their banks, citizens, corporations and governments are weighed down by debt and real economic growth is likely to become a distant memory.

In contrast, Eastern economies are in fine shape. Previous crises have ensured they have learned the lessons of excessive debt, their economies have recovered quickly, they have healthy current account surpluses with which to shore up their economies and their citizens are on the cusp of embracing consumer spending. The transfer of power looks assured – right?

There is plenty to support this argument. Western economies are now in the worst shape they have been in for many years. After hundreds of billions of dollars worth of stimulus was injected to prevent a complete collapse in the banking system and to resurrect growth, Western economies finally began to expand again in the third quarter of 2009. The US reported GDP growth of 3.5% between July and September with the eurozone up 0.4% over the same period. Of course, it was by no means universal, and the UK lagged other markets in emerging from recession.

Even though the recession ended for the majority of Western countries in the final few months of 2009, the outlook – certainly for the Anglo-Saxon economies such as the UK – is bleak. The figures are well known, but no less staggering for that. UK public sector borrowing was set to be approximately £165 bn in 2010 and only slightly lower in 2011, according to the British Chambers of Commerce. Savings rates have been near zero, and consumer debt levels vast. Western economies are driven substantially by consumer spending, so the widespread deleveraging and higher taxes that are likely to characterize the fallout from the crisis will impact them disproportionately.

The large economies of the eurozone, such as France and Germany, may fare better, having avoided the chronic consumer debt problems, housing bust and spending binge, but growth is still likely to be anaemic. Job losses will exert further downward pressure on asset values and growth.

High oil and commodity prices have also played their part. High demand in China pushed up prices for Western consumers. It could even be argued that a desire to preserve the supply of oil has led the US into some costly wars.

Why are these countries so weak? Many economists would argue it is because every time a recession has loomed, central banks have slashed rates, thereby creating more debt and putting off the economic consequences. As this pain has been deferred, the difficult deleveraging process has been multiplied.

Furthermore, the banks have, in many cases, lent recklessly and without sufficient supervision. The sub-prime crisis began because of the over-availability of capital. It spread because the resulting bad loans were sold on, disseminating "toxic" assets through the system. This was very bad news indeed for the credibility of the major investment banks, which had already been weakened by their involvement in the technology boom and bust, the Enron collapse and other corporate finance scandals.

"Companies in the developed world could be facing permanent exclusion from emerging markets," says Palmer at Gartmore. "During the global downturn, companies in the developed world fell behind in terms of launching new products into emerging markets. Meanwhile, in countries such as Brazil and China, local companies took market share."

Of course, Western companies still have financial firepower, so they may once more look to buy companies to gain a foothold in emerging markets. Ultimately, however, faith in Western institutions has been severely shaken. The central bankers look craven, governments look incompetent, citizens look greedy and companies look mismanaged.

In contrast, Asian countries – whether emerging economies such as Malaysia or the Philippines or more developed ones such as Singapore – appear to have learned their lessons from successive crises in the 1990s. They recognized their weakness lay in a lack of foreign reserves and grew their economies with a bias towards exports. They also recognized the problems of debt, particularly foreign denominated debt.

As such, the majority of Asian governments run with a current account surplus and large foreign exchange reserves. Estimates vary as to the extent of foreign exchange reserves, but most agree they were far better cushioned against any downturn than many developed economies. Russia, for example, is thought to have around $400 bn of reserves. It also has a $160 bn sovereign wealth fund while, for its part, China launched the China Investment Corporation in 2008 with about $200 bn.

These sovereign wealth funds have been an important part of that perception of a transfer of power and, as discussed above, the fear has been that they would use their economic might to buy influence. Until the credit crunch, they had been restrained, recognizing they had to ensure access to capital markets, which – to some extent – depended on the goodwill of Western institutions.

But they have come under pressure to be more activist and vigilant as many have seen huge losses from weak and/or poorly-run Western corporations. Having been the saviour of a number of Western companies during the credit crunch, it is possible that the experience has politicized many sovereign wealth funds into becoming exactly what the West has feared.

The Asian banks largely sidestepped the credit crunch and remained well capitalized and ready to lend as the economic environment improved. Furthermore, savings rates are high, GDP growth is robust and the lack of leverage means there is plenty of room for domestic consumption to grow.

The strength of the East has been in providing low-cost manufacturing (most obviously China), or services (most obviously India), to which Western companies could outsource and these levers to growth are still largely in place. Equally, as China and India urbanize and industrialize, it creates demand for commodities, which in turn creates wealth for commodity-rich emerging markets such as Brazil and Russia.

As we shall see in the next chapter, this economic growth is trickling down to the citizens of all the BRIC countries, creating a nascent consumer economy that has built demand for consumer goods such as mobile phones, cars, white goods and clothing.

Most emerging markets also have a better demographic picture than developed markets. India is perhaps the best of all, boasting around 25% of the world's under-25s, with 60% of the population below 30. This creates a vast group of potential consumers, which should support economic growth for many years.

Growth is also likely to be generated by infrastructure development. The Indian government, for example, has earmarked $400 bn to $450 bn for infrastructure development, which will include power, ports, roads and telecoms, and China, Russia and Brazil are planning similarly ambitious infrastructure projects. This is an area that has traditionally been seen as an Achilles' heel for emerging markets as creaking infrastructure hampered progress, but now it is just another investment opportunity.

In examining whether the decline of the West and the rise of the East are likely to become a permanent economic reality, it is necessary to judge whether all these factors are likely to remain in place. Emerging markets are not without their problems. Political instability remains a risk and, while many emerging markets have had stable regimes in place for some time, history suggests things can change very quickly.

For example, Venezuela in the 1970s looked as if it would be one of the emerging market success stories on the back of abundant oil reserves, but unhelpful politics has meant it has failed to develop. The same is largely true with Argentina. Many emerging market companies are still in development and their growth could be derailed.

Furthermore, while corporate governance in the West has been shown to be flawed and Asian corporate governance has improved, some emerging markets still have weak shareholder protection and a marked lack of transparency – with the Russian market in particular dogged by these issues.

Of course, the West may not prove to be as weak as some commentators expect. The US economy has shown itself to be resilient over time – not least because its labour laws are flexible and it is easy to set up businesses there. If the economy was thought to be too focused on finance, for example, it would not take long to switch that emphasis. Education and training are strong and the West is still home to world-class companies.

According to Peter Kirkman, manager of the J.P. Morgan Global Consumer Trends fund, Western markets may still be beneficiaries of the growth in the East. "Whenever you buy into emerging market consumption, you end up with a Western brand – Samsung, Hyundai, are the exceptions," he explains. "Asian consumers tend to buy luxury goods and sales of luxury goods doubled from 2004 to 2009." So Western companies still have a lure for Asian consumers while some established giants such as Unilever or Rio Tinto are significantly exposed to emerging market growth.

The shift in economic power from West to East is real and tangible. Harnessing this trend is important for long-term investment, particularly pensions, and many global fund managers are now building it into their portfolios. The West may well rise again from this gloom, but it has a battle ahead to retain its economic supremacy. It may be sensible to hedge your bets.

3.6 ARGUMENT 5: THE SUCCESS OF EMERGING MARKETS IS ASSURED

It is tempting to suggest the ultimate dominance of emerging markets is assured and that the economic world order will do a complete about-turn, leaving the US, Europe and Japan mired in debt and permanently chastened. While this argument has a number of factors to support it, it is important to recognize that very few emerging markets are likely to see a smooth path to industrialization and developed world status.

As we have just seen, the ascendancy of East over West has the potential to become the stuff of cliché. Everyone knows that on current growth rates China is set to overtake the US as the world's largest economy within 20 years, with Brazil and India hot on its heels. These are the new economic superpowers, the keepers of the global purse strings.

From the current perspective, this is undoubtedly the most likely scenario, but economics is perfectly capable of playing tricks. Financial modellers had the credit crunch down as a one in a million chance while, back in the 1980s, Japan was going to rule the world. So what could derail the success of emerging markets?

As much of the growth story centres on China, it is worth examining the risks to its economic growth story. Of course it has a lot in its favour, but its route to a fully industrialized economy is unlikely to be without speed-bumps. Much is premised on its smooth transition to a service-based economy with buoyant consumer demand, but a number of things have to happen before this is fully realized.

First, there has to be the effective implementation of a welfare state. People in China – and across Asia – hold onto their cash because to date there has been no provision for them in sickness, joblessness or old age. Much of the stimulus has centred on creating health care programmes so that people feel secure enough to spend some of their savings, thereby creating a service-led domestic economy that is less reliant on exports.

The chances are that this will happen, although China only has to look East for an example of where it has not. In Japan, repeated economic stimulus, welfare programmes and low interest rates have failed to persuade people to part with their savings.

Other risks such as the demographic time-bomb brought about by the country's one-child policy and indeed the political time-bomb of its assumed path from one-party state to eventual democracy are discussed in the next chapter alongside the degree to which international investors are able to trust the data emerging from China.

Although the numbers do appear to chime with companies' experience of doing business in the country, it is not unheard of for communist governments to flatter economic figures to present a better front to the world. China's risks are the global economy's risks and if the Chinese growth trajectory fails, it will take down a lot of emerging markets with it, particularly the commodity-focused countries.

Political risk has not disappeared elsewhere in emerging markets. Countries such as Venezuela and Argentina demonstrate how poor government can swiftly erode the benefits of abundant natural resources. In the Corruption Perception index devised by Transparency International, the majority of emerging markets still fall squarely in the bottom half of the table. The index amalgamates 13 different expert and business surveys and gives a score out of 10 for 180 countries. To take one key example, Russia is ranked 146th – at around the same level as Zimbabwe.

When markets are riding high, it is tempting to overlook this type of risk. Economic success often dampens revolutionary fervour anyway, but weak politics can speedily undermine faith in government and institutions. International money flows are prone to flee countries at the first sign of trouble, so the problems can become self-perpetuating. Otherwise solid emerging markets such as Malaysia have seen international investors pull out on the back of an uncertain political situation.

Another recent example of this has been Russia. In 2008, the RTS index fell 80% from peak to trough as international capital fled the country on political grounds. Admittedly, there were fears of economic weakness as well, but the catalyst was the military conflict between Russia and Georgia, when Russia sent troops into Georgia saying it recognized the independence of Abkhazia and South Ossetia.

Corporate governance also remains weak in many emerging markets. Churchill once described Russian politics as like watching dogs fight under a carpet and BP's experience of its joint venture with TNK suggests it may hold a similar view. That episode saw unseemly wrangling about the appointment of a chief executive and infighting between the domestic oligarch shareholders and those from abroad.

Much of the weakness in the Russian market has centred on the government's propensity to pinch assets from corporations and any further instances of this sort of monkey business can only serve to deter international investors even more. Reporting and accounting standards are often weaker. Transparency can be poor. Many fund managers take a "whites-of-their-eyes" approach to all corporate management.

Developed markets are weakened and chastened and many of their institutions have been exposed as flawed, but – for the time being at least – it is still their world. The governance structures, trade accords and regulatory and accounting regimes are all moulded by developed markets.

Global institutions, such as the International Monetary Fund, all sing to their tune and developed markets still have their hands on much of the best technology. This does not just mean the insides of a Nintendo Wii but sophisticated agricultural and manufacturing technology. It would be premature to write off the developed world just yet.

Ultimately, the world of economics and finance always has the capacity to surprise and the consensus is so often wrong in ways that no-one can see at the time. The emerging markets story is strong, but it is by no means assured.

3.7 ARGUMENT 6: EMERGING MARKETS ARE FAR HIGHER RISK THAN DEVELOPED ECONOMIES

Emerging markets periodically go through phases where investors throw caution aside in pursuit of the white-hot growth available. To most people's minds, emerging markets tend to fall squarely at the "risky" end of global investment spectrum but is this necessarily true? While it is easy to look at the historic performance of emerging markets and decry them as volatile, past performance has typically been a weak indicator of future growth or risk. To what extent are the risks greater in emerging markets?

Technically speaking, risk is a difficult concept to pin down. Volatility is the standard measure of risk in markets, but even this is imperfect as it is a historic measure and therefore takes no account of the changing risk profile of a country's stock market. Equally, if something goes up very quickly, it is deemed to be as volatile – and therefore as risky – as something that goes down very quickly.

There is no question that emerging market stock markets have been more volatile than those of developed markets to date. International fund flows have been erratic, tending to inject huge quantities of cash when risk tolerance is at its highest, only to withdraw it promptly as it evaporates. But if emerging markets' strength continues alongside developed market weakness then international capital is likely to stick around for longer and volatility will reduce.

Much will depend, therefore, on the economic prospects for emerging markets. This is extensively discussed elsewhere in the book but, in general, emerging market countries have less personal, government and corporate debt, better demographics, stronger growth, better capitalized banks and large foreign exchange reserves on which to draw in times of trouble.

This is by no means universal, particularly among those countries that have been pushed towards convergence with the developed economy model, such as those in Eastern Europe, but it applies to the vast majority of Asia, much of South America and, still, parts of Eastern Europe.

This century has already seen developed economies aiming to "cure" two potential recessions through the mechanism of cutting rates – in 2002 and 2008. While this has made debt servicing easier, it has not got rid of the debt itself. Deleveraging was always going to have to happen at some point and there are signs that people are increasingly reining in spending, increasing their saving rates and starting the painful process of debt repayment. This is a good thing for the longer term, but it will constrain growth.

The UK, for example, also faces some systemic problems. The banking sector is, to all intents and purposes, bust – or very nearly so. Government borrowing has exceeded all records and the UK government has faced the real prospect of having its debt downgraded by the rating agencies, which would increase the amount it has to pay to borrow. Much of the economy relies on consumption by already indebted consumers and, while it is tempting to see this as a government problem, UK companies must still function in this environment. As such, from an objective point of view, the outlook for many emerging markets may seem less risky than for the UK.

Even if you wanted to, it is extremely difficult as an investor to separate out emerging market risk as many companies will operate in multiple locations. US, Japanese and European markets all have emerging market companies listed on their stock exchanges and these are a legitimate investment target for managers ostensibly charged with investing only in their domestic market.

West China Cement, for example, is listed in London and has cropped up in the portfolios of UK smaller companies managers. Meanwhile Antofagasta is one of the largest companies in the FTSE 100, yet is entirely focused on copper mining and rail network services in Chile, Bolivia and Peru.

According to Marcus Brookes, head of multi-manager at Cazenove Capital Management, managers of funds investing in the developed world are looking to gain exposure to emerging markets through this type of company. As such, an investor in a supposedly plain or "vanilla" UK or US equity fund may in fact have a significant degree of emerging market exposure – which of course may or may not work for them.

The real difference may come down to corporate governance. Stocks listed in the developed world may have emerging markets exposure, but they will be subject to developed-world accounting regimes and regulatory scrutiny. This was traditionally seen as an advantage, but it has become fashionable to suggest that the corporate governance regime in developed markets may not be what it was. Many recent high-profile corporate crises – most notably Enron, WorldCom and Lehman Brothers – have happened in developed markets.

Some emerging market corporate governance regimes remain second to none, though this tends to be in countries such as Hong Kong and Singapore rather than giants such as China and Russia. Although there have been weaknesses in the corporate governance regimes of some developed markets and the system is, without doubt, imperfect, for the most part shareholders have clearly stated rights, which is not always the case in emerging markets.

"It is a case of caveat emptor when buying in China," says Stuart Parks, manager of the Invesco Asian fund. "There is not much regulatory protection in place if a company decides to pull the wool over your eyes." With that in mind, one of the key things Parks looks for in a company is that he can trust the management and he meets them a number of times before he invests. "We question them closely and have to be convinced their interests are aligned with ours," he adds.

Angus Tulloch, head of emerging markets at First State Investments, notes that that many Asian companies are majority controlled by the state or by a powerful family. The family may have interests outside the company and may try to further those interests through the company, which may not be in the interests of minority shareholders, and this may also happen with the government.

In developed markets, shareholder registers tend to be open and it is possible to orchestrate shareholder action to get rid of management. In Asian companies, Tulloch says, investors are often stuck with the management they are given and therefore have to be sure their interests are aligned.

As ever, investors have to weigh everything up. The risks in emerging markets are undoubtedly less than they were while the developed economies certainly look shakier in the wake of the credit crunch, so there has been some convergence. Furthermore, the growth outlook for many emerging market economies appears more secure than for many of the developed markets.

Corporate governance also remains an issue for a number of emerging markets and some notable corporate failures in developed markets should not distract from that weakness. Investors should not be lulled into thinking emerging markets are without risks, but – particularly in the context of the new global economic environment – neither should they overestimate those risks.

3.8 CONCLUSION

Investors may tend towards a polarized view but there are plenty of aspects of the emerging markets space that are not so easily compartmentalized. From many angles, the advance of the emerging markets appears unstoppable while the global credit crisis has had a far more adverse effect on the West. Even so, when faced with someone telling them the asset class is a one-way ticket to riches, investors would do well to retain an element of scepticism and remember that, in investment, certainty is the rarest commodity of all.

4

The "BRIC" Economies

4.1 INTRODUCTION

Brazil, Russia, India and China, the four giants of the emerging markets universe, are so central to the outlook and prospects of the global economy that they have received the accolade of being granted their own acronym – "BRIC".

There is a line of thought – possibly apocryphal, certainly cynical – that the idea of grouping this quartet together came about as a result of turning a necessity into a virtue. The story goes that cost-cutting by Western investment banks in the 1990s led to many of them operating just a handful of local offices within the emerging markets – say, Beijing, Moscow, Mumbai and Sao Paolo – and the rest is history.

Be that as it may, full credit for the term "BRIC" goes to investment bank Goldman Sachs, which published its paper "Building better global economic BRICs" in November 2001 and indeed has maintained its position at the forefront of thinking on the subject ever since, thanks to a regular stream of analysis, including "How solid are the BRICs?" (November 2005) and "BRICs lead the global recovery" (May 2009).

The term may be universally used but it is by no means universally loved. Critics point, for example, to the disproportionate importance of China, even within this illustrious grouping, and also to the absence of other large emerging markets such as Mexico and South Korea. Or, as Jerome Booth, head of research at Ashmore Investment Management, puts it: "BRIC? What about 'Cement' – the Countries in the Emerging Markets Excluded by New Terminology?"

Such criticisms are not without foundation, particularly from an investment point of view – after all, with such exciting growth potential on the upside and daunting risk on the downside, why would anyone want to restrict themselves to just four markets, even if they are the four largest? That said, there are some interesting comparisons to be made between the four and that is why – with apologies to Booth and others who may feel similarly – they are considered together within this chapter.

4.2   OVERVIEW

Champions of the BRIC concept argue it is the most exciting idea in emerging markets for the simple reason that it focuses on the four countries that dominate the emerging markets universe. They are among the 10 largest countries in the world, both by land mass and population, and indeed between them they account for more than 40% of the world's population. Furthermore, all are jostling among the top dozen countries in the world as measured by gross domestic product.

According to the IMF's figures for 2008, the US lay way ahead of the pack on $14.4 tn followed by Japan on $4.9 tn and China on $4.3 tn. Brazil was in 8th place, Russia 11th and India 12th. Fast forward to 2050, courtesy of projections by Goldman Sachs, and the pecking order of the top seven is China, the US, India, Brazil, Russia, the UK and Japan with China now expected to surpass the US in 2027, rather than in 2041 as the bank had first predicted in its October 2003 paper, "Dreaming with BRICs – the path to 2050".

Interestingly, while Brazil has been the leading stock market performer in recent years, with India second, followed by China then Russia, none of the four has monopolized first – or fourth – place on a calendar-year basis. Thus in the seven years from 2002 to 2008, Brazil, China and Russia have featured first and last between two and four times each while India has always featured in second or third place, once more underlining the importance of a diversified portfolio.

What really excites professional investors about the BRIC grouping is the four countries' huge domestic markets, a factor that has not only helped them enjoy strong growth momentum over the last decade – and, their champions argue, will do so over the decades to come as well – but has also helped them weather the financial crisis better than many of the more developed economies.

These huge domestic markets also help differentiate the quartet from other emerging economies because a successful business model can be replicated many times domestically. As such, a Brazilian or Russian company, say, can grow to a significant size at home before taking the risk of venturing into foreign markets whereas a similar company in, for example, the Philippines or the Czech Republic would very quickly reach a size where it would need to go abroad if it wanted to grow further.

Forgive the broad brushstrokes for the time being – yes, China is still seen as the production base of the world and exports remain hugely important, while Russia found itself more buffeted by the financial crisis than its BRIC counterparts – but the size of the subject means that while it will always throw up similarities, they will not always be precise.

As it happens, some commentators have tried to simplify matters further, suggesting that between them the four countries embody two of the globe's most powerful economic themes – thus, while China and India are two of the world's strongest domestic demand growth stories, Brazil and Russia are both leading commodity exporters.

Certainly the BRIC concept involves two very populous countries that need constant and growing access to both hard and soft commodities thus allowing the other members of the grouping to profit over-proportionately in providing them and meaning the outlook for all four is increasingly interlinked.

Although, in themselves, such basic facts are undeniable, the idea as a whole rather crosses the line from the simplified to the simplistic. Suffice to say that the quartet are the flagships of the three main emerging markets regions of Asia, Emerging Europe and Latin America and their importance to global trade over the coming decades is hard to overstate – not least in the way they interact with each other.

"If you think about the four, I have more confidence about China and Brazil because I think they are both sustainable – different but sustainable," says Richard Titherington, chief investment officer and head of the emerging markets equity team at J.P. Morgan Asset Management.

"For their part, both Russia and India might be sustainable or they might be cyclical and might have just benefited from the bubble of the first decade of the millennium. Certainly there are no grounds to prove that India has fundamentally changed – the political system is still very difficult, it's still a very hard place to operate, it's still very hard to build things. It's better and it might well be that it is sustainably so but it's not certain."

Undeniably there are risks associated with the BRIC grouping – whether they stem from internal politics, geographical neighbours, an over-reliance on commodities and so on – and these will be dealt with in more detail shortly on a country-by-country basis but market watchers have been greatly encouraged by the growing interdependence between the four.

China's rapid industrialization has substantially shaped investment markets over the past five years. Its voracious demand for raw materials brought about the vast boom in commodities that has been one of the most important investment themes since the turn of the century. This commodities boom has also had a profound effect on other emerging markets, bringing wealth to resource-rich countries such as Brazil and Russia.

Thus, for example, China's appetite for commodities has seen the Chinese government provide multi-billion-dollar loans to oil companies in Brazil and Russia to develop oilfields and production capability and Chinese steel companies investing in Brazil to build up steel capacity there alongside local operations. Unsurprisingly, in view of the heavy increase seen in agricultural imports, China has also been increasing its investment in the agriculture sector and instances of BRIC interaction only look set to become more widespread in the coming years.

One question worth addressing at this point is why these countries have not risen to global prominence earlier – or at least, in the case of China and India, re-risen to prominence after dominating all but the final century of the last millennium. After all, all four have always been very large and populous. The answer most likely lies in the shift in social and, especially, economic thinking that has come about over the last two or three decades.

The collapse of the Soviet Union saw the whole concept of socialism and the communist economic structure, if not disappear, then at least no longer look so attractive and indeed, since China first moved to institute free market reforms in 1978, all four BRIC countries have significantly altered their economic policies.

This is perhaps most obviously seen with Russia because the whole economic system collapsed there, leading to 10 years of great volatility and disorder and this has only recently started to become a slightly more orderly process. But India and particularly China have also seen their economies open up and the introduction of market reforms has unleashed the huge potential that has been present in these countries for many years.

Naturally the process took a while as, for example, capital markets developed and growth rates normalized after some initial volatility but some commentators now go so far as to argue that a virtuous circle has been created for the BRIC countries, where their economies have been opened up and market reforms have been introduced so that they can play a full role in the global economy while attracting plenty of external investment.

What is not in doubt is the ambition of the people of Brazil, Russia, India and China to achieve a similar level of wealth to that of, for example, the US and Western Europe and this is very much helping to drive their economies forward.

4.3 CHINA

Despite the impression you might gain from some commentators, China is not the only story in emerging markets but it sure beats what comes second. "If investors do nothing else, they need to spend 10 minutes trying to understand a little bit about this country because the ramifications of what's occurring there are going to be enormous," says Graham French, manager of the M&G Global Basics fund. "There is simply no single question that any industrial leader, CEO, fund manager or investor needs to ask in the next 15 years more than 'What is going to be the effect of China?' "

4.3.1 A Brief Economic History

In 1976, as Mao Zedong's death brought an end to the Cultural Revolution and its soviet-style "planned economy" lay in ruins, few can have imagined China was about to embark on one of the most extraordinary periods of change in its remarkable history – one that would see it, within three decades, breathing down Japan's neck in a bid to be the world's second largest economy.

The architect of this change was Communist Party stalwart Deng Xiaoping, who came to power in 1978 and set about bringing about free market reforms and seeking to attract overseas investment. One of his first actions was to break up the agricultural communes that had been collectivized by Mao, and the move to give each household an individual plot of land to farm saw significant increases in crops such as grain.

Commerce was similarly liberalized with citizens allowed to set up a business rather than be employed by the state. In 1990 Deng reopened the Shanghai Stock Exchange that Mao had closed in 1949 and the ensuing decades saw the privatization of a number of state-owned enterprises as well as the creation of many private companies.

Another Deng initiative that contributed towards China's boom involved the creation of so-called "special economic zones", where foreign companies could invest in order to take advantage of lower labour and production costs.

Foreign direct investment into China stuttered in 1989 as Western and Japanese companies withheld capital in the wake of the brutal suppression of the student-led pro-democracy demonstrations in Tiananmen Square in June. Nevertheless, according to the Ministry of Commerce of the People's Republic of China, external investment had grown to $11 bn in 1992 and, in the latter half of the 1990s, hovered between $40 bn and $45 bn per year.

Overseas investment surged again both in the run-up to and aftermath of China's accession to the World Trade Organization in December 2001, leading to the country becoming the most popular destination in the world for foreign direct investment in 2003. From 2005, foreign direct investment levels grew each year to peak in 2008 at $92.4 bn.

Deng died in February 1997, just months before sovereignty of Hong Kong was transferred from Britain to China on 1 July – a move that saw the country gain convenient access to Western capital markets – but his reformist policies have been continued by his successors within the Communist Party.

In 2009, the US State Department noted that China was "firmly committed to economic reform and opening to the outside world. The Chinese leadership has identified reform of state industries, the establishment of a social safety net, reduction of the income gap, protection of the environment and development of clean energy as government priorities.

"Government strategies for achieving these goals include large-scale privatization of unprofitable state-owned enterprises, development of a pension system for workers, establishment of an effective and affordable health care system, building environmental requirements into cadre promotion criteria and increasing rural incomes to allow for a greater role for domestic demand in driving economic growth."

The government's commitment to driving – or at least, at the time, sustaining – growth was underlined in November 2008 when it announced a 4 tn yuan ($586 bn) stimulus package to be spent over the following two years in a bid to pull the country through the global recession.

"People keep getting China wrong," says French. "For 15 years, Western commentators have doubted China's ability to succeed. They have taken every opportunity to knock it and yet every single time it has recovered and boomed again. At the beginning of 2009, the daggers were out for China once again but, because the commentators are generally from Wall Street, they don't understand this place. They simply don't understand this place of 1.3 billion people – the equivalent of five Americas."

4.3.2   The Investment Case for China

The global financial crisis found China at something of a crossroads. The explosive growth enjoyed by the country in the 1990s and early part of this century was built on a number of factors – a huge pool of cheap labour, an inexpensive currency, an apparently insatiable appetite for consumption in the West and, just as important, easily available credit to fund that appetite.

That represented a heady cocktail for growth but the trouble with cocktails is they are all too often followed by hangovers. As China lost its cost advantages, its currency came under pressure and the West lost its appetite for consumption as the true scale of the credit crisis hit home, it became apparent the country was in dire need of a more stable growth model.

"China's export market has collapsed and only the unprecedented injection of four trillion yuan has sustained the country's economic growth," says Jing Ning, portfolio manager on the BlackRock Global Funds China fund. "China's pockets, although deep, are not infinite and a new driving force is needed if the economy is to grow."

As it happens, professional investors specializing in the region believe that China – never a country to do things by halves – has found not one but two driving forces in the shape of domestic consumption and higher productivity.

Of the two, the productivity argument is perhaps the less intuitive – at least to those conditioned to see China simply as the manufacturing centre of the world. "People have an image that it's just millions of Chinese making shoes and televisions for the West," says French.

"However, the reality is fundamentally different. China is increasingly moving away from an export-led economy to one that is internally focused because the domestic demand is now there. It's estimated somewhere in the region of three to four hundred million Chinese are now 'middle-class'. That means the middle class in China is already greater than that in the US and that's why people are getting China wrong again."

Certainly the traditional idea of a low-end factory in Guangdong churning out basic goods with no added value no longer works. "Instead, cost inflation and government regulation are pushing Chinese manufacturing further up the value chain," says Jing, pointing to research from CICC, China's first joint-venture investment bank, that shows research and development budgets in China doubled between 1996 and 2005.

"While research and development spending does not yet rival that in the US, as an example of increasing sophistication, recent years have seen the establishment of high-quality medical research centres in China," she continues. "This is backed by a significant expansion in the number of Chinese college graduates – from around 1 million a year in 2000 to 5 million a year in 2006.

"China's government has recognized any emerging market can easily replicate a low-cost export model and yet it has the ability to build some intellectual capital and move into more sophisticated areas. This is harder to replicate and ultimately leads to more stable growth."

According to Jerome Booth, head of research at Ashmore Investment Management, China is certainly well placed to pull off the move towards a consumption model of growth. "Frankly that's not difficult," he says. "When you have a savings/investment rate of 60%, which has been artificially boosted to that level only in the last few years, it's pretty straightforward to have more consumption.

"It involves more welfare provisions to reduce the precautionary savings motive and also higher incomes – particularly in rural areas, which is really what the Chinese are focused on. Over the next few years, I think we're going to see a very marked change.

"Fiscal policy in China is completely different to fiscal policy in, say, the US. In the developed world you're talking about countries that have to deliver massively and so fiscal policy in that context is a palliative. It's to reduce the pain in the short term and spread it out a bit and, because there will be a cost later on, the debate is all about how much to do and what the efficacy will be because the multiplier effect is arguably extremely small. That's very different to giving more money to a rural farmer in China, who then goes and buys a fridge or whatever, because the multiplier in that instance is huge."

One could also turn the reduction in cheap labour into an upside for China and, more particularly, the Chinese, as the natural consequence of that is an increase in wages and spending power. "China's workers are aspiring to middle-class comforts and increasingly have the means to gain them," says Jing. "Over the next 15 years, Goldman Sachs estimates the proportion of the Chinese population with incomes of more than $3000 a year will rise from less than 20% to almost 80%.

"This dollar figure is crucial as evidence suggests that, above $3500 a year, spending on the discretionary comforts of middle-class life – for example, a washing machine, an air conditioner or a small car – really takes off. All this should lead to investment opportunities among

Chinese companies as similar consumption booms elsewhere in the world have turned domestic companies into global brands."

China has experienced massive social and economic changes in the space of a generation. The lives of older people in China were shaped and driven by the vision of Mao, which meant there was no scope for individualism or entrepreneurialism. The focus was almost exclusively on saving money rather than investing it whereas the middle-aged segment of the population has become more accustomed to making money, buoyed by Deng's progressive assertion that "to get rich is glorious".

"This generation sowed the seeds of capitalism and entrepreneurialism, investing in their own properties and starting to indulge in spending on consumer goods," says Charlie Awdry, manager of Gartmore's China Opportunities fund.

"Ultimately, however, the future of China's prosperity is rooted in the younger generation. Healthy, educated, fashion-conscious and technologically aware, they aspire to a good life. Predominantly a generation of only-children, these young people have been the focal point of their parents' attentions, and the inexorable rise of this massive group of aspirational individuals will continue to drive China's development forwards and upwards."

While incomes in both rural and urban China are on the rise, it is the latter set that has caught Awdry's eye. "Urban incomes are rising much more steeply, fuelling demand for consumer goods such as property, cars, fashion and information technology," he says. "What is more, this demand is built on cash, not debt, and this presents a huge vista of opportunities to financial services firms looking to grow and develop their presence in key emerging markets."

4.3.3   Industrialization and Infrastructure

Nevertheless, the dynamics of China's rural population should not be ignored – if only because of the numbers making the transition from country to city. "China is a very complex country," says Alan Gibbs, manager of the Waverton Asia Pacific fund. "It is a society that only 20 or 30 years ago was 90% agrarian and has shifted, over a very short period of time, to more like 40% in the cities and 60% in the rural environment.

"With that comes a completely different set of expectations – both political and economic. It's a precarious thing if a political system in some way lags its economic progress – if it doesn't keep up, it could well be storing up problems."

That is because of the need to create jobs, housing and infrastructure for the tens of millions of people moving to the cities each year, which in turn requires a minimum level of growth rate to fund it. "The main threat to the status quo for the Communist Party would be social unrest but, so far, they have been able to prevent social unrest with adequate economic growth," says Michael Konstantinov, head of global emerging markets equities at Allianz Global Investors' RCM.

"It is always in the interests of the Communist Party to create a certain growth rate and so we were actually quite positive on China when its government was the first to introduce a significant programme of fiscal and monetary measures in November 2008. We were comfortable they would achieve a growth rate of 7% or 8% in 2009 – even at the beginning of the year when people were almost predicting the collapse of the economy."

An extra dimension to the issue of China's growing industrialization takes the form of what might be termed the semi-permanent migrant worker – someone who heads to the cities looking for work, stays when there are jobs and, when there are not or the job has finished, heads back to the heartlands.

"That can go either way," says Gibbs. "You could have 20 million people displaced and then potentially you've got a problem. On the other hand, those 20 million people will have some savings and they have probably kept in touch with where they've come from over the years. Europe's industrial revolution was in the 19th century but China's has been in the last 20 or 30 years so most of the migrant workers who are going back to the country and readjusting would still have a live memory of where they come from, so it is different.

"What's more, there have of course been technological advances and the power of the mobile telephone is huge. The migrant population are in constant touch. They may be back on the farm but they're continuously working out where the next opportunity is and where their friends are – and probably the opportunity of the moment is more likely to be in the construction and capital formation businesses than the export sector."

However you look at it, China is going through a massive development phase that takes in all the aspects of the virtuous circle of urbanization, industrialization and infrastructure spending discussed in Chapter 2. "China is rolling out into the middle part of the country the industrial-ization and modernization programmes that have been so successful in the Eastern cities," says Khiem Do, head of Asia multi-asset at Baring Asset Management.

"That is exactly what happened in America in the late 1800s and the early part of the last century – this time it's just faster and it funds itself. That is a great theme to invest in because it is a multi-year theme. When you embark on that sort of project, it's a 10- or 15-year theme – especially when you can self-fund it and you're not too scared about having to face the foreign funding question, in the way Russia and India are having to.

"If a country has a problem with funding its long-term projects, then that will definitely have a negative impact on its investments and so its growth will be confined to a sub-par profile. But the growth path of China will likely surpass everyone else in the BRIC grouping.

"It has very ambitious programmes to complete over the next three to five years and they include a lot of infrastructure development, including railways in the north, south, east and west as well as more roads. In addition, there's not enough water in the north-western part of China, where the minerals are, while in the south there's a good river system so you need to pump the water up to the north west and bring the minerals down south. Whichever way you look at it, you need a road system or a pipe system and so China is building more.

"It will take years to do it but not only can China fund it itself, government debt as a proportion of GDP is only in the high teens and that's a most enviable position to be in. I dislike that ratio because it's based on a flawed concept but the thing is, in times of trouble that counts. The banks always borrow short and lend long, which means it all comes down to confidence.

"This is not to say infrastructure projects are more profitable in China than the other BRIC countries – very possibly it's the other way around. But, after the credit crisis, the banks are so short of capital that even if you dangle a profit in front of them, they might say they are unable to invest in a particular country. They might already have enough exposure, say, to Russia and so they can't do more."

4.3.4 Country-specific Risks

A constant theme of investing in emerging markets is that reward is always accompanied by risk and since China offers many reasons for optimism these must be tempered with a similarly long catalogue of reasons to be careful, which range from the macroeconomic to the company-specific, taking in demographics, politics and the sustainability of natural resources along the way.

Starting with the short term, China's goal of continued growth with more stability is by no means a done deal. In the short term, the government is attempting a delicate balancing act as it strives to achieve annual economic growth near 8%, on the basis this figure is enough to absorb those 20 million or so new workers each year while maintaining social stability.

In late 2008 and the first half of 2009, the government only maintained this rate by way of a flood of cheap credit to offset the collapse in export demand – much of it funding speculation in stocks and property. "The possibility of short-term assets bubbles must therefore be acknowledged while economic overheating can also be a concern once inflationary pressures build," says Jing. "The government is wary of both, once again concerned over the effect on social stability and, although its near-term focus is on sustaining growth, it has talked down the market – with some signs of success."

On a longer-term basis, technical factors along the lines discussed in Chapter 2 should come into play with analysts at Macquarie Securities Group projecting China's representation in the MSCI All Country World index will grow from 2.3% in 2009 to 11.7% in 2013. "As it becomes a key player in the MSCI index, so it will play more and more of a part in investors' asset allocation decisions," says Jing.

Looking even further into the future brings the question of China's demographics into play. The country has recently enjoyed the benefits of the baby-boomers of the 1960s and 1970s entering the workforce but, over the longer term and not least as a consequence of its one-child policy, the country will have to contend with an ageing population and the burden that then places on those who are left working. "The government's major challenge here is to establish adequate social security systems over the next 30 years to ensure an ageing population is cared for without stymieing growth," says Jing.

China does enjoy the advantage of being free of legacy problems – that is to say, there is currently no pension system in place, so it does not have to address the sort of pension crisis that is plaguing the developed economies. Nevertheless, the situation cannot help but constrain the government's plans for the welfare state and corporate pension provision.

In addition to maintaining its extraordinary annual growth rates, avoiding asset bubbles and coping with some unusual demographics,

China's government will be keeping a wary eye on its neighbour North Korea as well as a watching brief on the state of its natural resources – not least water.

"It's not so much a domestic issue but industry uses a lot of water," says Do. "Industrialization is very water-intensive and there's a big water problem in parts of China. As a result of that, maybe agricultural production becomes a problem because rice production is also very water-intensive. Supply is the key with all natural resources – it's very hard to find new supply examples of hard commodities while, with soft commodities, industrialization means less land available for agricultural purposes."

And if all those were not enough headaches for the government, there is the eventual question of China one day becoming a democracy – and therefore what happens to the Communist Party itself. "They haven't made the transfer to democracy," says Angus Tulloch, head of emerging markets at First State Investments. "It will happen, but no political party gives up power voluntarily. It will probably happen after a leadership crisis and, from an investment point of view, it will be a good buying opportunity but it is very unlikely to happen peacefully."

There is certainly a degree of irony about a communist regime overseeing a massive period of growth and expansion and the biggest threat to all that being the regime's demise through the introduction of democracy. In the meantime, however, how "free" is China at present and what sort of investment risk is involved there?

"I've talked to Chinese friends about how they perceive freedom has developed over the last few decades under the Communist Party," says Konstantinov. "If, for instance, you look at travelling abroad or meeting other people or criticizing the government or creating new businesses, the scope for all that has tremendously increased and therefore, in terms of freedom, the country has come a long way.

"Obviously you still cannot officially criticize the Communist Party and there are still political prisoners but it's certainly not the situation of 20 or 30 years ago. There are a lot of different views on China but so far its policy of growth has certainly worked."

Back on the subject of growth, there is no doubting China's desire to achieve its annual targets but, over the years, some commentators have questioned how the country has managed to hit those numbers so consistently.

"It's always disputed whether China really grows at 8% or 9% or not," says Konstantinov. "It's difficult to verify the absolute number but, if you look at specific areas such as iron ore input or electricity production, these are numbers you cannot really manipulate. So there has been tremendous growth and probably therefore these figures of 8% or 9% are relatively realistic.

"If you look back at the industrialization phase of Japan or the rebuilding of Germany after the Second World War, it was not unprecedented to have growth rates of 7%, 8% or 9%, so why not in China? It's just that because it is such a huge country with so many people involved, it has a much larger impact on the global stage."

How much one can trust China's headline growth figures naturally leads on to how much one can trust the country's companies but, for his part, Do is reasonably phlegmatic. "Whereas the Indian market will always be an interesting one for professional investors because they respect capital, in the case of China, the respect for capital will only come slowly," he says.

"However, at least the risk of fraudulent cases in China is very small while the global investment banks have taught the management of China about cashflows, profits, return on equity and return on capital employed. So, over the last five years, they have done the right things – increased dividends, respect for cashflow and so on.

"Finally, unlike the Western world where stock options are all the rage, in China they are extremely limited. So the management of Chinese companies are not working to manipulate shares. If people try that, they can do really stupid things to get the shares up – and we know what the consequences of that are."

4.3.5   China's Stock Market

China actually boasts three independent stock exchanges – Hong Kong, Shanghai and Shenzhen – which, if combined, would overtake Tokyo as the largest in Asia. The three use a mini-alphabet of letters to denote the tradability and accessibility of various shares to domestic and foreign investors, with the most important categories being A, B and H.

A shares, which are denominated in local currency on the Shanghai and Shenzhen exchanges, are only available to domestic investors and a limited number of approved foreign investors. B shares, which are denominated in foreign currency and are on the two mainland exchanges, are far more thinly traded than A shares and indeed H shares, which are those of mainland Chinese companies listed in Hong Kong.

"Taken together, China is a huge capital market," says Konstantinov. "It has a lot of companies listed from many different industries and is very dynamic in terms of IPOs, so there are plenty of new companies coming on-stream. It is also a market where the state or a city or a region can be a major shareholder and therefore have a massive influence on individual companies so, while there is a thriving purely private sector too, that is a driver that makes China slightly different to some other markets."

While essentially broad-based, China's stock market is dominated by energy producers such as PetroChina, which was ranked second in the *Financial Times'* list of the world's largest companies in 2009, and Sinopec (24th), banks such as Industrial & Commercial Bank of China (4th), China Construction Bank (13th) and Bank of China (21st) and telecommunications groups, such as the Hong Kong-listed China Mobile (5th).

China Mobile is the largest telecommunications provider in the world while Industrial & Commercial Bank of China is the largest bank and this suggests investors need a different mindset when approaching the market. As an illustration, by the end of 2008, the latter had close to 400 000 employees, more than 16 000 branches, 190 million personal clients and 3.1 million corporate clients. "I'm always amazed by the numbers in China," says Konstantinov. "Whatever you know from other countries, you almost have to multiply by 10 to get a properly representative number for China."

The relative fortunes of China have been reflected in the performance of its stock markets. For example, the FTSE Xinhua B35 index, which monitors the largest stocks in the B shares universe, rose 282% in the three years to its peak in 2007 and then slumped 75% to its trough in 2008. The market then rebounded quickly with the prospect of global recovery.

Despite the strong rally of 2009, Jing does not believe Chinese equities were overpriced towards the end of the year, arguing instead that the equity market was trading around mid-cycle valuations. "China underperformed Taiwan, India, Thailand and Indonesia over 2009 and, on a return on equity-adjusted price-to-book basis, had been trading at a 20% discount to the region – its largest since 2003," she says.

"What's more, in our view, the massive expansion of credit in China is not a threat to the stability of the country's banking system, which is still owned by the government and backed by its reserves. Record loan growth has been accompanied by record growth in deposits, so ratios are not at dangerous levels and indeed loan growth should normalise to somewhere in the region of 15% to 17%, which is healthy for an economy growing at 8% to 9% a year."

Company focus: Tencent Holdings

Tencent Holdings, which is based in Shenzhen, South China, has grown into China's largest and most widely used Internet service portal since it was founded in November 1998. The company, which went public on the main board of the Hong Kong Stock Exchange in June 2004, describes its long-term development plan as "future, innovation and nationally oriented" and, to that end, more than three-fifths of its employees work in research and development.

According to data compiled by Bloomberg towards the end of 2009, Tencent's market value of $35 bn was more than double the $14.8 bn of Baidu, China's biggest search engine, as well as being ahead of the $30.3 bn capitalization of eBay, the US's most-visited e-commerce site.

China actually overtook the US as the world's largest Internet market in 2008 and, by June 2009, the number of registered users of Tencent's QQ Instant Messenger platform had reached 990 million while active users numbered 448 million. As such, the company offers businesses around the world the opportunity to reach a huge number of new consumers through online advertising.

4.3.6   Conclusion

Many emerging markets are coming out of the economic crisis with power, influence and capital and China is right in the vanguard. Looking ahead, the country will be impossible to ignore, whether that be in terms of investment, business or politics.

While the world's increasing interaction with China could lead to instances of friction as well as opportunities – as the managements of, for example, Google and Rio Tinto are well aware – the country looks set to present investors with significant chances to tap into real growth. "China is a classic emerging economy in that people are coming off the land and industrializing but it is happening in a hell of a hurry, which does bring risks," says Bob Yerbury, chief investment officer of Invesco Perpetual. "Nevertheless, it should be part of people's thinking and probably their portfolios too."

The idea that the ideogram or written Chinese word for crisis is made up of the ideograms for "danger" and "opportunity" runs its own risk of becoming something of a cliché on investing in China but it has some resonance with regard to the biggest threat – and opportunity – facing the country and indeed the whole of Asia over the coming years.

"Quite a substantial adjustment is going to have to take place," says Gibbs at Waverton Asia Pacific. "For the last 10 years at least, the whole business model of the region has been about coping with Western demand and providing manufactured goods for a Western world that has been prepared to borrow heavily to buy them – and a Western world that has been happy to help finance the capital formation process.

"Now, because of the credit crisis, that has come to an end – it was always going to end one day – and the emphasis is going to have to change. In particular, Eastern demand is going to have to grow at a rather faster rate to meet Eastern supply because, if that doesn't happen, then we're going to see, I would think, a very pronounced slowdown in global growth. That in a nutshell is Asia's – and China's – challenge."

4.4   INDIA

Few would deny the theoretical money-making opportunities offered by India with its billion-plus population, attractive investment themes such as consumer demand, outsourcing and infrastructure and a stock market that boasts some world-beating corporate names. However, investors in India have heard all this before and, despite the country's exciting poten-tial, the jury is still out. "India's performance before the financial crisis might have been a cyclical bubble," says Titherington at J.P. Morgan Asset Management. "On the other hand, it might effectively go down the same path as China."

4.4.1   A Brief Economic History

In common with the other BRIC countries, India began to take shape as a free market economy in the early 1990s. In 1991, following the prospect of the country defaulting on its debt obligations and a $1.8 bn bailout loan from the IMF that came hand-in-hand with a demand for reforms, the then government moved to liberalize the economy. Con-sequent reforms included the termination of various public monopolies as well as import, industrial and investment licensing, thereby enabling the automatic approval of foreign direct investment into many areas.

Since then the economy has moved slowly but surely towards a market-based system, with better economic policy and a revival of economic reforms after the start of this century helping to accelerate India's growth rate. According to the IMF, India's real GDP grew at an average rate of 5.6% per year in the 1990s, rising above 9% in each of 2005, 2006 and 2007.

Although real GDP growth fell to 7.3% in 2008 and was projected to be 5.4% in 2009, this can hardly be portrayed as a disaster given what was going on in the rest of the world at the time. If this period can be seen as a test of the relative strength or weakness of an economy, then India certainly passed.

One of the main reasons for that is the Indian economy is largely dependent on domestic demand. Some 85% of GDP comes from local production and the local market, with exports accounting for the rest. This helps to insulate the country from any global slowdown, meaning that – in direct contrast, say, to Russia – growth in India gets to be a little less volatile than most global markets.

The country's banking system also passed the tests provided by 2008 and 2009, because the toxic assets that proved such a problem for the Western economy were not an issue in India. Over this period, the percentage of non-performing loans in the Indian banking system as a proportion of assets was around 2%, a figure of which most Western banks could only dream.

On the whole, India's economy has improved steadily since 1991 regardless of which political party has been in power but the result of the general election that took place in April and May of 2009 may come to be seen as a watershed moment.

The key feature of the victory for the Congress Party-led United Progressive Alliance was that, to form a government, it would not have to rely on the Communist Party-led grouping, which had dragged its heels on reforms over the previous five years. Unlike in 2004 when the United Progressive Alliance won only 218 seats and had to court the support of the left, 2009 saw it just 10 shy of the 272 seats necessary for an overall parliamentary majority, a shortfall it could easily make up from minor parties and independent legislators.

"The decisive result offers hope that economic and governance reforms will now move forward, although the huge budget deficit will continue to present a major challenge, with public opposition to subsidy cuts remaining strong," says Hugh Young, managing director of Aberdeen Asset Management Asia. "However, the easing of foreign restrictions in the areas of banking, insurance and pensions now seems more likely, as does the privatization of selected state-owned enterprises."

4.4.2 The Investment Case for India

The foundations on which India's growth has been built – and which seem set to continue for the foreseeable future – can be divided into three aspects. One is infrastructure, an area in which the country has not obviously been a leader so far but in the wake of the 2009 election could be expected to do better; another is outsourcing, which in essence boils down to the country's export potential; and a third is the Indian consumer.

India's population is crucial to its investment outlook. It is the second most populous country in the world and, aside from China, the only one to boast more than a billion citizens. By the end of 2009, just over 17% of the world was living in India and the country grows, in population terms, by the equivalent of one Australia every year.

"This demographic profile is very positive and arguably one of the best in the world," says Anup Maheshwari, head of equities and corporate strategy at DSP BlackRock Investment Managers. "Some 60% of the population is under the age of 30, which means it has really yet to start working – thereby increasing its income over time and increasing consumption as well. This also ensures growth will not just be restricted to the next few years but can continue for the next couple of decades."

The Indian market is also highly underleveraged – that is to say, the Indian consumers are not used to borrowing in order to go shopping. As of 2009, the typical Indian household had five times more assets than liabilities. However, with a combination of falling interest rates and an increase in the availability of financial products, this trend is changing and thus a combination of higher incomes and more leverage should help to drive consumption.

Already market watchers are pointing to evidence to support this view. For example, in 2009 mobile phone subscriber growth in India was more than 50% and some 11 million new mobile phone users were subscribing to networks every month – in absolute terms, the largest number to be found anywhere in the world.

Meanwhile, 1.2 million passenger cars were sold in the first seven months of 2009, representing year-on-year growth of 29%, while 132 million tons of cement – another instructive indicator of economic activity – was dispatched in the first eight months of the year, equating to an 11% gain, year-on-year.

When discussing consumer demand, analysts, the media and other commentators tend to focus on India's cities, in the process ignoring the rural economy, which is a combination of agriculture and other rural infrastructure and still accounts for about 70% of the country's population. Yet this sector turned out to be one of the most resilient parts of the whole Indian economy in 2008.

One reason India's rural economy is faring well is because of the National, Rural Employment Guarantee Act, which came into force in 2005 and aimed to provide a minimum amount of employment – at least 100 days a year at a basic wage – to every household whose adult members volunteered to do unskilled manual work.

"Oddly enough, this is probably the most important reason why the government was voted back into power in 2009," says Maheshwari. "The Act had a dramatic effect with regard to both the working population and income levels in the rural economy. Furthermore, thanks to the higher prices of agro-commodities over the last five years, we have noticed this spread into physical incomes in rural India while the rural infrastructure has also grown, which has again contributed to the rural economy doing very well."

4.4.3   Infrastructure and Outsourcing

Even so, in comparison with its BRIC counterparts – particularly Brazil and China – India has not excelled with regard to building infrastructure and, with capital so hard to come by, this track record did not get any better in 2008.

However, market watchers believe matters are set to improve, with the catalyst being the presence of a more stable government, which should be able to make the most of a clear five-year window to implement many of the ambitious power, road and other transport projects that had become stuck on the runway, as it were, under the previous coalition. Indeed, the Indian government has stated it plans to spend more than $500 bn on infrastructure projects between 2007 and 2012.

"India is heading in the right direction but clearly the political system prevents the sort of a quick and fast execution that is being seen in, for example, China," says Konstantinov at Allianz Global Investors' RCM. "In India, you have a fairly reliable legal system so, if someone doesn't like something, they use legal means to challenge it.

"At the same time, a democracy obviously means you have changes of government so everything moves a little more slowly. However, the election outcome in 2009 was surprisingly positive, meaning there was pretty much a clear mandate for a reformist government to continue economic and structural reforms."

The politicians may finally be getting their act together but they have some way to go to match the zeal, endeavour and hard work of India's entrepreneurs and business community, who have helped raised the country's profile globally through its reputation as a key destination for outsourcing.

Information technology tends to be the first sector that springs to mind in this regard – and with good reason. For example, some four-fifths of Fortune 500 companies outsource their information technology work to India, which immediately demonstrates not only is it a well-established model, it also means any firm looking to outsource their information technology around the world has to consider India.

However, outsourcing as a key investment theme is no longer limited to information technology. The pharmaceutical industry is increasingly looking towards India, with global giants such as Pfizer contracting local companies to manufacture particular drugs, while similar developments are taking place in the engineering and automobile sectors.

Maheshwari points to the $2.2 bn purchase of Jaguar and Land Rover by Tata, India's largest vehicle maker, from Ford in 2008 as an interesting extension of this theme. "This is very typical of what a lot of Indian companies have been trying to do over the past few years," he says. "They want to go out, make global-sized acquisitions and then try and leverage the domestic low costbase to facilitate that acquisition and try and cut the overall cost.

"Generally we saw a bit of a blip in outsourcing in 2009 because, at the end of the day, it is linked more to the global economy and, when you have a big financial meltdown in the US, it will affect business for, say, Indian information technology companies. Nonetheless, outsourcing companies still managed flattish growth in 2009 and we're expecting that to pick up again in the coming years."

4.4.4 Country-specific Risks

We have already seen how India's political system and tendency towards bureaucracy can hold back its development and indeed late 2009 saw the publication of an OECD report that said the country needed to strengthen and liberalize its regulatory framework and invest more in infrastructure in order to attract increased foreign direct investment.

According to the OECD's *Investment Policy Review of India*, the country has designed policies to encourage investment as part of market-oriented reforms since 1991 and these have paved the way for improved prosperity. "Restrictions on large-scale investment have been greatly relaxed," it noted. "Many sectors formerly reserved to the public sector have been opened up to private enterprise. Import substitution and protectionism have been replaced by an open trade regime.

However, the report went on to note that further reforms are needed as India's policy framework for foreign direct investment still remained restrictive compared with most OECD countries. At the same time, added the report, the country's investment needs remained "massive", with poor infrastructure holding back improvements in both living conditions and productivity.

That said, it is not just India's internal politics that may give investors pause for thought. The country's relationship with Pakistan has historically tended towards the tense – degenerating as far as a nuclear stand-off in 1998 – while its vulnerability to terrorism was starkly illustrated by the Mumbai attacks in 2008.

At a more company-specific level, in early 2009 the collapse of Satyam Computers – as a result of a billion-dollar fraud at India's then fourth-largest software firm – once again raised unwelcome questions about emerging markets' standards of corporate governance.

The affair certainly tarnished the reputation of Indian industry overseas but comparisons with Enron, while highlighting the extent of the scandal, also served to underline that poor corporate governance can no longer be seen as the sole preserve of emerging markets.

"Satyam wasn't actually a complicated fraud," says Young at Aberdeen Asset Management Asia. "It was more Lesson 1:01 of accountancy – after all, if you can't believe the cash a company has in the bank, that's a fairly basic aspect of investing. Usually a fund manager misses something – a bad smell or a complicated structure – but that wasn't the case here. Investors lost money and learned nothing but they didn't do anything wrong."

4.4.5   India's Stock Market

As has been noted earlier, it is all very well for an economy to do well but investors are not able to buy the economy – they have to participate through the underlying stock market. With that in mind, to what extent is the Indian stock market synchronized to the country's whole economic profile?

Excluding Japan, at the end of 2009, India was the third largest market in the Asia grouping, after China and Hong Kong, with companies totalling some $1 tn in market capitalization. Foreign investors owned about 21% of the Indian market – significantly less than the proportion in the region as a whole, thereby leaving plenty of scope for foreign ownership to increase over time.

At the same time, the country boasted a number of companies that were of a good size for investment, with 150 in the $1 bn-plus range, while the market capitalization to GDP ratio was of a similar order to China's at about 90%. Daily turnover was in the region of $19 bn – a figure that equates to a highly liquid market – and the average 10-year forward price/earnings multiple was about 16.25 times.

India's price/earnings multiple has always been a little higher than the rest of Asia, principally because the profitability of Indian companies has tended to be higher than their counterparts in the rest of the region. Return on equity for many years has ranged around the 20% level while earnings growth has also been reasonably consistent – even including 2008 when, on average, companies still managed to post some positive earnings growth.

It goes without saying – though it will continue to be noted – that past history is no indication of future performance but over the 25 years from 1984 to 2009, the Indian market delivered a positive return in 90% of all five-year periods. What is more, the median five-year return in this period was 17%, primarily because Indian companies have grown at an average of about 15% consistently over very long periods of time. If they can maintain that level of growth, India's stock market should continue to perform well on a medium-term view.

India's highly entrepreneurial mentality has led to the creation of potentially interesting companies with, again, the best-known example being the information technology sector, which really developed out of nowhere in a very short space of time from the mid-1990s.

"While China has some huge companies, there are none that we would say were great yet," says Young. "However, India has some really great companies, such as Tata Consultancy Services, Housing Development Finance Corporation, the Indian operation of Unilever and Infosys, which is the icon of corporate India. It has grown from nothing and, while it is very entrepreneurial, it is very professional too."

What's more, as can be seen with Tata Motors' acquisition of Jaguar and Land Rover, a lot of these companies have ambitions to become global players in their individual sectors – whether that be information technology, automobiles, engineering and so forth. It seems only a matter of time before a number of Indian companies become more prominent on a global scale.

Company focus: Infosys Technologies

Infosys Technologies, which is based in Bangalore and employs more than 105 000 people in more than 50 offices around the world, is India's second-largest software exporter and now ranks among the top 10 information technology companies on a global basis. Its shares are listed on the Bombay Stock Exchange, the New York Stock Exchange and the Nasdaq 100.

Set up in 1981, it is now widely regarded as one of the best-managed companies in India. Infosys' business model is based on outsourcing information technology services to India and servicing clients globally, using its low but well-qualified costbase of Indian engineers.

This strategy has resulted in high operating margins, which has allowed the company to challenge well-established information technology giants such as Accenture and IBM. Despite the global recession, 2009 saw net income recovering and revenues continuing to grow. Indeed over the 15 years to 2009, revenue growth was impressive – increasing from $9 m in 1994 to $121 m in 1999, then to $1.06 bn in 2004 and $4.66 bn in 2009.

4.4.6   Conclusion

The Indian stock market is well diversified and efficient and, on the back of themes such as outsourcing and infrastructure, long-term corporate earnings growth should support equity market returns. Furthermore, while, in the past, India could be said to have prospered in spite of its government rather than because of it, a more stable legislature at least offers some cause for optimism.

"A stable and supportive government at the centre will clearly facilitate growth," says Maheshwari. "For the longest time, we've had politics and economics working at loggerheads. Now is the first time in many years where both aspects are fairly well synchronized. That is going to be very important in attracting international flows and sustaining what's been happening."

There does appear to be evidence that the country's leaders are more aware of what is needed to continue India's rise to global prominence. When he made the keynote address at the 2009 India Economic Summit, Prime Minister Manmohan Singh spoke of the need for India to develop long-term debt markets and to deepen corporate bond markets.

"This, in turn, calls for strong insurance and pension sub-sectors," he continued. "We need to improve futures markets for better price discovery and regulation and we also need to remove institutional hurdles to facilitate better intermediation." The theme of the summit was "India's Next Generation of Growth", which just leaves the little matter of the country's political and financial leaders matching words with deeds.

4.5 RUSSIA

Winston Churchill may have famously described Russia as "a riddle wrapped in a mystery inside an enigma" but in investment terms it has been a good deal more straightforward. Its close relationship with the fortunes of the commodities sector – and in particular the oil price – means it is more than usually exposed to the whims of global supply and demand. Unless Russia finally succeeds in diversifying its economy, the country and its champions will be praying China and India retain their appetite for energy.

4.5.1 A Brief Economic History

Since the Soviet Union collapsed in 1991, Russia has looked to build a market economy with a view to achieving consistent economic growth. However, the move started inauspiciously as the radical reforms instituted by President Boris Yeltsin from October of that year and encouraged by the US and the IMF led to economic collapse, hyperinflation and millions being plunged into poverty.

Yeltsin's controversial privatization plans also went awry with ownership of the largest state-owned companies passing for far less than they were worth to just a handful of individuals – the so-called "oligarchs" – whose great wealth allowed them to wield a similar degree of political influence. This coincided with a significant flight of capital as billions of dollars worth of cash and assets were taken out of the country.

The nascent economy hit its low point in 1998 as Russia's dependence on short-term borrowing to finance budget deficits and difficulties in implementing tax reforms aimed at raising government revenues was exacerbated by a decline in investor confidence as a result of the Asian financial crisis, which had begun the previous year, and a simultaneous drop in the price of oil and other raw materials, the country's major exports. Russia's own financial crisis kicked in on 17 August 1998, leading to a rapid decline in the value of the rouble, delayed debt payments, a crippling outflow of foreign investment and, once again, the threat of hyperinflation.

Vladimir Putin's arrival in power on the eve of the new millennium coincided with a change in Russia's economic fortunes – this time for the better – although this was again linked to the world's appetite for commodities. Unlike China and India, whose new-found wealth has been built on the back of providing outsourced manufacturing and services at a low cost, Russia's growth has been founded squarely on oil.

As the price of oil drove up to a high of $147 a barrel in July 2008 (from a modern-day low of $19 dollars a barrel in January 1999), the country built up vast reserves of cash, which began to filter their way down into a growing consumer economy and increased prosperity.

However, this secondary development did not happen quickly enough and, as the oil price tumbled, so did Russian GDP and the country was to endure its second financial crisis in almost exactly a decade. Having grown at a healthy 8.1% in 2007 and 5.6% in 2008, the IMF forecast the economy would slide into negative territory in 2009.

Despite another huge devaluation of the rouble and the Russian parliament approving a massive stimulus package to help banks hit by the financial crisis towards the end of 2008, the Russian economy was only expected to grow at an anaemic 0.5% in 2010.

4.5.2 The Investment Case for Russia

Of the four BRIC countries, Russia is arguably the least complicated – at least from an investment, as opposed to social or political, point of view. The market is highly correlated to commodity and oil prices and despite initiatives to reduce this reliance over time – for example, the then President Putin said back in 2006 that diversification was the major task of that year – the 18 months to the end of 2009 clearly proved this correlation still holds.

This high exposure to commodity and oil prices and the consequent lack of balance among other industrial sectors – energy companies account for a little over half of the Russian stock market – is also the primary reason why the country is still perceived by investors as the most volatile market within the BRIC economies.

The commodities angle colours every aspect of Russian finances. Thus, for example, for many years the huge inflows of "petrol dollars" meant significantly negative real interest rates, where inflation was running at more than twice the level of nominal interest rates. For the man on the street, that meant it was not really practical to try to save money in a bank account but it also had an influence on many other areas such as asset prices.

"That has now been corrected and it has been a very important and positive result of the crisis," says Konstantinov at Allianz Global Investors' RCM. "Clearly, if money is available at too cheap a price, you'll also get a lot of misallocations within the economy. Now we're in a situation where the allocation of capital will be more rational and, hopefully, this will lead to more sustainable growth in areas other than energy.

Even so, with Russia the second largest producer of oil in the world – it is within touching distance of global leader Saudi Arabia – the oil price is likely to remain a dominant factor within the economy for a while yet. From an investment point of view, therefore, investors need to have an opinion on commodity and energy prices and, if they are positive on that, they can almost automatically become positive on Russia.

"Russia is the most paradoxical of the four BRIC countries," says Titherington at J.P. Morgan Asset Management. "It is the most highly developed, the most urbanized and the most advanced so it should be the best positioned of the four. But it wasted its five or so good years.

"It didn't develop or diversify the economy and it didn't strengthen political, legal and financial institutions – in fact, as the tsunami of the crisis swept through, those institutions were all found to be pretty weak. That is its major problem and so it has reverted – or at least people perceive it as having reverted – to being an oil-dominated economy, which means if oil goes up it will be fine. You shouldn't write it off because if you believe in the enormous demand for energy from India and China and consequently rising oil prices and 'peak oil', Russia will be a huge beneficiary of that."

4.5.3   Consumer Demand

We have already seen that the growth in consumer demand is a key part of the outlook for China and India but what about Russia? Once again, the fortunes of commodities are a key consideration and will clearly provide some impetus when demand is on the up. "If you were to analyse in detail the creation of wealth in Russia, you would come to the conclusion that, statistically, the country has seen the strongest increase in real wages over the last seven or eight years," says Konstantinov.

"If you have 15% inflation plus some real wage growth, you can get to a 20% or 25% wage increase every year. Over seven or eight years that can create a lot of purchasing power and indeed it has in the past. The devaluation of the rouble in 2008 hurt a bit but it is still the case that Russia has a growing middle class – especially if you were to compare it with five or 10 years ago. So that's an important aspect that should, over time, give more stability to the Russian investment case and is certainly something we can play on the stock markets as well."

Even so, with the IMF expecting the economy would contract in 2009, leading to increased unemployment and poverty, consumer demand cannot help but be hit, if only in the short term. "The Russian middle class, as measured by household consumption, is likely to shrink by about 10% or some 6.2 million people," says Elena Shaftan, who has run Jupiter Asset Management's Emerging European Opportunities fund since 2002.

"But the large stimulus package, the gradual recovery of oil prices and lower inflation should bode well and the Russian economy could return to modest growth in 2010. However, given the weak global demand, the external environment for Russia will continue to be difficult over the next year or two and short-term policy emphasis continues to be warranted for social assistance, infrastructure and small and medium-sized enterprises.

"With a more constrained financing environment for the government and the private sector in the post-crisis period, Russia should accelerate structural reforms aimed at raising productivity and improving diversification and competitiveness."

Market watchers also believe the devaluation of the rouble in 2008 – which came after a number of years of stability against the euro and the US dollar that was ultimately unsustainable if Russian companies were to remain competitive – may prove a positive move by the government.

Russia undoubtedly has the ability to be a self-sufficient economy with regard to food production, consumer goods, pharmaceuticals and so forth. However, while it has never been reliant on Western capital – arguably it is better for Russia that the financial downturn happened when it did rather than two or three years later when that might not have been the case – recent years have seen the country grow more reliant on Western companies.

"The trouble with Russia is that it hasn't learnt, for example, to wash and package its own potatoes and so it imports them from Belgium or wherever," says Shaftan. "Domestic manufacturing has therefore declined in recent years but the devaluation of the rouble should rebalance that.

"Western companies that sold to the Russians could be in trouble as a sort of 'soft protectionism' emerges, with companies being encouraged to look inwards. As a result, domestic manufacturing would pick up and people would buy local potatoes, thereby encouraging domestic production."

Another advantage for Russia, in common with its BRIC counterparts, is that there is not much household debt. "Household debt is only around 10% of GDP – compared with around 50% in Western Europe," says Shaftan. "Thus while households in other countries will have to cut back on borrowings, in Russia household spending can keep going up. It supports domestic consumption and allows Russia to decouple globally. That said, the country is still leveraged to oil and oil remains leveraged to the global economy."

4.5.4   Country-specific Risks

There are, of course other aspects to the investment case for Russia beyond commodities – not least political considerations. Events such as the short-lived conflict with Georgia in August 2008 or the long-running uncertainty over precisely who has control of BP's Russian joint venture TNK-BP do not fill potential investors with confidence. Certainly, in the aftermath of the credit crisis, investors want transparency above everything else and there remains a feeling that Russia's institutions and corporations are still relatively opaque compared to those of other emerging markets.

However, it is the arrest of the oligarch Mikhail Khodorkovsky that arguably still sums up why potential investors can continue to think twice about directing money towards Russia. At the time Khodorkovsky was arrested on his private jet at a Siberian airport in October 2003, he was Russia's richest man and owner of petroleum giant Yukos.

His arrest and subsequent prosecution for fraud caused consternation both in Russia and abroad but it also sent out a clear message to the country's other oligarchs. It was no coincidence that Khodorkovsky's arrest followed three years of political stability and economic success as this gave the government the power to wrest back control of the country's industrial sector. Many of the remaining oligarchs saw the writing on the wall and fled the country to avoid a similar fate to Khodorkovsky – an eight-year term in a prison camp that began in 2005.

Indirectly or otherwise, the Yukos affair and decline in the power of the oligarchs created a vacuum in Russian industry that the government swiftly filled. The biggest beneficiaries were the two state-controlled energy giants Gazprom and Rosneft – the former finding itself clear to acquire oil company Sibneft, after a proposed merger with Yukos fell through, while the latter was able to pick up a number of key Yukos assets in the government auctions that followed the seizure of Khodorkovsky's wealth.

However, while the pair have come to dominate Russia's commodities market and are now seen as "national champions", they have also come to embody the dilemmas facing anyone planning to invest in Russia – the influence of volatile commodity prices on the economy and the influence of politics on business.

That said, what one fund manager described as "the strong hand of Putin" can be portrayed as having an upside. To his credit the former President has at least been fairly consistent in his dealings with companies, meaning they know where they stand and can plan for the long term. What's more, they know that if they do not behave properly, they will be penalized. Nevertheless – and perhaps ironically – some investors see government-owned companies as a safer prospect from a corporate governance point of view.

The Corruption Perceptions Index, which is assembled on an annual basis by Transparency International as a measure of domestic, public-sector corruption, sees Russia faring very badly compared to the other three BRIC economies and indeed most of the rest of the world. The 2009 table had it scoring just 2.2 out of a possible 10 and 146th out of 180 countries – up one place and one-tenth of a point on 2008's showing.

By comparison, Brazil was 75th with a score of 3.7 (up five places and two-tenths of a point on 2008); China was 79th with a score of 3.6

(down seven places though with the same score); and India was 84th with a score of 3.4 (up one place though with the same score).

4.5.5   Russia's Stock Market

The Russian stock market has reflected the country's fluctuating fortunes. Micex, the country's leading stock exchange, tripled over the course of three years to peak in May 2008 before plummeting by two-thirds by the end of that year. By the end of October 2009, the market had doubled from that point but still faced a long climb to reach its former heights.

Whereas in the early days of the free economy the Russian stock market was heavily dominated by oil and gas, utilities and telecommunications companies – much of it government-owned – a significant number of more consumer-oriented companies have since come to the market. Examples would include the high-growth, high-margin mobile telephone operators, such as MTS, and Magnit, the so-called Wal-Mart or Tesco of Russia. However, while some have gone from strength to strength, others have faded without a trace.

"A lot of formerly privately-owned companies have been successful only up to the point at which they choose to list," notes one fund manager who specializes in investing in Eastern Europe. "Sometimes the owner or majority shareholder may realize that growth is peaking or they just want to go and fish in the South of France and don't care what happens to the company next. A lot of these companies should really remain privately-owned. They come in on too high a multiple, factoring in very high growth rates. You have to be careful as these shares can be too expensive and too illiquid."

Company focus: Magnit

Magnit, which is based in Krasnodar in Southern Russia and has shares listed on the RTS and Micex stock exchanges in Moscow as well as on the London Stock Exchange, is the second largest food retail network in Russia after X5 Retail Group.

As of September 2009, the chain consisted of 2960 convenience stores and 21 hypermarkets in almost 1000 locations around the country, with approximately two-thirds of its stores located in cities with a population of fewer than 500 000 inhabitants. The company has been described by analysts as the most effective Russian retailer, not only because of its growing purchasing power but also because of the extensive investment it has made in internal improvements, such as information technology and logistics.

Magnit's management has promised to continue to focus on developing its logistics system and plans to build additional distribution centres and expand the retailer's fleet of vehicles, while continuing rapid construction of convenience stores and hypermarkets. Again as of September 2009, the company operated an in-house logistics system consisting of nine distribution centres, employing automated stock replenishment systems and a fleet of almost 1400 vehicles.

In October 2009, shortly after celebrating the opening of its 3000th store, Magnit raised $527 m in an oversubscribed secondary share offer that attracted strong interest from international investors. The company then announced it planned to use the money raised to expand further, with analysts suggesting that its budget format could prove attractive to cash-strapped consumers.

4.5.6 Conclusion

Russia's economic past and present have been inextricably linked with the fortunes of oil and other commodities but its future will depend on whether the country has now learned some painful lessons from its experiences of the last decade or two.

Putin's crushing of the oligarchs and global demand for commodities saw the country able to build up vast reserves of cash but, when that commodities boom came so abruptly to a halt in July 2008, not enough had been done to diversify its reliance on oil and gas revenues nor had money filtered its way down sufficiently into a growing consumer economy and increased prosperity for the average citizen.

"It's always important to keep in mind the main drivers for the Russian equity market," says Konstantinov. "It remains primarily the commodity and energy side although many are now trying to make the case that it is on a more sustainable and diversified path."

Admittedly, Russia's high correlation to the global economy works both ways so that, as things stand, whenever a sustainable recovery looks to be on the horizon, it represents a potentially dynamic market that is worthy of close consideration.

Nevertheless, most people investing for the long term in Russia will hope that those making claims of improved sustainability and greater diversification follow up their words with action sooner rather than later so that the country is finally able break away from its reliance on the commodities markets and its consequent position as a hostage to the vagaries of the global economy.

4.6 BRAZIL

Resources-rich Brazil may have built up a reputation as an export-driven commodity producer but the growing significance of its domestic economy means it is better insulated from global shocks than Russia, the BRIC country with which it is most often compared. For decades Brazilians would wryly observe that theirs was the country of the future – "and it always will be" – yet Brazil now appears set to fulfil its potential and take its rightful place as a major player on the global economic stage.

4.6.1 A Brief Economic History

Brazil's recent economic history might be categorized as a recurring boom-bust cycle, punctuated by some fairly spectacular crises. The last real crises – and the ones most likely still to give nightmares to those involved in the first wave of emerging markets investing in the 1990s – came in 1994 when the forced devaluation of the Mexican peso also dented confidence in South American markets and the 1997 Asian financial crisis and 1998 Russian bond default led investors to desert the emerging markets in droves.

Essentially Brazil became trapped in a vicious circle where a crisis would lead to risk aversion on the part of investors and thus capital flowing away from the country. However, since the government was dependent on foreign capital for its debt financing it would then have to raise interest rates in order to keep money in the country. Raising interest rates would then collapse the local economy, thereby collapsing tax revenues and the whole budgetary situation would deteriorate further – leading to the prospect of another financial crisis.

Brazil's resurgence can be traced back to the Plano Real (or Real Plan), a set of measures that aimed to break this vicious circle by stabilizing the economy and, in particular, combating the hyperinflation – that is to say, inflation that is very high or on occasion out of control – that had afflicted the country for decades.

The plan was instituted in the spring of 1994 by Fernando Henrique Cardoso, then the country's minister of finance and later Brazil's

President for two terms. While economists argue about its long-term effects, the Plano Real certainly succeeded in its primary aim of killing off hyperinflation. In June 1994, the month before the plan came into effect, monthly inflation averaged 31% – or a total of almost 2300% for the year. In 1995 inflation declined to an annual rate of 26%, falling to 16.5% in 1996.

The Cardoso administration can also be credited with establishing the Brazilian real as a stable currency, overseeing a number of large privatizations and initiating the country's fight against poverty by introducing a national version of the Bolsa Escola, which provided financial aid to poor families on the condition their children attended school.

Brazil suffered another wobble in 2002 – what one fund manager describes as "more market-induced psychosis than a real crisis" – when concerns over the likely successor to President Cardoso, the left-leaning Luis Inácio Lula da Silva, and especially fears he would default on the country's debt led to yet another attack of nerves among investors.

President Lula was duly elected in January 2003 but ultimately those concerns proved unfounded as he consolidated and then expanded on his predecessor's initiatives. "What Lula gets credit for is that he's a very pragmatic man with a lot of common sense, who understands that Brazil is a fundamentally capitalist and entrepreneurial culture, and he built on his predecessor's achievements by being extremely consistent," says Urban Larson, director of emerging equities at F&C Investments.

"What Lula has done is essentially take a lot of issues out of the political arena by saying they are now consensus. So he did not invent so much as maintain what was already in place but that was crucial because, until he did so, there was a lot of doubt as to whether Cardoso's changes were permanent or not."

By the time Lehman Brothers failed in September 2008, Brazil's economy was operating at full capacity, growing at some 7% a year and very underleveraged thanks to a banking system required by its regulator to maintain solid reserves and capital adequacy ratios.

Arguably Brazil might have survived the global recession without entering into one itself but, by now, the country had grown used to dealing with a crisis – regardless of whether it was of its own making. So when Lehman failed and credit lines were suddenly cut off around the world, previous experience told Brazil's corporate sector it should cease production, stop orders and shut everything down.

"They panicked and turned off the switch," says Larson. "Suddenly you had a recession from an economy that had been accelerating a week before. It's both a weakness of emerging markets companies and a strength that they react very quickly to crises.

"There's a lot of room for debate on whether Brazil actually needed to have a recession. In a sense, it was a corporate overreaction to global events but, in general, it's probably that healthy emerging markets corporations are so good at handling crises. That is how they stayed out of trouble this time and why they were ready to come back quicker."

And yet while corporate Brazil ground to a halt, the country's consumers appeared not to notice. "There wasn't really a significant slowdown on the consumer side of the economy at all," continues Larson. "Consumers were still coasting on the wave of prosperity – on low inflation, low interest rates, easier credit and so on – and they kept right on going. Within a year, both the real and unemployment had returned to pre-Lehman levels, lending had been reactivated and the economy bounced back. Investors are used to a Brazil that is very volatile but this is a new Brazil."

4.6.2 The Investment Case for Brazil

At the start of this chapter we touched on how some commentators have tried to simplify the BRIC story by suggesting China and India are consumer growth stories while Brazil and Russia are commodity plays but arguably Brazil is able to combine the best of both these worlds. Brazil's supporters point out that, while it may be a resource economy, not only is it a much more diverse and flexible one than the oil-and-gas dependent Russia, it also has great domestic growth potential.

While Russia had Gazprom (36th) and Rosneft (76th) among the top 80 of the *Financial Times'* list of the world's largest companies in 2009, Brazil boasted oil producer Petrobras (17th) and iron-ore giant Vale do Rio Doce. However, in addition to oil and iron ore, the country's other natural resources include manganese, bauxite, nickel, uranium, gemstones, timber and aluminium. In addition, Brazil enjoys vast agricultural resources and is a major producer of beef, wheat, rice, corn, coffee, soybeans and sugarcane.

A by-product of Brazil's sugarcane production is that the country is by far the world's largest producer of sugarcane ethanol, which can be used to power cars. Initially stirred into action by the oil crisis of 1973, Brazil is now seen as the first sustainable biofuels economy.

China's appetite for both hard and soft commodities has seen it grow in significance as a destination for exports and in May 2009, Brazil's

Ministry of Development, Industry and Exterior Trade published statistics that showed China had replaced the US as the country's biggest trading partner, gate-crashing a relationship that dated back to the 1930s.

According to Brazil's official statistics, the bilateral trade volume between Brazil and China reached $36.4 bn in 2008 – an increase of 55.9% from 2007. Broken down, this meant Brazil's export volume to China was $16.4 bn and its import volume $20 bn, respectively up 50.8% and 56.9% on the previous year. Even so, Brazil's trade minister announced the country was looking to diversify further its exports to China, which till that point had principally been soya, cellulose fuel and manufactured products.

Brazil's diversified economy also extends to an industrial base that dates back to the development programme of the 1960s and 1970s when the country's government invited a number of multi-national companies to start up operations there. As a result, Brazil's automobile industry has been boosted by the likes of Ford and Volkswagen manufacturing cars both for domestic consumption and export while Siemens was involved locally in building the generators for Itaipu, the largest operational hydroelectric power plant in the world.

"The commodities side of Brazil gets a lot of coverage at the expense of the domestic side," says Larson. "People forget that Brazil has approximately 190 million people, which is some 50 million more than Russia, and they also forget that commodity exports, even at the peak, were at most 15% of the country's GDP.

"Brazil is really a domestically driven economy – for example, it's got a very big service sector and a very well-developed financial sector. The commodity story is part of what makes Brazil attractive and that's certainly helped bring investment into the country but what has been interesting about Brazil is the unleashing of the domestic market from a combination of forces over the last 10 years, starting with inflation."

4.6.3   Post-hyperinflation

Brazil's decades of hyperinflation, which saw annual inflation regularly above 1000%, have had a significant effect on the thinking of consumers and companies alike. For a start, since the memory of hyperinflation is still so fresh, the country's central bank needs to maintain a very responsible monetary policy, both to keep inflation in check and also to knock down some psychological barriers.

On the other hand, the experiences of and challenges posed by hyperinflation have led to many of Brazil's corporate management teams being extremely flexible and quick to adapt to circumstances – almost by definition, those who enabled their companies successfully to negotiate the financial crises of the 1990s and early 2000s deserve respect.

"The central bank has succeeded in entrenching low inflation expectations," says Larson. "So, for example, when the currency weakened so sharply in late 2008, everybody feared prices would rise and inflation would return but that didn't happen. This was partly because companies had built up a lot of inventory in the expectation of a strong fourth quarter and so they just sold this down and partly because companies were well aware that the central bank would react very quickly to any sign of inflation."

Even so Brazil's political and financial leaders had to battle for the best part of a decade to tame inflation and bring about a virtuous circle where interest rates could start to come down. Furthermore, victory came at a high cost and took the shape of extremely high real interest rates. Clearly, in the early part of this century, for example, inflation of 30%-plus and consequent real interest rates of around 45% were not supportive of the economy.

"President Lula's administration has done a very good job of continuing the structural reforms of the previous governments," says Konstantinov at Allianz Global Investors' RCM. "The central bank has been left pretty much independent and has been very successful in bringing down the inflationary numbers and real interest rates to single digits. That has certainly been one of the major successes in Brazil.

"Also, from a social point of view, the best economic policy for the poor is low inflation because it is normally they who lose out with inflation – for example, they do not have bank accounts so they can't compensate for high inflation that way. So lower inflation, along with some other policy measures, has resulted in a slow but steady uplift in incomes for many Brazilians."

4.6.4 Consumer Demand

Under the Lula administration – thanks to initiatives such as the Bolsa Família, which extended the Bolsa Escola so that poor families receive financial aid if they prove their children are vaccinated as well as attending school – the gap between rich and poor may have narrowed but demographically Brazil is still a country of extremes.

On the one hand Brazil has a lot of social infrastructure that should help it over the long term as it develops. For example, it enjoys a free press, courts, the protection of property and the rule of law and all within a vibrant democracy. It has regulatory agencies and a very capable layer of bureaucrats who manage all of these processes and it has a good domestic education system and universities that produce their fair share of Nobel Laureates.

"It is all fairly advanced among the top tiers of society," says Chris Palmer, head of emerging markets at Gartmore. "But then there is this very undeveloped and disenfranchised population as well – and that's really where the growth opportunity is. Brazil has a very large proportion of its population living in some form of near-poverty but they are the consumers and the household creators of the future. They are the future car-owners and the future magazine buyers, who aren't yet because they are on very low incomes.

"Then there are large parts of the country that are underdeveloped and being used for extremely low productivity or not being used at all. I'm not talking about the Amazon here but huge amounts of underutilized, underinvested land – resources that nobody has really got at yet. So you have that as well as the people and a population that is still growing, which is why Brazil is such an exciting place."

Furthermore Brazil is experiencing a theme common to all the BRIC economies – a growing middle class. Thus when commodity prices fell in the second half of 2008, Brazil's domestic economy was able to pick up the slack, with the country even seeing a small increase in consumer spending in the tumultuous first three months of 2009.

Any weakness came more from a tailing-off in corporate investment rather than from the consumer and yet, according to World Bank figures, penetration of consumer goods remains relatively low. For example, in 2006, there were 52 mobile phone subscriptions per 100 people in Brazil, a figure that climbed to 63 in 2007. By way of comparison, those rates in the US and Western Europe work out as more than one mobile phone subscription per person.

4.6.5   Country-specific Risks

It is only a matter of years rather than decades since Brazil was crippled by hyperinflation and stumbling from one financial crisis to another so it is not unreasonable for investors to be wary of the country slipping back into the bad habits and policies that contributed to that environment in the first place.

Most pertinently therefore, since Lula is not going to be president for ever, investors must contemplate the possibility his successor may have a slightly different agenda. Furthermore, there is the eternal spectre of corporate governance standards.

However, Palmer is hopeful on both counts. "Everybody generally agrees the direction the country is going in and it will be impossible to govern Brazil without the buy-in of the parts of the population that have recently become enfranchised under Lula," he says. "The battle against poverty, improved education and children's issues are all political issues in Brazil now.

"What's more, the standards for public leadership have risen dramatically so there's been improvement in public policy in terms of people, corruption and so on. I'm not going to say any platitudes but Brazil's leaders have made progress, that progress is tangible and they have put themselves under a lot more scrutiny, which has been part of their success. Even where they have been successful, Brazil is now advanced enough as a society that it can go back and question that success – question whether the country did things right or whether it needs to take another look – for example, at the oil industry."

One potential risk facing many emerging markets – though Brazil is an obvious example – was identified by British academic Victor Bulmer-Thomas as the need for "backward integration" – essentially that when resources and goods are exported, the exporting country needs to ensure there is investment back into its infrastructure, systems and so forth.

"What we are seeing in Brazil is a continued improvement and sophistication of the overall economy and a good example is Lula's policy that a certain portion of investment into the oilfields should have local content," says Palmer. "This may sound like protectionism but I think it's a fair trade-off between a country allowing a vast amount of development to occur and asking its partners to make sure some of that is reinvested in local companies and the communities. As a result there has been a big upswing in investment, property, infrastructure, job creation and visitors because the oil industry is responding to that local content. It's not the oil the matters, it's what happens after the oil."

4.6.6 Brazil's Stock Market

The principal indicator of the Brazilian stock market's average performance is the São Paolo-based Bovespa index, which has seen a similar trajectory to other leading emerging markets in recent years. Having almost tripled from May 2005 to its peak in May 2008, it then plummeted by almost three-fifths in the last few months of 2008 and early 2009. However, it reached its nadir significantly before many other markets and then enjoyed steady gains.

There is no denying the Bovespa index is still dominated by commodities companies or, more precisely, a pair of commodities companies. At the end of 2009, energy company Petrobras and iron ore producer Vale were both more than twice the size of the third biggest company in Brazil, Itaú Unibanco, and accounted for almost 30% of the entire index.

Even so, the Brazilian market can no longer justifiably be portrayed as a pure play on commodities. It is growing very quickly as more and more companies come to the market in search of capital that will help them to expand their operations further and has seen significant developments and dynamic new entrants in sectors such as health care, information technology, real estate and retail.

"In Brazil – together with probably China – we are seeing the greatest dynamic in terms of IPOs," says Konstantinov. "The market is growing very quickly and so there are a lot of interesting new areas to play. The market has become much more diversified than five or 10 years ago and is therefore offering many more investment opportunities."

Brazil's taming of inflation has been transformative for the country's stock market. Thanks to resulting lower interest rates, not only does it unlock consumer credit that would otherwise have been unaffordable, it also unlocks credit to the corporate sector – and particularly to small and medium-sized businesses.

On one level, this means a lower hurdle rate for investments – that is to say, a lower level of required return before institutional and private investors agree to commit money – and consequently a longer time horizon for investments. This is all very positive in itself, but much lower inflation has a more direct effect on the stock market too.

In 2009, Brazilian institutions had some $800 bn in assets under management domestically, of which approximately two-thirds was in mutual funds and one-third in pension funds. "Historically that money has overwhelmingly been invested in fixed income – at times as much as 85% or 90% – and in many cases the hurdle rate for pension funds is inflation plus 6%, which would give you about 10%," says Larson. "Historically, you could make that on government paper without even thinking but you can't any more – you have to work for it."

As such, Brazil's pension funds now have longer-term incentives to start moving money into equities and the same goes for the country's private investors. They too have been used to receiving high returns on fixed income and so, when they invested in equities, they tended to be extremely value-conscious and also very short-term in their outlook.

"With lower interest rates, you open up long-term equities investing for the retail market," Larson continues. "This is a major structural change for the market and, while it is not something that will happen overnight, it is clearly on the way. The market has already become a lot more liquid and, if that continues, then you will get a market increasingly driven by domestic institutional money and thus much more stable. Over the coming years you will see the volatility of the Brazilian market fall substantially because of that."

Interestingly, Brazil's significant banking sector traditionally made a lot of money out of the volatility that was part and parcel of the country's economy but it is now having to rethink how it does business. Brazil's banks became very adept at trading government bonds, trading the currency and moving money extremely quickly – and usually managing to do even better in times of crisis.

With volatility largely a thing of the past, the banks – led by the country's big three of Itaú Unibanco, Banco Bradesco and Banco do Brasil – are now making the transition towards a more classical banking business model. In other words, they are focusing more on lending to consumers, on credit analysis and cost-cutting, none of which much interested them in the past.

Brazil's banks also have a history of outwitting and outperforming foreign competitors to the extent that there are only a handful of non-domestic banks left in the country. "The Brazilian banks are extremely sophisticated, run by very smart people, very well capitalised and they are both quick to seize opportunities and very conservative in their risk management," says Larson. "There was a time in 2008 when the market capitalisation of Itaú was bigger than Citibank and UBS combined and I asked the management why they didn't just buy Citibank. They simply felt it was too risky to invest outside Brazil."

Company focus: Localiza Rent a Car

Localiza, which is based in Belo Horizonte, Brazil, and listed on the New Bovespa Stock Exchange, is the largest car rental and fleet rental company in Latin America. Established in 1973 with six Volkswagen Beetles that were bought on credit, the company now commands a 30% share of the Brazilian car rental market.

Renting cars primarily through sites at airports, Localiza owns and franchises locations in Brazil and the rest of Latin America as well as offering fleet management services and selling used cars. Its successful business model has allowed it to survive through Brazil's numerous financial crises.

The company reacted to the global credit crunch by reducing the growth of its business to a level that was cashflow-neutral while increasing prices in late 2008 and selling part of its car fleet to strengthen its balance sheet. In June 2009, it went on to announce it would invest some $763 m to renew its rental-car fleet

Already benefiting from a strong market position against a number of financially weak competitors, Localiza enjoyed another boost as one of the Brazilian companies picked out by investors as likely to benefit from the announcement that Rio de Janeiro would host the 2016 Olympic Games and the consequent influx of tourists.

4.6.7 Conclusion

Brazil is a relatively advanced society with a less advanced economy that looks to be coming to terms with achieving a balance between resources and other exports leaving the country on the one hand and inward investment in local companies and communities and a growing domestic economy on the other.

"Brazil has a huge amount of natural resources, no doubt about it, but I would suggest the country's GDP is still relatively undeveloped," says Palmer. "The country's mining and oil industries can loom large over the overall GDP figure but that doesn't mean that balance couldn't shift over time. Having the advantage of a lot of natural resources didn't hold back the development of other parts of the US economy over the last 100 or more years – it's what you make out of that that is important."

The comparison with the US is an interesting one because, while China may have edged its way between the two long-time trading partners, Brazil and the US look set to dominate the Americas for decades to come. "Within a Latin American context, Brazil is becoming increasingly dominant," says Konstantinov. "That's most visible on the equity market as some three-quarters of the overall Latin American market capitalization is in Brazil. But also if you look at some of its economic measures, then when people look at the whole of America, they are going to look at the US and Brazil and the rest will have to somehow group around these two regional giants."

5
The "Emerged" Emerging Markets

5.1 INTRODUCTION

For a number of Asian markets the tag of "emerging" or "developing" hardly fits. Hong Kong, Singapore, South Korea and Taiwan all have per capita GDP approaching or exceeding that of developed markets. Hong Kong and Singapore, in particular, have some of the most well-established and sophisticated capital markets and business practices of anywhere in the world. Even so, when considering the topic of investing in emerging markets, it is instructive to examine those that have been there, done that and are now waiting in the queue to buy their T-shirt.

5.2 OVERVIEW

Whether Hong Kong, Singapore, South Korea and Taiwan are categorized as technically developed or developing varies depending on the criteria of the assessing organization and it is difficult to find many that still classify the first two in the list as emerging. The major index providers FTSE and MSCI classify them as developed and only *The Economist* still lists them both as emerging.

According to the World Bank, Singapore has a gross national income per capita figure higher than Spain or Italy and while this is not the only criterion, in the absence of significant structural problems, deeming it as "emerging" seems something of an anachronism.

Taiwan and South Korea draw more varied assessments, largely on issues such as ease of access and shareholder and corporate governance considerations, although by the start of 2010 MSCI had South Korea "on watch" for an upgrade. Per capita gross national income is also lower in both countries – Taiwan is around $17 000, while South Korea is around $21 000, compared to $34 760 for Singapore and $31 420 for Hong Kong.

However, all these countries may be seen as providing a blueprint for development in the rest of Asia. They have moved up the value chain from being low-cost manufacturing bases, as China or Vietnam are now, or trading centres. Hong Kong and Singapore now have more service-based economies, Taiwan has specialized in sophisticated electronics manufacturing and South Korea houses manufacturing giants such as Samsung.

At the same time they have developed sophisticated capital markets, which have been a distribution point for the disbursement of capital round Asia. Before China had a developed stock market, its biggest companies would list in Hong Kong and international investors were willing to invest there because of its strong corporate governance codes and shareholder protections. With Chinese corporate governance still seen as relatively weak, many international investors would still rather channel capital through Hong Kong when investing in China.

Although the emerging economies of Asia now have their own stock markets, some of which are large and dynamic, these countries still have the largest and most liquid markets in the region. "Corporate governance in places such as Hong Kong or Singapore is as good as anything in the West," says Stuart Parks, manager of the Invesco Perpetual Asian fund. "They rank extremely highly for ease of doing business and the strength of their codes. However, places such as China have a long way to go – it is really a question of caveat emptor when buying shares there."

Of course, there is also a good long-term investment case for these countries in their own right. If the Asian growth story is to be believed, with China at its heart, these regions are potentially the strongest link between Asia and the rest of the world. This has already brought capital to the region and indeed, in some cases, fears of bubbles. In November 2009, the World Bank warned that Hong Kong and Singapore were vulnerable to asset price bubbles after increases in equity and house prices across the region.

Such fears draw a mixed response from investors in the region. Andrew Beal, manager of the TR Pacific investment trust, points out that although lending rates have grown, they are still vastly below those in developed markets. Asset prices have undoubtedly increased but this is from a low base and on the back of an improvement in the economic fundamentals for the region.

For his part, Mike Kerley, manager of the Henderson Far East Income trust, believes asset bubbles are a risk, but adds that investors could make a lot of money on the way up. He explains that as the Hong Kong dollar is pegged to that of the US, the former effectively imports US monetary policy, so rates there will remain artificially low, which may create excess liquidity and therefore asset bubbles. Parks meanwhile takes the view that Asian markets trade at fair value for around "a millisecond on the way up and a millisecond on the way down" so investors have to ride these waves.

Singapore and Hong Kong consistently rate among the top few countries in the World Bank's ease of doing business survey and, in 2009, they were first and third respectively. They generally have sound, hands-off governments, committed to business development. China, which ranks a lowly 89th in the survey, has not yet been tempted to meddle in Hong Kong recognizing that much of its success depends on it being seen as a reliable and transparent place to do business. South Korea and Taiwan are 19th and 46th respectively in the survey.

The growth rates available from these four countries rival those of many genuinely "developing" economies. The IMF expects all four to deliver GDP growth in excess of 3.5% in 2010. Certainly Taiwan, Hong Kong and Singapore all saw a difficult start to 2009 but bounced back strongly in the second half. South Korea barely even registered a dip.

Unlike some of developing Asia, all these countries already have established domestic consumption markets. Per capital wealth is higher and the consumer infrastructure is in place. This provides a different set of consumer growth opportunities than in, say, China, which is at an earlier stage in its development. Singapore consumers may be demanding Gucci, while the vast majority of Chinese consumers want white goods. It also means potential growth is lower.

All of which suggests that this quartet does not have the demographic advantages that characterize many other Asian countries. "Population growth tends to slow down as countries develop," says Chris Palmer, head of global emerging markets at Gartmore. "Greece and Portugal are the most recent countries that moved from being 'emerging' to 'developed' and their population growth is practically zero. As such, the gains from wealth creation and household income growth tend to be smaller. That said, countries with very high wealth creation, such as Singapore, can transcend this."

On the upside, investors should not forget that it is these markets where they will often pick up their dividend yields. The Hong Kong market, for example, has had an average dividend yield of around 3% since 2000, though this had reached as high as 5% at the end of 2008.

Investors will tend to pay a premium for the stronger corporate governance and higher liquidity available in these markets compared to some Asian markets. That said, Chinese shares that are dual-listed in Hong Kong and Shanghai tend to trade on lower valuations in Hong Kong because of the greater liquidity. As the markets are larger and more sophisticated, there will tend to be fewer pricing anomalies.

According to the FT, the Hong Kong and Singapore markets in November 2009 traded at around 18.5× and 18.9× earnings respectively. At the same time, the Philippines market was trading at 16.4×, the Indonesian market at 17.2× and – for a broader comparison – the UK market at just 12.6×. Taiwan has consistently tended to trade on higher valuations – at the same time, it was trading at 28.8× earnings.

5.3   HONG KONG – A BRIEF ECONOMIC HISTORY

It is symbolic of Hong Kong's commitment to capitalism that it has a chief executive rather than a president. When it became a "Special Administrative Region" of China in 1997, many feared the influence of a forceful, authoritarian government, but Hong Kong has been a significant beneficiary of the relationship, becoming the frontman of Asian growth rather than a has-been Communist lackey.

Hong Kong is often not considered an emerging market at all – index providers MSCI and FTSE classify it as a developed market although *The Economist* still considers it emerging. Either way, its proximity to China has been crucial to its development. At times of Chinese isolationism it has acted as a conduit between China and the rest of the world and it is now benefiting from its giant neighbour's ongoing industrialization.

Hong Kong has always been a regional centre for financial and commercial services, attracting shipping, merchant and banking companies. Its success has come from the consistent pro-business environment provided by the government – taxes are low, employment laws are lenient and free trade is a mantra.

As agreed under the terms of its lease with China, the British had been in the country since 1898 and, under their administration, Hong Kong had emerged as one of the "Asian tigers" during the 1970s – a term also used for the regional powerhouses of Singapore, South Korea and Taiwan. Their economies boomed on the back of growth in high technology industries and financial services and each country saw rapid industrialization.

Hong Kong became a leading financial centre and indeed is still ranked third in the world for ease of doing business. But the spectre of the handover to China cast a lengthy shadow, particularly after the massacre at Tiananmen Square in 1989. Eventually, with Chris Patten as governor, the two countries agreed a "one country, two systems" formula, which meant Hong Kong would become part of China, but retain its capitalist infrastructure and economy for at least 50 years.

The Chinese government can still veto changes to the political system, which has frustrated reformers as Hong Kong remains only partially democratic, with its government elected by an electoral college. They see Beijing as blocking reform and pro-democracy demonstrations are still a regular occurrence.

Unfortunately the handover to China came just ahead of the economic fallout from the Asian financial crisis – indeed, some suggested the handover may have precipitated the crisis. Certainly, the devaluation of the Thai baht that marked the start of the crisis happened only a day after the transfer of sovereignty. However, this is an isolated view as there were undoubtedly many other factors at work in the region such as high foreign-currency denominated debt and weak governance.

Either way, although the crisis had started in Thailand, Hong Kong could not avoid "Asian contagion". With the currencies of its customers and competitors devaluing rapidly, its exports could no longer compete. On 27 October, the Hang Seng sold off 5.8% in one session on rumours it would abandon its peg to the US dollar and this triggered a global crash in stock markets.

In the event, it maintained its peg, thanks to its strong reserves. The dollar peg had been a key tenet of economic policy since "Black Saturday", when the then floating Hong Kong dollar was sold off to unprecedented lows on news of the handover from Britain to China. Hong Kong's fierce defence of the peg also sent a message to currency speculators that lingers even now.

However, in protecting its currency, Hong Kong was forced to raise interest rates savagely to maintain global investor interest. The Hong Kong Monetary Authority also bought domestic shares worth up to $15 bn to deter speculators. The government ultimately made a profit from the shares, but it was only able to take this action because of its strong governance to that point and it was not an option open to other countries in the region.

The combination of high interest rates, a weakening stock market and depleted government coffers led to a slump, from which Hong Kong did not begin to recover until 1999. It received additional setbacks from the dotcom fallout of 2000 and 2001 and the SARS outbreak in 2003. GDP growth just remained in positive territory, but was only 0.5% for 2001, 1.8% for 2002 and 3% for 2003.

The years leading up to the Lehmans crisis were Hong Kong's salad days. It has proved a useful public face for China to the rest of the world and has significantly benefited from Chinese growth. According to the IMF, its GDP rocketed 8.5% in 2004, 7.1% in 2005 and 6.4% in 2006 while GNI per capita rose from $26 570 in 2000 to $31 420 in 2008. Inflation was under control, employment was high and the country built up a significant current account surplus of $18.5 bn – or 36.6% of GDP, according to the Statistics office of Hong Kong.

These years were important as well from a legislative point of view. Under chief executive Donald Tsang, plans for full democracy were unveiled and, in late 2007, the Chinese government said Hong Kong would be able to elect its own leader in 2017 and parliament by 2020. The timescale disappointed pro-democracy campaigners, who went on to win a third of the seats in the legislative elections, thereby significantly improving their position.

But Hong Kong could not remain immune to world events. Although its leading banks – such as HSBC – emerged relatively cleanly from the banking crisis, its position as a global financial centre left it exposed. Its fifth largest lender, the Bank of East Asia, saw a bank run – the first since the Asian crisis. Its GDP dropped 7.8% in the first quarter of 2009 and 3.8% in the second quarter from the corresponding period the year before and the IMF was expecting an overall fall of 3.6% for the whole year, among the weakest in Asia.

5.3.1 The Investment Case for Hong Kong

Hong Kong had its major financial crisis in 1997 and spent the next 10 years deleveraging. As such it did not have many of the structural imbalances of developed economies going into the credit crunch. Its banks, most notably HSBC, avoided the worst of the subprime crisis and emerged as among the best capitalized and strongest in the world. However, its open economy meant it got hit through trade during the crisis – trading and logistics still contribute more than a quarter of GDP. Exports were down 7.2% in the third quarter, with domestic exports – as distinct from those coming from China – hit particularly hard.

The IMF has predicted a strong bounce-back for the country. China absorbs almost half of Hong Kong's exports and its growth remains robust, which should serve to shore up the economy. Private consumption expenditure is recovering after a weak first quarter in 2009 that saw a drop of 6%.

In the longer term, Hong Kong is geographically blessed and should continue to be a significant beneficiary of Chinese growth. China is growing as an export partner while, as of 2009, Europe and the US took 13.7% and 12.5% of exports respectively – which may be an advantage or a disadvantage depending on the outlook for the global economy. After all, the US consumer may not remain chastened forever.

There are opportunities for Hong Kong to integrate further into China. "Hong Kong is first and foremost part of China's Guangdong Province – they are all Cantonese," says Alan Gibbs, manager of the Waverton Asia Pacific fund.

"It's a remarkable thing given what's happened with China; how long it's taken Hong Kong to get together with Guangdong Province, both physically – the road and the train and the bridge systems are still pretty poor – and in the way they don't talk to each other very much. They're pretty zealous of their own independence. So the first step towards Hong Kong's full integration into China would be closer ties with Guangdong Province, which is happening."

Hong Kong does not have the industrialization story that makes so much of the rest of Asia attractive nor is it likely to see a domestic consumption boom. Per capita GDP is already high and is unlikely to expand as it will in other Asian countries. That said, a property boom remains a real possibility.

Hong Kong's real attraction for an investor lies in the companies listed there, which may not necessarily reflect the economy. The Hong Kong Stock Exchange remains the main route into China. This is something of a historical accident. Before China opened its own stock exchange its largest and strongest companies tended to list in Hong Kong. Some of the companies are listed in both countries now, but many international investors prefer the corporate governance and regulation that exists in Hong Kong. So-called "red-chips" are shares of Hong-Kong-registered companies that have large interests in China.

There have been fears that as the Shanghai market expands, Hong Kong will lose its usefulness but Philip Ehrmann, manager of the Jupiter China fund, does not see that as a significant possibility for the next 20 years or so given Hong Kong's pre-eminence as a trading centre. The Shanghai exchange remains relatively opaque and, for the time being at least, valuations are higher.

In common with much of Asia, Hong Kong companies do not have significant borrowings. The market also contains some of the largest and/or fastest-growing companies in the world. There is no shortage of internationally recognized brands, such as Bank of China, Cathay Pacific, China Mobile and HSBC.

For the time being, its biggest risk may be not so much its weakness, but its strength. Hong Kong has been attracting attention for some eye-popping real estate prices, to the extent that many are starting to worry about an asset bubble. In late 2009, Sun Hung Kai Properties, the world's biggest property developer by market capitalization, brought flats to the market for HK$75 000 (US$9700) per square foot.

The Hong Kong dollar is pegged to the US dollar, so the country effectively imports US monetary policy. If Hong Kong raised its rates significantly higher than the dollar, money would move in and push up the value of the Hong Kong dollar and vice versa, so Hong Kong has to keep its rates in line with the US. This means interest rates are likely to remain artificially low for some time as the US recovers, even though Hong Kong's relative economic strength means it does not need low rates. This can create excess liquidity and, in turn, bubbles in asset prices.

If bubbles do emerge, people will make a lot of money on the way up, but they will need to know when to get out. The main Hong Kong index, the Hang Seng, rose more than 40% in the 10 years since the turn of the century, compared to a 25% fall in the FTSE 100, but it is prone to accelerating and then crashing.

Between them, Hong Kong and Singapore are Asia's safe pair of hands. Corporate governance is strong, markets are open and transparent and both are well-established, internationally recognized trading centres. Hong Kong's strength will remain its position as the gateway to China. Investors should beware of bubbles, but in the short term the good times are likely to keep rolling.

Stock market focus: Hong Kong

The main Hong Kong index, the Hang Seng, is the largest index in the region with, as of the end of 2009, a market capitalization of $1390 bn. It is comprised of 45% in Hong Kong ordinary shares, 39% in H shares and 16% in red-chips. At the end of 2009, financials was by far the largest sector, with around 50% of the index, followed by energy, property and construction and telecommunications at some 10% each. HSBC was by far the largest stock, with a 14% weighting.

5.4   SINGAPORE – A BRIEF ECONOMIC HISTORY

Singapore was among the first into the recession following the global financial crisis. Its open economy left it globally exposed and vulnerable to external shocks and its GDP took a sharp lurch down in the immediate aftermath of the credit crunch.

Up to that point, Singapore's approach had served it well. It is consistently rated the top country in the world for ease of doing business. Its economy had returned to robust growth in 2002 after the Asian crisis and by 2004 had picked up sufficient steam to deliver a 9.3% rise in GDP. This strength continued for the next three years with GDP growing 7.3%, 8.4% and 7.8% in 2005, 2006 and 2007. In fact, some economists argued the downturn was welcome to cool things down.

It has moved, apparently seamlessly, up the manufacturing value chain. Like many Asian countries it started out as a manufacturing base, but that seems a long time ago now. Manufacturing still makes up around 20% of GDP but it is in areas such as sophisticated electrical components, marine engineering or biomedical firms that it has found its niche. One fund manager described it as "the shipyard and maintenance" for the Chinese economy.

However, Singapore's real strength is in services. Almost 30% of its GDP is from business and financial services and these saw only marginal falls as a result of the credit crisis and then a strong rebound over 2009. The hard-hit sectors have been wholesale and retail trade, hotels and transport and storage.

The former British colony was built on trade, as the home of the East India Company. It achieved independence in 1959, though it did not emerge as a significant player on the world economic stage until well into the 1960s. Its Economic Development Board was set up in 1961 and had considerable success in building an industrial base and drawing in foreign investment with tax incentives. The sector evolved on the back of industrialization to producing higher-value goods. The now all-important service sector grew on the back of the needs of shipping companies using Singapore as a port.

Its road to riches has not been without its speed bumps. Nick Leeson's antics on the Singapore Stock Exchange in 1995 exposed a somewhat too freewheeling approach to capitalism in the region. In 1998, the country suffered in the Asian crisis and it slipped into recession for the first time in 13 years.

5.4.1   The Investment Case for Singapore

Given its global clout it is easy to forget Singapore is only around 700 square kilometres in size. In GDP terms, however, it is the world's 47th largest country, with a total GDP of $238 503 m. According to the World Bank, its per capita GNI was $34 760 in 2008, up from $22 960 in 2000, but still some way off that of the US at $47 580.

Come the end of 2009, as Western governments worried about reviving their flagging economies, Singapore's leaders had different problems on their hands. That year saw money flooding into its property and stock markets as investors sought a stable, high-growth home for their wealth, forcing the government to worry about a potential bubble.

Singapore's property market rose some 15% in 2009 although there were pockets that rose even further – S&P research showed Singapore real estate investment trusts surged 63% in the second quarter of the year. While the property market has not yet hit the giddy heights it reached in 2007, it has been enough for the government to intervene to ban interest-only loans though, as yet, it has shied away from full-blown monetary tightening.

The sector is being given a boost by Russian money, which is also filtering through to Singaporean private banks, property funds and luxury services companies. International fund flows into the country tailed off after significant growth in 2006 and 2007, but had returned to pre-crunch levels by the end of 2009.

There is logic behind the flow of money into the country. The economy staged a remarkable bounce-back over the course of 2009. The third quarter economic data from the Monetary Authority of Singapore showed a 14.9% seasonally adjusted, quarter on quarter annualized rise in GDP. Having previously predicted an overall contraction for 2009 of 4% to 6%, the authority said the contraction was more likely to be nearer 2.2%. Output in 2009 rose 0.8% year on year yet consumer prices remain low and employment is rising. These are figures to make a Western premier drool.

For international investors looking for a safe home for their cash, Singapore looks the picture of health – it is exposed to the Asian growth story, has a strong and stable government, world-class companies and a sound economy.

It is not even as if international fund flows are particularly needed. Singapore was among the first into the sovereign wealth fund game – Temasek Holdings was established in 1974, while the Government of

Singapore Investment Corporation (GSIC) was established in 1981. At the end of 2009, Temasek was worth some $120 bn and, while GSIC does not disclose its fund size, *The New York Times* estimated it to be in the region of $265 bn even though it suffered heavy losses in 2008.

These sovereign wealth funds offer an important stabilization mechanism. GSIC is run with a 20-year time horizon and aims to "preserve and enhance" Singapore's foreign reserves. The government has not had to call upon it to release reserves during the crisis. GSIC invests globally while Temasek, which manages the Singapore government's direct investments, is focused almost exclusively in Singapore and the rest of Asia.

But Singapore's strength is also a danger – too much money sloshing around the system can be carelessly spent – companies invest without thought, banks dole out too much to consumers and the economy overheats. Equally, it can make things extremely expensive, including share prices. Singapore's growth is strong but it is not worth any price.

"Singapore's government policies and economic development have been one of the great success stories of the region but it all changes very quickly according to global circumstances," says Andrew Gillan, manager of the Aberdeen Asian Income fund. "It is often forgotten alongside China and India, but there are good opportunities for Singapore companies. A lot of Singapore's companies are truly regional."

Stock market focus: Singapore

The main index in Singapore is the Strait Times index, which covers the country's 30 largest companies. By the end of 2009, it had a total market capitalization of $114 bn and, while well diversified, had concentration points in banks (27.5%), general industrials (17%), telecoms (14%) and real estate (11.5%). Singapore Telecom is the largest company, at $14.7 bn. The market peaked at 3831 in October 2007, dipping to 1513 at the height of the credit crunch. It swiftly recovered by around 1000 points.

5.5   SOUTH KOREA – A BRIEF ECONOMIC HISTORY

South Korea's path to political and economic stability has been chaotic. The government has intervened heavily in the economy, leading to some significant imbalances and unintended consequences. For example, it engineered a forced rationalization of many of the country's industries in the 1980s in an attempt to address imbalances that had built up over the previous decade. It merely succeeded in creating monopolistic or oligopolistic conglomerates or "chaebols", whose excessive debt contributed to the crisis of 1997.

Each decade aimed to address the problems of the last. Even when the country appeared to reach a "Goldilocks" point in the mid-1990s – with stable inflation, GDP growth and low unemployment – it was soon exposed by the Asian financial crisis of 1997. At that point the won sank against the dollar and South Korea's foreign reserves were quickly depleted in trying to shore it up. The country's debt problem was laid bare with both the government and domestic companies laden with short-term external debt.

The fallout was painful. Corporations went bust – even among the chaebols – and that had a knock-on effect for the banking sector, which was swamped with non-performing loans. In a familiar tale, banks tightened their lending criteria just as corporations needed it most. The country finally agreed terms for IMF bailout loans in December 1997.

Nudged by the conditions laid out by the IMF, South Korea's government has learnt its lesson and has made few mistakes in policy since. Monetary policy has been tight, with interest rates reaching as high as 20% at one point. Public sector spending has been kept in check with the civil service rationalized. The financial sector was re-engineered with the Non-performing Asset Resolution fund set up in late 1997 to house weak assets away from banks' balance sheets. The banks were recapitalized.

South Korea's companies were also in need of a clear-up to reduce their levels of debt and improve their corporate governance structures. But the government had learnt its lesson about the unintended consequences of interfering too heavily in the corporate sector and let it do its worst. A notable casualty was the giant chaebol Daewoo, which was dismantled by the government in 1999 due to excessive debt.

Among the corporate governance structures that came in was legal protection for minority shareholders. Accounting rules were introduced, conforming to internationally recognized standards. The restructuring reduced the power of the chaebols, as the government committed to end the cronyism that had seen them pick up preferential contracts. The crisis also broke some of the union strength that had hampered labour market flexibility. Unemployment rose from 2.6% in November 1997 to 7.6% in July 1998.

This action proved effective and much of the growth that has characterized the decade since the Asian crisis has stemmed from those policy decisions. The economy also proved itself more flexible than its detractors gave it credit for. Then, as now, its highly skilled population served it well and this remains a key swing factor in South Korea's competitiveness over the longer term. Its education system produces a skilled and motivated workforce with strong scientific and mathematical suits.

5.5.1   The Investment Case for South Korea

Were it not for its volatile neighbour to the north, South Korea would occupy an enviable place among the global economies. It currently sits a surprising 13th in the world GDP charts. It has seen nearly a decade of strong GDP growth, boasts world-beating companies such as Samsung and Hyundai and is developing a strong consumer economy. It's just that unwelcome missile threat...

As with the other countries in this chapter, some debate remains as to whether South Korea is genuinely an emerging market. Its GNI per capita was $21 530 in 2008 and the IMF lists it as a developed country. MSCI has it on its watch list for "promotion" although it remains as an emerging market for now. MSCI said it had made the decision because the country's currency wasn't fully convertible and its stock market's real-time data didn't meet requirements. However, it is set to be reconsidered in 2010.

In September 2009, FTSE said South Korea would now be classified as a developed market for the purposes of its indices. Although the minutiae of why it may or may not be a developed market is of little concern to potential investors, its movement from one index to another can potentially have an impact.

FTSE estimates that around $3 tn is benchmarked against its indices worldwide, mostly in developed markets. South Korea has already benefited from an increase in fund flows since the change was announced and more are likely to follow once the change has been implemented. Such developments tend to provide a natural short-term support to markets.

"Its position as an emerging market is more a reflection on its business and market practice than any comment on its economic development," says James Syme, head of emerging markets at Baring Asset Management. "Corporate governance and accounting are always quite tricky in South Korea. As a result, the market tends to look cheap because investors have to price in the risk."

The criteria on which the index providers are basing their judgements tend to be economic development, market size and liquidity, a free and well-developed foreign exchange market, free delivery settlement, and off-exchange transactions. In all these things South Korea has come a long way in the past 25 years. Its first free parliamentary elections were as recent as 1988, though its economic transformation had started in the 1980s.

When the Lehmans crisis reared its head, many thought South Korea would be among the hardest hit. The region had seen debt increase once again and, according to the FT, its country's banks have been Asia's largest borrowers outside Japan in cross-border markets. The won was among the weakest of all major currencies against the dollar. It moved from 1118 for $1 pre-Lehmans in September 2008 to 1469 for $1 by the end of November 2009. Equally, it was a significant exporter and with global growth slowing, the country was always likely to be hit hard.

It was undoubtedly painful and even in September 2009 the export sector was still struggling, not helped by the resurgence in the currency as international fund flows were drawn back in. But October saw the country move up with a vengeance as rising demand from China restored export growth and helped the economy deliver its fastest growth in seven years for the third quarter of the year.

The weakness in the won was beneficial, but the gains were a tribute to the robustness of South Korea's products. Samsung, for example, saw net profit triple in the third quarter of 2009 on the back of higher microchip prices and strong sales of flat-panel TVs and mobile phones. China is the country's biggest export partner, taking a fifth of overall exports.

South Korea had maintained a positive current account balance every year since the Asian crisis and, while this record slipped in 2008, it looked set to hold for 2009. Consumer price inflation has remained stable at around 2% to 3% over the same period, only rising in 2008. Real GDP has remained in the region of 4–5%.

The country has a few other factors in its favour. Syme labels it the most advanced economy in the emerging world, adding: "Its technology is second only to Japan. It is super-competitive in steel as well." For his part, Angus Tulloch, head of emerging markets at First State Investments, has held department store Shinsegae and electronics group LG among his biggest holdings.

Even so, Bank of America Merrill Lynch's fund manager survey for October 2009 showed emerging market fund managers were still not keen on South Korea. Why? Syme believes the biggest problem for the country lies in its debt burden. Although the government has been prudent, the same cannot be said of consumers and companies, who have built up debts equivalent to that of developed markets such as the US or UK.

"One in four transactions in the economy is funded by debt and it is difficult to get very optimistic about the country," he says. "I don't see that there will be a big liquidity crisis, but there will be a period of sub-trend growth while personal and corporate balance sheets rebuild." South Korea also tends to be a cyclical market, so there are naturally good and bad times to invest.

As mentioned earlier, South Korea lives with the threat from its northern neighbour and stock markets largely factor this in. However, it is vulnerable to the withdrawal of international investment if its political situation worsens and its debt burden will hamper growth. On the bright side, the country has a relatively stable economy and some global leaders among its companies. The South Koreans' legendary work ethic should also keep it competitive.

Stock market focus: South Korea

The main index in South Korea is the Kospi, which at the end of 2009 had more than 700 underlying stocks and an overall market capitalization of $712 bn. There are also Kospi 100 and 200 indices that focus on the larger stocks. Some of the larger companies in the index will be familiar to many – Samsung is the largest, with Hyundai and LG also in the top 10. The index moved up from 870 at the start of 2005 to peak beyond 2000 in October 2007. Peak to trough, it lost around 50% of its value during the crisis, but by the end of 2009 had recovered to about 20% below its previous high. At that time, information technology made up around 30% of the index, with semiconductors second at 20%, then banks (11%) and autos (8%).

5.6 TAIWAN

Taiwan has built much of its economy on the provision of sophisticated electrical components to technology companies. As such, it was at the coalface of the economic downturn. Exports were hit significantly and the last three months of 2008 saw an annualized drop in GDP of 27% – the highest on record.

Taiwan is, to some extent, defined by its relationship with China. Relations have historically been fraught, with China claiming sovereignty over Taiwan since 1949, but the latter considering itself an independent state. President Ma Ying-jeou took office in March 2008 and has presided over a thawing of relations. This should expand the already buoyant market for Taiwanese goods in China and the stock market has surged on this expectation. "Chinese Taiwanese relations are improving dramatically," says Andrew Beal, manager of the Henderson TR Pacific trust. "They have never been this good – ever."

The Taiwanese government has now lifted its historic ban on Chinese investments into stock and futures markets, which has brought a valuable new source of capital into Taiwan. In April 2009, the Chinese government made its first investment into a Taiwanese company as it took a 12% stake in Far EasTone. The investment led to the largest gains in one session for the Taiwanese main Taiex index in 18 years.

The motive behind these moves is just as politically expedient as it is economically so. "This is a deliberate policy," says Mike Kerley, manager of the Henderson Asian Income fund. "Taiwan needs growth for political stability. Without growth there is social unrest and they will do anything to avoid that."

Although the credit crunch was painful – the IMF forecast a 4.1% slide in GDP for 2009 – the bounce-back has been swift and resolute. The third quarter of 2009 saw an annualized rise in GDP of 7.66% and it is forecast to return to its steady growth rate in 2010. Inflation is under control and Taiwan has maintained a healthy current account balance for many years, now standing at around 8% of GDP.

In addition to the influence of China, Taiwan's recovery has been buoyed by strength in domestic consumption, which has come in spite of continuing rises in unemployment. In fact, Taiwan is one of the few Asian countries to have had problems with excessive credit card debt. This has picked up some of the slack from the export sector, which has still not performed as well as expected. Although its human cost was devastating, Typhoon Morakot did little to derail the economy in August 2009.

Historically, the country's growth has been steady rather than spectacular, ranging between 4% and 6% from 2001. With a national income per head of around $17 000 a year, Taiwan is certainly not "developing" in the traditional sense of the word and indeed it has already achieved what many of the smaller Asian countries hope to do. It has moved to being a skilled manufacturing base with a good domestic demand story.

Stock market focus: Taiwan

Taiwan's stock market is relatively broad but it is still dominated by technology stocks. It tends to trade on higher multiples than its Asian peers and at the end of 2009 was on 28 times earnings, with a total market capitalisation of almost $600 bn. The main index is the Taiwan SE Weighted index. The market is largely driven higher by the potential for closer relations with China and lower from weakness in the technology sector. Despite their technology bias, Taiwanese stocks tend to pay higher dividends than elsewhere.

Company focus: Taiwan Semiconductor

Founded in 1987, Taiwan Semiconductor, which manufactures semiconductors for global companies, was the pioneer in its sector and now operates across China, India, Japan, Korea, the Netherlands, Taiwan and the US. The Taiwanese market is very information technology oriented, but quite a few companies pay high dividends. As recently as 2004, the company wasn't paying a dividend but it now yields around 5%. The reason why it is able to do this is that it is the dominant player within its market.

According to Richard Sennitt, manager of the Schroder Asian Income fund, the company has reached the sweet spot in terms of size versus its competitors. "It can spend a lot more on research and development," he explains. "It generates more free cashflow and can then invest in more research and development. It is one step ahead of its competitors and is very disciplined when it comes to shareholder returns."

Many of its companies can compete on a world stage. Taiwan Semiconductor, for example, is the world's largest contract chip maker, with around half the market. Taiwan Mobile announced towards the end of 2009 that it would acquire Carlyle Group's local cable TV business, making it the island's largest pay-TV provider.

Taiwan's problem from a competitive point of view is that, compared to many of its Asian peers, it remains a tricky place to do business. Although the IMF considers it an advanced economy, its corporate governance and business structures are one step behind. In a World Bank survey at the end of 2009, it still scored relatively poorly for ease of doing business, particularly when compared to Hong Kong and Singapore.

Its political future is also a negative for the country. It does not have a seat at the UN and China will not allow independent diplomatic relations with Taiwan, so the country only has formal diplomatic relations with a handful of countries. China is simply too powerful for global governments to challenge. Despite the recent improvements, its relationship with China remains relatively fragile, with Taiwan's defence ministry warning about China's military strength in 2009, saying it was far more than it needed for self-defence and was a threat to the region. US arms sales to Taiwan have also caused considerable friction with China.

Taiwan is also still reliant on a couple of sectors. The microchip industry is vital for the economy and has tended to attract the heavy-handed intervention of the government, which in 2009 created the Taiwan Innovative Memory Company with the aim of acquiring foreign technology and reforming the industry. However, the industry viewed this as a competitor rather than a saviour and still has some structural difficulties. It is seeing consolidation, which should help in the long term, but it is a cyclical business. Taiwan needs to ensure its long-term competitiveness while simultaneously diversifying its economy.

"Taiwan is interesting," says Syme at Baring Asset Management. "Although many things are broadly negative – for example, technology is facing big challenges and the banks are weak – there is increasing interest in pressing detente with the mainland. This could have a significant impact on the economy and particularly on property and asset prices.

"In Hong Kong, when China began to allow visitors across the border, a million visited in the next 12 months. If Beijing wants you to be happy, you can be happy. But overall, the increased level of visitors and investors will be good for property and asset-rich firms."

5.7 INVESTING IN THE REGION

All these markets will feature significantly in a pan-Asian portfolio because of their size. Active and passive funds are available on individual markets as well, though investors should be aware that each market has its own sector biases, which will affect the overall diversification of their portfolio. Because of their size and liquidity, they are unlikely to have the same pricing anomalies as less developed markets. However, for the most part, they will have stricter listing rules and better corporate governance.

5.8   CONCLUSION

While developed Asia still looks a great story, everyone knows it and, if everyone knows it, it is in the price of shares. Asset bubbles are undoubtedly a risk although it is in the nature of bubbles that investors will make a lot of money on the way up. If investors bear that warning in mind, the markets of Hong Kong, Singapore, South Korea and Taiwan can offer a more defensive way to access Asian markets.

6

The Rest of Asia

6.1 INTRODUCTION

Western economists have a long history of underestimating the resilience of the Asian economies and the global economic downturn has proved no exception. Received wisdom suggested they were too reliant on exports to failing Western economies, their currencies were weak and their fragile economies would ultimately bow under the strain. Decoupling was a myth – China simply did not have the might to carry them on its own. But how wise was received wisdom?

6.2 OVERVIEW

For a while, it looked as if received wisdom might have got it right. In the first quarter of 2009, output and then GDP sank for many of the Asian economies – for example, Thailand's GDP dropped 7.1% over 2008. But the rebound since then has been astonishing. In the second quarter of 2009 China's GDP grew by 15% on the first quarter, South Korea's by almost 10%, Singapore's soared by 21% and Indonesia's by 5%.

In October 2009, the IMF doubled its forecast for Asian growth for 2009, saying that just as the region's export dependency had caused a sharp slowdown initially, it was now generating a swift upturn as global trade resumed.

China, the engine for the region, delivered 8.7% GDP growth in 2009 – and it brings its neighbours with it. For example, the collective forecast for the five large developing economies of south-east Asia – Indonesia, Malaysia, the Philippines, Thailand and Vietnam – was raised from 2.3% to 4%. The IMF added that the region had been given a boost by a swift and effective policy response from Asian governments.

But there is more to it than this. First, Asia started in a better position. "During the credit crisis, there has been a clear difference between Asia and the rest of the world," says Mike Kerley, manager of the Henderson Far East Income trust. "Asia went into the downturn in a strong position.

"The credit crunch was a developed – rather than emerging – market phenomenon. Irrational credit and creative banking practices have created this problem. Asian markets had their pain after 1997. Asia blew itself up and spent the next 10 years deleveraging. Banks and industrials are not highly geared and Asia has been hit because of trade rather than any domestic phenomenon."

This has been perhaps the most important factor in Asia's recent resilience – they have been through it before. This meant that corporations felt justified in ignoring Western analysts who told them to gear up their balance sheets. It also meant consumers had a healthy fear of excessive debt and governments knew when to stop borrowing.

However, the downturn in the global economy forced Asian economies to reassess their economic priorities. The biggest problem in the Asian crisis had been a lack of foreign exchange reserves, so many economies in the region built up a strong export base with the aim of addressing that weakness. But the downturn exposed the vulnerability of an economy built on exports and generated some policy momentum behind a development in the economic model for Asian countries.

Governments have realized the ultimate goal has to be a strong domestic consumer, which will generate self-sustaining growth for the region and reduce its reliance on demand from foreign consumers. The strength of the savings ratio across Asian countries has been a boon so far, but governments will have to break the habit if the region is to continue its strong growth. "Domestic consumption has held up pretty well, but people are still saving rather than spending," says Kerley. "It's a legacy issue and a number of the governments' stimulus packages have been aimed at mobilizing consumer spending."

Asian populations have traditionally saved a high proportion of their income because they have had no social safety net, particularly pensions and health care. A lot of the stimulus measures are aimed at implementing a welfare state, encouraging people to spend and thereby allowing the domestic consumer economy to flourish. Interest rates are being kept low, which should deter savers. Those determined to continue saving are likely to put more money into equities. Either way, it should mean better news for the Asian economies.

When – if – the expected consumption boom comes, it could be huge as, even outside China and India, many Asian countries have huge populations. According to the World Bank at the end of 2009, Indonesia had 228 million people, the Philippines 90 million and Thailand 67 million.

To bridge the gap, many of the Asian economies have been pouring their enviable surpluses into infrastructure spending, led by China as we saw in Chapter 4. This has a number of purposes – to create jobs and boost internal economic momentum, to keep the economies motoring until domestic demand emerges to take up the slack, and to move these countries on the next stage of their development – accommodating urbanization.

To support infrastructure spending some of these countries have had to run down the surpluses they built up in recent years or, in the case of Malaysia, extend their budget deficit. However, in general, these stimulus packages are much more affordable for the Asian economies than they are for, say, the US or the UK.

Market watchers hope both infrastructure spending and the emergence of a domestic consumer will lead to a greater measure of decoupling from the growth of the rest of the world. In an Asian context, decoupling means that, instead of the region relying on exports to developed markets, increasing intra-emerging market trade will support exports and therefore growth. These countries would then be in charge of their own economic destiny and so their growth rates would not slavishly follow those of the West.

During the downturn, decoupling became a dirty word – of course, the naysayers suggested, no region was immune from a global slowdown, the US was still the largest consumer in the world of just about everything and its weakness was everyone's weakness. Those who had argued in favour of decoupling looked somewhat naïve.

But, whisper it quietly, is it possible that some measure of decoupling is in fact taking place? Otherwise, how to explain the phenomenal growth in Asia, while the US's growth had yet to recover? The economic pick-up in the Asian countries started in February 2009, but was only seen in the latter half of the year for many Western countries. Far from the US leading the world out of recession, as has happened in the past, Asia has been firmly at the forefront of the global recovery.

The pessimists have been quick to attribute this to re-stocking, but there has also been a bounce in domestic demand. This had been constrained by high commodity prices and agriculture prices in 2008, but grew stronger throughout 2009 – for example, South Korea's private consumption rose by an annualized 14% in the second quarter. The Asian economies are doing it for themselves.

Intra-regional trade patterns are changing. According to Goldman Sachs, intra-emerging market exports had leapt to 44% by 2009, with the US making up just 19% of the total. "There has been a significant rebound in exports to China for places such as South Korea," says Ewan Thompson, manager of the Neptune Emerging Markets fund.

"They may be selling smaller flat-screen TVs, but they are selling more of them. There is a shift in the export focus. Retail sales in China are climbing by about 20% per year. In the past Asian exporters have had to rely heavily on the health of the US consumer. US strength, however, is no longer a necessity as a new structural demand source emerges – namely China."

This development is crucial to the long-term success story in Asia. The extent of government debt in Western economies means they are unlikely to recover their hunger for Asian exports any time soon. To maintain the growth momentum, Asia has to look inwards.

Historically, plenty of overly optimistic assumptions have been made about the development of domestic consumption – most notably with regard to Japan – and Asian consumers keeping their hands in their pockets remains a risk. Still, they are showing signs of an increased willingness to spend.

The region also has, for the most part, demographics on its side, particularly in countries such as India, which has a large and well-educated young population and an emerging middle class. This helps both in terms of consumption and economic stability. The population working and paying taxes is sufficient large to support its dependants.

Of course, in the longer term, there are risks. There is a risk that governments don't rein in their stimulus measures quickly enough and inflation results. International money has to go somewhere and for a while Asia seemed like the safe haven – though it has already seen the prices of some assets spiral upwards.

There is also a risk the global recovery could stall and the current positive spiral could become a negative one. But if this were the case, Asia would be at less risk than elsewhere. Many Asian countries could afford their stimulus packages several times over without ever reaching US or UK debt levels.

Perhaps the biggest risk for the region is also its biggest strength – China. Without the influence of China, the remainder of Asia could look weak. India is more domestic in its focus but China provides demand for goods and services across Asia and has substantially supported the rebound in growth. For example, Korea's 65% climb in exports from trough to peak in the crisis was led substantially by Chinese demand for consumer electronics and cars.

Nevertheless, the path to industrialization does not always run smoothly and the credit crunch showed the vulnerability of even the strongest economies. The World Bank warned in November 2009 about the effects of inflation and particularly asset price bubbles in China, Singapore and Hong Kong on the back of rapid increases in equity and house prices across the region.

The developing countries in the region also have to make their way up the value chain, which may in turn reduce their dependence on China. They need to expand their service sector, which will take an increase in internal migration and improvements in education.

The credit crunch altered the make-up of many of these markets and, in every country except South Korea, exports now make up a smaller proportion of the overall economy. To some extent the credit crunch has done what governments have been trying to do for a while.

For investors, there have also been significant improvements in corporate governance. As we saw in the previous chapter, in the more developed Asian economies, corporate governance is second to none, with the majority of companies adopting developed market accounting standards and practices. The demands of global investors have ensured companies do not neglect the views of minority shareholders, among other historic bad practices.

However, weaknesses remain and investors still need to exercise considerable caution when investing. "In Asia, companies tend to be owned by the state or by families and you always have to be aware of the agenda of the controlling shareholders," says Angus Tulloch, head of emerging markets at First State Investments. "In developed markets, there are open registers and you can always do something about bad management. It is not the same in Asia, so you have to make sure they are going in the same direction as you."

6.3 INDONESIA

Indonesia has fallen in and out of favour with international investors depending on whether the region's seductive growth story or fear at its endemic political corruption has won the day. Fund flows and the currency, in particular, have been wildly volatile. Much of its future will depend on whether it can rebuild its crumbling political and social infrastructure and therefore make the most of the growth opportunities available to it.

Indonesia breezed through the credit crunch in much the same way as Vietnam. It did not record a single quarter of negative growth and was expected to grow at around 4% in 2009 – and this in spite of having more to deal with than most, as an earthquake in October 2009 left thousands homeless. Corporate profits remained resilient as companies that were focused on the large domestic consumption economy took the reins from commodity producers who suffered from weaker prices.

The domestic economy was supported by private spending and, in particular, the election campaign in the first half of 2009 while government spending took the baton in the second half. From then on, the region saw exports recover relatively rapidly as key trading partners such as Japan, Singapore, the European Union and US emerged from recession.

The country also benefited from its trade and current account surpluses. Debate remains as to whether the external debt level is an issue for the country but, by most measures, debt has reduced exponentially since the Asian crisis and Western debt levels dwarf those in Indonesia. Debt servicing as a percentage of GDP has dropped consistently.

The early depreciation of its currency served Indonesia well. The rupiah has recovered against a weakening dollar but, in common with much of Asia, the Indonesians learned their lessons about foreign-denominated debt in the Asian crisis of 1997. Although the government still issues the occasional dollar-denominated bond, it has found sufficient demand for its local currency-denominated bonds as well.

Loan growth has remained flat, in contrast to strong growth at the beginning of 2008, but the banking sector is in good shape, with relatively few bad loans to drag down growth as the global economy recovers. Interest rates were cut around 3% to support growth, but at the end of 2009 remained at 6.5%, although the government has committed to keeping them low for the near term. As in developed markets, the cuts have not necessarily filtered through to loan rates.

Unemployment in the country is high, at more than 8%, but it actually fell during the downturn. Where there were layoffs it affected a few regions very badly – mostly those concentrated on agricultural exports – but this meant domestic demand remained largely intact. It was supported by some fiscal stimulus during the crisis, but not as much in percentage terms as other Asian regions. The IMF is rarely seen encouraging fiscal laxity, but actually encouraged Indonesia to widen its fiscal deficit to maintain economic momentum in July 2009.

The strength of domestic demand is likely to be of key importance going forward. Indonesia has a huge population of 226 million, which is currently growing at 1.2% a year. Although per capital gross national income is lower than that of China ($2940 versus $2010), consumer confidence remains high. Growth prior to the crunch has been solid rather than exciting by Asian standards, running at around 5%, but this may also insulate it from the risks of higher-profile countries.

Indonesia has strength in commodities, which was a hindrance during the global slowdown when commodities prices fell off a cliff, but should be a long-term strength if China continues its growth trajectory. Its strongest areas are thermal coal and palm oil, but it also has reserves of copper, oil, gas and gold.

The country's big bugbear is its political make-up and the recent arrest of the former chairman of the anti-corruption agency for murder has done little to improve its reputation. President Susilo Bambang Yudhoyono came into power on an anti-corruption ticket, promising to bring foreign investment into the country with a crackdown, but his reformist credentials have been called into question. There are a number of well-respected ministers in government, notably the finance and trade ministers, but Indonesia has a long way to go to shake off its reputation for graft.

Also the left-leaning politics don't please international investors. The country's infrastructure is decrepit and requires huge spending, but the government is committed to some chunky social spending programmes. The remaining structural weaknesses for Indonesia centre on inflation, which remains stubbornly high. It was 11.1% at the end of 2008 and although that dropped to 4% in 2009, the IMF was expecting it to head up to 6% or higher in 2010.

A big problem for investors is the lack of companies that can compete on a world stage. The country lacks any big domestic brand names, which leaves it vulnerable to the locals developing a taste for foreign goods. The worst situation would be for foreign companies to mop up the newly created domestic demand from 226 million – and counting – consumers.

Investors have periodically become very excited about Indonesia – for example, in late 2009, Standard Chartered Bank issued a report entitled "Indonesia: Asia's emerging powerhouse". Investors have periodically become very excited about Indonesia – for example, in late 2009, Standard Chartered Bank issued a report entitled "Indonesia: Asia's emerging powerhouse". Interestingly, the IMF has called to bracket it with the BRIC giants. It is, after all, the 16th largest country in the world according to World Bank estimates, ahead of Australia, Poland and the Netherlands.

Stock market focus: Indonesia

The main index in Indonesia is the Jakarta Composite, which fell from peak levels of 2830 in January 2008, to 1245 in March 2009 – a 56% drop that put it in the middle of Asian stock markets for performance. The index has substantially recovered its previous strength as the global economy moved upwards. Financials make up the largest share of the index, but are more structurally sound than many developed markets' banks. Energy and telecoms also feature highly with materials providing a significant share.

6.4   MALAYSIA

Malaysia has already started its ascent from a raw materials exporter to a sophisticated, value-added economy, but seems to have got stuck en route. Nor does it seem likely to resume its growth path any time soon. It has been among the hardest hit of the Asian economies with exports down heavily year on year in 2009. But it still has high household savings, a current account surplus and its government is promising a liberalization of the service sector and boosts for private investment. Will this economic strength help it recover faster?

Malaysia has been a victim of the so-called "Wal-Mart effect", whereby global consumers came to prefer unbranded cheap goods, such as those produced in Vietnam or China, to the more sophisticated electrical components and automobile parts in which Malaysia now specializes. Exports fell around 30% year-on-year from January to July 2009 and although growth has resumed, demand from the European Union and Japan remains subdued.

Japan in particular has been an important trading partner for Malaysia and its weakness has rubbed off. According to the World Bank, there are 1300 Japan or Japan-related companies in Malaysia and these Japanese multinationals have been vital in building up trade. The electrical and electronics sector, which makes up 38% of exports and 9% of GDP, will be vital in the pick-up of the economy. That said, Singapore is the country's largest overall export partner (with 14.7% of exports), and its strength should offset some weakness elsewhere.

Thus far, the Malaysian economy is one of the weakest in the region, with a 3.6% drop in GDP in 2009 (IMF estimate). This is lower than any other major East Asian country, including Thailand, which fell 3.5%. This is mostly a reflection of the huge early hit Malaysia took from the credit crunch, as growth resumed in the second quarter. However, it has not returned with the tailwinds that have been seen in some parts of Asia and 2010 growth is expected to be a relatively anaemic 2.5%. Although these are figures that many of the developed economies would envy, it remains weak compared to many of Malaysia's neighbours.

With a chunky current account surplus, Malaysia had the firepower to inject some stimulus into the economy. In the end, the announced stimulus measures were around 10% of GDP, though the World Bank has suggested not all of that may have been spent yet. It has also suggested the country's stimulus measures had not been as effective as elsewhere in Asia.

Political uncertainty has also affected sentiment towards Malaysia and caused a reversal in some of the foreign direct investment that had supported the country to date. In early 2008, the ruling coalition lost its two-thirds majority in parliament for the first time since independence in 1957.

Ratings agency Standard & Poor's downgraded Malaysia's credit rating on the back of the ensuing turmoil from "positive" to "stable". There have also been concerns about the increasing "Islamisation" of government institutions and Sharia courts are becoming more extensive, an issue that troubles global investors.

However, politics aside, some of the things that have weakened the economy thus far may also play a part in its resurgence. Production was cut fast in response to the global slump in demand, but Malaysian companies were reluctant to lay off skilled or semi-skilled workers as they worried about being able to rehire them when growth returned. There is still a lack of skilled labour to call upon. As a result, it was largely contractors and foreign workers who were laid off and unemployment rose by just 0.1% in the recession. The struggle has been to re-hire workers quickly enough as demand has improved.

This has had a number of effects. First, Malaysia hasn't witnessed the huge rises in poverty seen in other parts of Asia. It also hasn't seen the drop in domestic demand. People remain cautious, but they have always had high household savings and relatively low levels of debt. This gives a good base from which to build the recovery. Domestic demand is not expected to be a significant engine of growth for the country, but at least it is not providing a headwind.

Foreign exchange reserves remain strong, at around $94 bn at the start of 2010. Although lower than 12 months previously, it means holdings of foreign debt are well covered. According to the IMF, while the country runs with a healthy trade surplus of around 13% of GDP, which is again expected to drop, it remains among the highest of all Asian countries. The banking sector is also in good health, so companies and consumers are unlikely to feel the same liquidity pinch as is being seen in developed markets. On the corporate side, debt remains relatively low at just over 26%.

Malaysia's focus on higher-end manufacturing is unlikely to be a disadvantage for long and its reasonably diverse export sector should help longer-term growth. Ultimately, it is politics and racial tensions that are likely to derail the Malaysian growth story. International investors loath instability.

Stock market focus: Malaysia

Malaysia has traditionally been seen as a "low beta" – traditionally less risky – market and has proved more defensive than other Asian markets during sell-offs. This is because there are reasonably high levels of local institutional ownership of equities. This concentration on domestic investment has been even more pronounced since political uncertainty in 2008 led to the withdrawal of foreign capital. The local stock market is also supported by high domestic savings ratios.

The main index is the FTSE Bursa Malaysia KLCI – formerly the Kuala Lumpur Composite Index – which comprises the 30 largest listed companies and totalled $113 bn in market capitalization at the end of 2009. It dropped 44.85% from its peak in January 2008 to its trough that December, but recovered quickly from March onwards.

Company focus: Aeon Co

Aeon Co is a leading Malaysian retailer. It was incorporated in 1984, after the Malaysian government asked parent company Aeon Japan to help modernize its retail sector. Aeon now has a chain of department stores across Malaysia, mostly in suburban residential areas, catering to middle-income households.

> The company saw revenue growth of 19% from 2007 to 2008 and pre-tax profits growth of 11%. Its strong growth has been led by the development of the consumer economy in Malaysia and may accelerate as the economy develops. At the end of 2009, it was one of the top ten holdings for Hugh Young, managing director of Aberdeen Asset Management Asia, in his Aberdeen Asian Smaller Companies fund.

6.5   THE PHILIPPINES

The Philippines managed to avoid a recession in 2009. This doesn't make it unique in Asia, but the reason it avoided it does – it was supported by consumer demand. The country has one of the highest per capita incomes in developing Asia at $11 880 and it loves to shop. It is home to the third largest mall in the world.

There were other reasons for the Philippines' continued strength. Remittances sent home by the 8 million-plus Filipinos living and working abroad had reached their highest level ever by mid-2009. This is both a curse and a blessing for the country's economy. The remittances are welcome – and the diversity of their sources has helped ensure their consistency – but the widespread migration of a large proportion of the well-educated population has slowed growth.

Consumer spending still forms around two-thirds of the local economy – as high as that of the UK – and its quarter of negative growth at the start of 2009 was its first since the 1980s. Consumer confidence remained high even in the face of the typhoons and flooding that hit Manila.

This may sound like a good thing – after all, much of the rest of Asia is trying desperately to encourage its citizens to spend – but the government of the Philippines recognizes there needs to be some rebalancing in the economy. Exports of goods, however, were significantly weaker in the first two quarters of 2009 and only recovered towards the end of the year.

Manufacturing is the main alternative source of economic growth, and production has been weak with levels significantly below its pre-crisis peak – so much so, in fact, that many Filipinos fear a double-dip as manufacturers lay off swathes of workers. The Philippines has always been a country with disparate wealth levels, but this may become even more of a problem.

The country's export picture does have some things going for it, however – around 70% of its exports to China are in value-added electronics and electrical components, which should be a strong area of growth for an industrializing country.

The Philippines is building something of a speciality in business process outsourcing, covering back-office administration, engineering and financial services. As global companies reassess their cost base, particularly in hard-hit areas such as banking, there is a second wave of outsourcing emerging. The country has managed to establish itself as an alternative venue to India for outsourcing, which has helped the services sector weather the global economic slowdown.

The economy has some basic strengths too. Having learnt its lesson from the 1997 crisis, it had strong foreign exchange reserves and no debt problems going into the global financial crisis. This enabled the government to shore up the economy by spending and real GDP was expected to rise 1% in 2009. Furthermore, the country still has a current account surplus of more than $3 bn.

It has grown in a modest but unexciting way since the end of the Asian crisis with growth ranging from 4.4% (in 2002) to 7.1% (in 2008). Inflation has generally been well controlled but did show signs of becoming a problem in 2008 when it hit 9.5%. The downturn brought it back in line.

In the corporate sector, according to the World Bank, profits grew 12% on average in 2009 – the highest in the region – compared with a drop of 28% in 2008. The stock market, however, remains perilous for investors. Attempts in late 2009 to halt trading in the Benguet Corporation reinforced international investors' negative image of the country's stock exchange.

This saw a huge insider trading and price-rigging scandal in 1999 and a new securities law and better corporate governance legislation was launched on the back of it – but scepticism remains about the strength of the reforms. Some of the major global pension funds have periodically struck the Philippines from their list of permissible investments on the back of these doubts.

The Philippines population of 90 million does not offer the potential economic firepower of Indonesia, but its propensity to spend is a huge advantage. The country's economy is generally in good shape and it is already making its way up the development curve. The biggest problem, as with Indonesia, is likely to be political, and the extent to which investors believe their capital is safe. The country still has some way to go.

Stock market focus: the Philippines

The Philippines Stock Exchange remains relatively small with a market capitalization of $127.6 m, as of the end of 2009. Daily liquidity is light – for example, in November 2009 it varied between $106 m and $159 m – so getting in and out can prove costly. Like Vietnam it is a market that favours locals, who can source liquidity on stocks and negotiate the market's foibles.

The main index is the Manila Composite, which is almost entirely comprised of domestic focused stocks, such as property developers, banks and retailers, so an investment is a pure play on the local economy. Electronics and other major exporters do not tend to be listed. There is a reasonable spread of sectors, but financials are still the largest stocks, with industrials, services and property in support.

6.6   THAILAND

Before the 1997 crash, Thailand had a brief moment as the economists' darling. In the run-up to the crisis, GDP was growing at around 8% for 10 years, money flowed in and the good times rolled. Since its currency devaluation and economic slump at the end of the 1990s, it has never quite recovered its economic verve. Growth has been stable but unexciting and investors have been put off by continued political instability.

The credit crunch did it no favours either. Around two-thirds of Thailand's economy is in exports and a substantial chunk of that is the export of car parts. Many of the large Japanese companies used Thailand as a manufacturing base, which skewed its exports towards automobiles and electronics. This made Thailand uniquely vulnerable to declining global growth and the downturn hit hard.

Unemployment rose significantly in the automobile sector while GDP fell 3.5% in 2009. Of the major Asian economies, only Malaysia was expected to do worse. Nevertheless, 2010 looked brighter, although the country's fortunes truly seem to rise and fall with those of the global economy.

Political instability has done little to endear Thailand to the global investment community. A state of emergency was declared in December 2008 as anti-government protesters took over Bangkok's two major airports. As further civil unrest in 2010 confirmed, tensions remain between the rural poor and the Bangkok governing classes. The 2006 coup is also relatively fresh in investors' minds. Ultimately, domestic harmony always seems a relatively fragile and temporary state.

"So much depends on how these countries have reacted to the growth of China," says Stuart Parks, manager of the Invesco Asian fund. "Countries such as Thailand are having a difficult time because they set themselves up as a cheap manufacturing base and they've been replaced by China. As yet they haven't found anything to take the place of those exports."

Thailand – in common with much of the rest of Asia – hopes that ultimately domestic demand will fill the void left by cheap manufacturing exports. The first stimulus package to be put in place after the credit crunch was aimed at promoting domestic demand through private consumption and the second at infrastructure development.

The World Bank has spoken of the need for Thailand to avoid the "middle income" country trap by taking early action on bottlenecks in infrastructure, education and improved competition in manufacturing and services. With exports likely to remain weaker as key developed markets struggle to resume growth, Thailand needs to find another source of growth.

As yet, there is relatively little sign of this happening. Household consumption rose 0.8% in the second quarter of 2009 and consumer sentiment improved but consumption was hit hard at the start of 2009 and the country has a long crawl back to health. Manufacturing had not recovered to pre-crisis levels by the start of 2010. While tourism, which comprises up to 10% of the Thai economy, has recovered, it has also been dented by the political tensions.

Does Thailand have anything going for it from an investment point of view? Its growth was stable, if unexciting from 2002 to 2007, ranging from 4.6% up to 7.1%, and it is expected to bounce back quite strongly in 2010. The IMF was predicting a solid 3.7% growth, which was higher than the forecasts for Malaysia and the Philippines. The country also has a current account surplus – not as strong as those of China or Malaysia, granted, but a surplus is a surplus. This gives it leeway and should ensure some stability in the currency.

Equally, if it is successful in improving private consumption and expanding infrastructure through its stimulus programmes, then – with a strengthening export base – it could have a good story to tell. But this is going to be difficult to implement effectively with an unstable political regime. Ultimately, Thailand has a long way to go and that needs to be reflected in the price of shares. There are relatively few companies that can stand on their own merits to defy the wider Thai economic environment and tempt investors.

Stock market focus: Thailand

From peak to trough in the credit crunch, the main Thai index, the SET Composite, fell 56%. The market had never quite kept up with other Asian stock markets and the same was true in the recovery phase at the beginning of 2009. The stock market also lacks rich pickings for investors. Most of the companies listed are micro, small or medium-sized businesses – there are few world-beaters among its ranks – and this has been reflected in stock market performance.

6.7   VIETNAM

Vietnam has been a roller-coaster ride for investors in recent years. The country attracted record foreign investment in 2007, which created a speculative boom and significant overcapacity in the economy. The crash, when it came, was savage with stock markets down over 80% from peak to trough. It may put many people off investing for some time to come, but Vietnam's economy has proved resilient and has not seen a single quarter of negative growth.

Prior to 2008, Vietnam had been averaging 7%-plus annual growth since 1991. Even for 2009, it was still expected to deliver 4.6% growth – not as high as China, but still stronger than much of the rest of Asia. Its exports have proved surprisingly resilient – seeing single-digit falls – which may well be because the type of low-cost, non-branded goods in which Vietnamese manufacturers specialize have become more popular as global consumers have been squeezed. Exports have also been supported by a weakened currency.

There have been stimulus measures as well. The Vietnamese government has provided a 4% interest loan subsidy for businesses, which helped improve the availability of capital and support Vietnamese enterprises. Over $20 bn has been lent under the scheme and credit expansion is approaching the government's target of 30%. The government also instigated a liberalization of consumer lending, which enabled banks to lend to consumers at better rates.

This expansion in domestic demand growth is likely to be the most important support for Vietnamese growth in the years ahead. The Vietnamese have proved themselves willing and able consumers with retail sales growth of more than 20% in 2008 and market research group RNCOS suggests it may double between 2008 and 2012. As such, there is real scope for Vietnamese consumer-facing companies to build brand strength.

Vietnam has a few other factors on its side too. It has a relatively young and well-educated population. It has a good export base with strength in agricultural machinery and consumer goods. Inflation has historically been a problem – consumer price inflation ran at 23% in 2008 – but the downturn has brought it back under control and it was expected to be around 7% by the end of 2009. Urbanization is running at around 3% a year, which should support growth in the longer term.

There remain structural imbalances in the economy, however, with the trade deficit nearly tripling in the credit crunch. The Vietnamese tend to import higher value-added goods and export lower value-added goods, but its import bill did not lower in step with its export income during the downturn. The unexpected strength of exports has protected the country to some extent in the short term, but the gap is still widening and will need to be addressed.

Also, there are problems of corruption. The government introduced anti-corruption legislation in May 2009 but it will take some time for the effects to be felt. Corruption directly hits investors and many prefer to use local investment groups as they are in a better position to negotiate the insider dealing and front running to which markets are prone. There are also legislative hurdles for foreign investors, which domestic fund managers can overcome.

The economy is still vulnerable to liquidity squeezes, as was seen during the credit crunch. Vietnam does not have the healthy foreign reserves of many of its Asian neighbours on which to rely in difficult times. However, less government paper is held offshore post-crunch, so it is less vulnerable than it has been in the past.

The stock market, in theory at least, should be expanding and diversifying. Vietnam joined the World Trade Organization in 2006 and, as part of its participation criteria, must sell some of its state-owned assets. Early "equalizations" – "privatization" being considered too loaded a term in socialist Vietnam – have taken place with Vietcombank and Vietnam Airlines.

However, with the government inclined to put too high a price on the assets, these have not been a resounding success and have tended to attract only local rather than international interest. They have also placed onerous legal requirements on investors signing up for deals, forcing them to commit to a potentially unknown price. The government may wise up to the demands of foreign investors in future flotations, but these have not yet provided the opportunity they should have done.

Government controls remain a thorn in the side of all foreign investors in Vietnam. For example, the transportation sector should, in theory, represent a good investment opportunity, with demand high and supply low, but government controls weaken the growth story. Again, this may change over time, but it remains a problem in the short term.

The Vietnamese dong has also had a tempestuous time although the currency is likely to stabilize – providing the government keeps a lid on inflation and the deficit remains manageable, particularly as the dollar is expected to weaken against most global currencies in the near term. Interest – around the 7% level at the end of 2009 – will go higher if the trade deficit widens significantly.

The question for investors, therefore, is whether all these elements are in the price of shares. Vietnam has seen its stock market boom and bust and at the time of writing was a long way off its highs while trading at a discount to many of its Asian peers. It is likely that, until it matures as a market, Vietnam is more likely to continue to attract speculative investment at certain points in the cycle.

Certainly it polarizes the opinion of experts. "Vietnam has a lot of things going for it – for example, lower wages per head than China," says Stuart Parks, manager of the Invesco Asian fund. "However, it overexpanded leading up to 2008 and built up a relatively large current account deficit. When the global economy slowed, it was left with a huge import bill, which put pressure on the currency.

"Vietnam saw huge growth and that brought banking lending expansion. Its economy grew too quickly and inflationary pressures emerged. This is different to the rest of Asia where, by and large, inflationary pressures are under control. In the long term, Vietnam is a strong story, but it is not as attractive as the rest of Asia at the moment."

But the country also has its high-profile fans. "Vietnam will play an important part in the region," says Angus Tulloch, head of emerging markets at First State Investments. "It is low-cost, very entrepreneurial and very determined. Let's face it, over the past century, they've fought France, the US and China, and won." At the very least that says something for the resilience of the Vietnamese spirit.

Stock market focus: Vietnam

The main index in Vietnam is the VNI, which comprises 188 companies with an overall market capitalization of \$433 bn at the end of 2009. It has a wide range of sectors, including fisheries, cement and insurance but there are still restrictions on foreign ownership. The market has traditionally provided a bumpy ride for investors and at the end of 2009 remained 50% off its highs of February 2007.

6.8   INVESTING IN THE REGION

As the latest "hot" market, there are myriad ways to invest in developing Asia on both the active and passive side. Pan-Asian funds will include the larger markets of Hong Kong, Singapore, Taiwan and Korea, which may dominate as the companies tend to be larger. Some funds will also include Australia and/or New Zealand. Then there are funds that specialize in income, which again are likely to focus on the more developed markets in Asia.

There are country-specific funds too. For example, it is possible to invest in Vietnam either through trackers or through active investment trusts. Van Eck launched a Market Vectors Vietnam exchange-traded fund in August 2009 and db x-trackers offers a FTSE Vietnam Index ETF. Such vehicles have the advantage of being cheap and liquid, but will focus on larger companies.

There are also a number of Vietnam specialists with closed-ended funds – VinaCapital and Dragon Capital – which are actively managed funds and so should offer more protection as and when markets head south. However, they are vulnerable to market sentiment and may trade at a discount to net asset value.

If the domestic growth story is of greater interest, smaller companies are likely to represent a "purer" play than larger companies, which generate earnings from around the globe. "Rising domestic consumption is a key attraction of emerging markets," says Hugh Young, managing director of Aberdeen Asset Management Asia.

"Young and increasing populations with expanding workforces and developing middle classes will boost earning and spending power in emerging market countries and this in turn will drive domestic growth.

With its wide range of domestic growth-focused companies, the smaller companies sector offers greater exposure to this developing consumer story than the large-company universe. Furthermore, because smaller companies tend to be more exposed to domestic rather than overseas activity, they are less vulnerable to external slowdowns."

Emerging markets for income?

Emerging markets have traditionally been a no-go zone for income investors. Paying dividends was not a priority for companies in the early stages of development but, as markets have matured, there has been more choice for the income-seeker in the region.

International investors have demanded improved corporate governance, pushing companies towards returning profits to shareholders. Also, as Asian companies tend to hold less debt, they have more free cashflow to return to shareholders.

Recent years have seen a number of Asian income funds launched to take advantage of this trend, including UK offerings from Aberdeen, Henderson, Newton and Schroder. According to Andrew Gillan, manager of the Aberdeen Asian Income fund, the group saw more companies offering higher yields and more choice coming to the market. The fund launched with a 4.5% target yield, which it has maintained up to the time of writing.

As with Western economies, income investing in Asia naturally lends itself to certain types of sector and certain countries. For example, Singapore and Malaysia are key markets with strong banking and property companies. Telecoms, tobacco and brewing all tend to be strong dividend payers in the region too. Utilities, which make up a mainstay for Western income funds, are less attractive because they cannot pass higher costs onto the consumer.

The dividend mindset has not yet penetrated countries such as India and South Korea, but Gillan believes it will start to do so over the next few years. He also believes dividends should be more secure than in many developed market companies. Asian companies tend to have low debt-to-equity ratios and strong earnings growth and so are in a good position to maintain their payouts.

Opting for income-generating companies can also be an effective way to manage risk. Income stocks in the region suffered less in the downturn in stock markets at the end of 2008 although they also rose more slowly in 2009 as markets re-embraced risk.

6.9   CONCLUSION

It is tempting to associate Asia with economic turbulence. It has historically seen significant booms and busts and there remain fears among investors that each lurch up is only the precursor to a painful lurch down. But its position – at least in the short term – as the engine of world growth, is likely to encourage more stable fund flows to the region and may smooth out its historically bouncy ride for investors.

The Rest of Emerging Europe

7.1 INTRODUCTION

The early arguments for investing in emerging Europe were clear. As the Iron Curtain collapsed and Eastern European countries won their independence from Moscow, they would move closer to Western Europe, capitalism would have more influence and economic prosperity would grow. But emerging Europe revealed its vulnerabilities during the credit crunch, with some countries even requiring help from the IMF. To what extent is the region's growth story still intact?

7.2 OVERVIEW

Emerging Europe's problems have been severe and in October 2009 the IMF revised down its GDP forecasts for the year for much of the region. The previous April it was predicting an overall fall of 3.7% for Central and Eastern Europe as a whole but this fell to 5% in the latter survey. The weakest areas remain Latvia, Lithuania and Estonia, which were staring down the barrel of 18%, 18.5% and 14% contractions in GDP for 2009 respectively.

The three Baltic countries in particular, though not exclusively, fell prey to that now familiar weakness of running up debts in foreign currencies when their revenue streams were in local currencies, leaving them vulnerable to currency devaluation. Those devaluations, when they came, were savage, with many currencies down 40% or more as international markets priced in Armageddon. In some countries, currency markets had priced in an eventual move to the euro and when the downturn rendered this unlikely – at least in the short term – the currencies paid the price. The debt burden grew in proportion to the decline in the currency.

The only real pocket of strength in Eastern Europe over this period was Poland, which did well compared both to other countries in emerging Europe and also the developed economies. For example, the Polish National Bank was still expecting GDP growth of 0.8% in 2009, one of only two European Union member states forecasting growth for that year – the other being Cyprus. The IMF was even more optimistic, forecasting growth of 1%.

The weakness in the Baltics was expected to continue into 2010, with the region as a whole delivering anaemic 1.8% growth, and this should be set against a forecast of 7.3% in developing Asia and 2.9% in Latin America. Emerging Europe has delivered some stellar returns for investors over the past 10 years, but has it had its day?

It has been suggested that part of emerging Europe's problems have stemmed from the fact that they haven't experienced this type of crisis before. Asia had its problems in the late 1990s and knew the evils of over-borrowing. Latin America had also suffered the pain of debt crises and its corporations, governments and consumers had learned to resist the lure of freely available credit. If this argument is true, after a period of pain, emerging Europe's economies should emerge stronger – as Asia's and Latin America's have done.

According to Peter Elam Hakansson, head of portfolio management at East Capital, experience of previous crises suggests there will be large scale reforms over the next two to three years and things will pick up quicker than expected. The loans the IMF has extended in the region – to Romania, Belarus, Serbia and Latvia – have come with conditions. East Capital suggests this means that the crisis will not be "wasted".

Furthermore, it is possible the debt crisis may not prove to be as bad as billed. The IMF may have compounded the crisis by overstating the debt figures for some of the countries in the region and East Capital sees it as a "refinancing" problem rather than a structural debt issue.

What's the difference? In the West, we have a structural debt issue because consumers, governments and corporations are all over-borrowed. The overall debt levels across emerging Europe are much lower. In this context, the weakness of emerging European currencies is likely to be an advantage in the short term, giving exports a boost and making imports more expensive, thus increasing demand for domestic produce.

Overall, however, perhaps the key issue is that the convergence story that has supported emerging European stock markets and economies remains in place. It is tempting to see many of the countries that joined the European Union in 2004 as already "converged", but some emerging European analysts believe there is still some way to go.

"Convergence is a long process," says Elena Shaftan, manager of Jupiter Asset Management's Emerging European Opportunities fund. "It was happening 15 or 20 years ago and there is still some room to go. Credit card penetration, for example, is still a fraction of what it is in Western Europe. Household debt is around 20% to 30% in the larger Eastern European countries but it is around 50% in Western Europe."

She admits that Eastern Europe is no longer the font of cheap labour it was immediately post-Communism – particularly before the devaluation of many Eastern European currencies during the credit crunch. However, she says that pre-devaluation, you could still employ about five Polish workers for the price of one German worker and this gap has widened again.

Emerging Europe's economies have a long way to go in terms of wealth levels. According to the World Bank, Germany had a gross national income figure of $42 440 per head in 2008 while for even a relatively small European power such as Greece it was $28 650. Poland and Hungary, perhaps the top of the tree in terms of economic development in Eastern Europe, have gross national incomes of just $11 880 and $12 810 per head respectively.

Perhaps the main factor that remains in favour of emerging Europe is low expectations. Everyone expects Asia to be the engine of world growth. Everyone expects commodity-rich Latin America to be a key beneficiary of the rise of China and India. Emerging Europe has been the emerging market laggard, which has kept valuations low and stalled fund flows.

This suggests emerging European stock markets may remain cheaper than those in Asia or other developing economies. For its part, East Capital believes current estimates for the growth of Eastern European economies are too low and, if GDP growth estimates were to be revised upwards, this would represent good news for emerging Europe's stock markets.

7.3   A BRIEF HISTORY OF EMERGING EUROPE

It is easy to forget how far the economies of emerging Europe have come. According to the World Bank, in 1988, per capita income in Western Germany was 5.6 times that of what was then Czechoslovakia. Indeed, many emerging European countries had per capita income levels closer to those of Latin America than Western Europe.

These economies, the World Bank noted in its 1991 paper, "On economic transformation in East-Central Europe: a historical and international perspective", were characterized by "macroeconomic imbalances, obsolete and uncompetitive product capacities, a lack of modern infrastructure, underdeveloped factor markets and weak institutions".

Economic transformation did not come without pain although Central and Eastern Europe did approach financial reform at a gentler pace than Russia. Countries split the former state banks into a central bank and a number of large, government-owned commercial banks, with the view that these would eventually be privatized. As a result, support for unproductive companies making products few people wanted continued for longer than it did in Russia, which took a more radical approach to reform. These banks also had an overhang of bad loans from the Communist era.

Equally, the transformation to a market economy was not linear. As late as 1999, a survey of more than 3000 East European companies by the World Bank and European Bank for Reconstruction and Development (EBRD) showed continued state influence in business decision-making, coupled with corruption and factionalism.

GDP growth in the major emerging European countries – Poland, Hungary and the Czech Republic – began to turn around in the early 1990s and, although economic development has had to endure occasional teething troubles along the way, it has seen steady growth since then.

Much of this was on the back of Western European companies outsourcing manufacturing to the region. Japanese carmaker Suzuki started the trend, building a plant in Hungary in 1990, and Renault, Fiat and Volkswagen followed shortly after.

According to PricewaterhouseCoopers, from 1991 to 2006, Western carmakers shifted around $20 bn worth of production to the region, boosting its share of global car manufacturing from 5% to 6.8%. Labour in the region was cheap, relatively productive and more than compensated for the additional transportation costs.

However, the swell of emerging European GDP improvements didn't start until the mid-1990s as the economic ripple effect from these countries moved further East. International investors started to grow more excited about the region as membership of the European Union became a realistic prospect for many of the countries.

In reality, preparations had begun almost immediately after the fall of the Iron Curtain. The Phare Programme, for example, was put in place in 1989, initially to enable Poland and Hungary to shake themselves free from Communism. It was ultimately extended to include other emerging European countries and was followed by Sapard, an agricultural programme. Phare and Sapard allocated around $4.5 bn a year for Eastern European countries to move towards European Union membership.

In 1998, negotiations started for a dozen emerging European countries to join the European Union. Of the 12, 10 were due to join in 2004 – the Baltic states of Estonia, Latvia and Lithuania, the Central European countries of Poland, the Czech Republic, Slovakia, Hungary and Slovenia and the islands of Malta and Cyprus.

Bulgaria and Romania began negotiations at the same time, but with further to develop, they were only ever going to join in 2007 or beyond. This was an unprecedented expansion for the European Union and would take it from 15 to 25 members in 2004.

Investors were interested first because membership brought with it considerable cash – the European Union allocated $32 bn for members that joined in 2004. But more importantly, they looked at how accession to the European Union had put a rocket under the economies of Ireland and Portugal. Ireland, for example, saw GDP accelerate and its stock market soar. House prices boomed, employment surged and businesses flocked to the region.

The idea was that the new members would see a similar phenomenon as the criteria laid down for membership would force structural reforms that would in turn expand the economy. These countries could use their position as a manufacturing base for Western European companies to grow domestic industry. As a result, these regions would see the expansion of sectors such as financial services, technology and retail.

For the most part, accession to the European Union has had the desired effect in emerging Europe. Household consumption has grown and a nascent domestic consumer economy has developed, driven by rising employment and wages.

According to the World Bank, Poland, for example, saw annual GDP growth averaging 3.8% between 1997 and 2007, rising to 6.5% in 2006 and 6.6% in 2007. Services made up 60% of the economy in 1997. By 2007, this had risen to 65.9%. Household consumption rose from 3.5% between 1997 and 2007, but had accelerated to 5.2% in 2006 and 5.5% in 2007.

This pattern is repeated across emerging Europe. According to the EBRD, the region grew by almost 7% in 2007 and by more than 4% in 2008. However, the credit crunch has undoubtedly derailed growth in a number of emerging European countries, particularly those that have grown too fast and taken on too much debt. Latvia is probably the best example of that – at the end of 2009 its current account deficit sat at 22.9% of GDP, the highest in the EU.

7.4 REGION-SPECIFIC RISKS

The competitiveness of their labour force remains a key concern for emerging European countries, particularly in the Baltic states. Although their economies have broadened out, their ability to provide cheap labour still underpins their economic development.

Inflation has also been a big issue for many countries in the region. Latvia, again, has been among the hardest hit, with inflation hitting 16.7% for the year to July 2008. But it is by no means alone – Lithuania reported inflation at 12.2% for the same period. Among the more developed emerging European markets, Hungary has been vulnerable to inflation, which hit 8.5% in 2008. In general, wage inflation has been a by-product of rising food and energy costs, leaving emerging European labour less competitive.

These issues will be helped by currency devaluation. There are also signs in countries such as Latvia that workers are taking lower salaries. East Capital's Elam Hakansson says these countries have been through tough times before. The privations of the Communist regime are still a relatively recent memory for much of the population, which means they should be able to cope with public spending cuts without the social unrest that has accompanied, for example, Greece's attempt at reform.

Each country faces its own hurdles in its bid to accede to the European Union. For the major economies, becoming part of the single currency is the next step and the big risk is that this doesn't go to plan. In 2009, Poland admitted its bulging post-credit-crunch deficit meant it was unlikely to fulfil the criteria for membership in 2012.

Further down the line, the final wave of European Union membership should be Turkey, Croatia and the rest of the Western Balkans but that membership is by no means assured. Turkey opened accession talks in 2004 and is still apparently no nearer membership, although Prime Minister Recep Tayyip Erdoğan appointed a full-time negotiator early in 2009 and said membership remained a "top priority" for the country. The European Union is demanding the country improve its democratic profile – more specifically, safeguarding free speech, ensuring the rights of minorities and curbing the power of the armed forces.

Finally, Eastern Europe is still dependent on Western Europe to buy its goods. Although some areas of Western Europe – notably France and Germany – have been quick to move out of recession, the UK, Spain and the Netherlands are all weaker. The recovery is fragile across the developed markets with a double-dip recession a real possibility. If Western Europe takes another lurch down, Eastern Europe cannot remain immune.

7.5 THE INVESTMENT CASE FOR POLAND

Poland has been the great success story of the European Union's expansion. After the fall of the Iron Curtain, it was the first Eastern European country to receive the attention of Western Europe, who saw that its large well-educated population and proximity to the rest of Europe gave it natural advantages. Now it sits on a par economically with much of the wider European Union.

It has not all been plain sailing, however. Poland's plan to join the euro in 2012 has had to be scrapped as the country's budget deficit has expanded beyond its target for entry. The European Commission expected Poland would have a deficit of 6.6% in 2009, well in excess of the euro entry target of 3%. Inflation remains a concern too and rose as high as 4.8% in the year to July 2008, with some evidence this was coming through in wage demands. This has now dipped to 3.6% for the year to June 2009 and interest rates have come down from highs of around 6% to 3.5%.

The desire to keep public debt below 55% of gross domestic product has led to some unfortunate policy choices. The most recent has been the decision to raid private pension systems with the government planning to cut the percentage of employee salaries going into the private system, adding the difference to existing contributions to the public system.

But in general Poland has embraced capitalism in a skilful and measured way. GDP growth has been steady but significant and has continued even as the country has matured – Poland was still growing at 6.6% as recently as 2007. The global slowdown has slowed that growth, but the IMF still expected Poland to grow in 2009 and expand by 2.2% in 2010.

Poland's advancement has been built on the strength of its labour force. With a young, well-educated population of 38 million, it became the ideal outsourcing partner for Western European manufacturing companies. As recently as 2007, according to Eurostat, Polish hourly labour costs were a quarter of Germany's.

Productivity may not have been as high, but Polish labour still worked out considerably cheaper. Furthermore, productivity has been steadily improving and the złoty has significantly devalued against the euro, leaving labour rates lower post-credit crunch. This will continue to be a strength for the country.

The growth of Poland has also been supported by strong corporate profits, European Union funding and foreign direct investment. According to the EBRD, the last of these reached a peak of $27 bn in 2007 and a continuing worry for the future growth of Poland is whether this level of investment can continue. It dipped significantly during the downturn and there is a danger it will not return to those 2007 levels for some time. Foreign direct investment did tick up in 2009 but is well off historic highs.

As employment and wages have increased, so domestic consumption has emerged as a source of economic strength. The country has also benefited through remittances from Polish workers abroad, though again this diminished during the downturn.

The country has managed to avoid some of the worst excesses of its neighbours. There has been no housing boom or explosion in credit. The currency has free-floated, allowing it to undergo a hasty devaluation and improving the situation for Polish exporters. It also benefited from the German government's scrappage scheme, which helped prop up its ailing car manufacturing industry when Western demand slumped. Another encouraging aspect for investors is that Poland's corporate governance framework was brought into line with OECD Principles in preparation for European Union accession.

Poland's biggest challenge now is its fiscal deficit but the convergence story is intact with joining the euro still top priority for the country's government. This should ultimately reduce the economy's volatility and enable it to access financing at lower interest rates.

Poland was one of the only countries in the European Union to deliver growth in 2009 and, as a cheaper, skilled manufacturing base, it should be a beneficiary of Western European companies looking to cut costs. Ultimately if it can navigate its economic challenges, it will continue to lead emerging Europe's economic development.

Stock market focus: Poland

The Warsaw Stock Exchange is broad, with almost 400 companies listed on the main market and a total market capitalization of $240 bn by the end of 2009 – although the 25 foreign companies listed on the exchange make up almost half of that figure. It has come a long way from the five listed companies it had in 1991 and is expected to expand further still. It remains a popular choice for IPOs. The main index is the WIG, which lists 311 companies, but there are 13 other indices on the market.

As an exporter to Western Europe in the middle of a vulnerable region, Polish share prices were hit hard in the downturn. They were also hit by the devaluation of the currency. The WIG lost 51.1% in 2008, after years of double-digit growth. In the four years from 2003, the market grew 44.9%, 27.9%, 33.7% and 41.7%. Even in 2007, it grew by more than 10%.

The markets were supported by the prospect of Poland joining the euro, which promised to iron out various corporate governance issues and structural imbalances that had emerged. However, by the time it became clear that euro entry was not an option, some rationality had returned to global markets and Poland's relative economic strength became clear. The WIG's performance in 2009 was much punchier and it had recovered by half by the end of the year.

7.6 THE CZECH REPUBLIC AND HUNGARY

The differing fortunes of the Czech Republic and Hungary amply illustrate the importance of sound policy-making. On the one hand, the Czech Republic looked set for a brief dip in GDP in 2009, with good growth resuming swiftly afterwards. On the other, Hungary appeared likely to record a 6% dip in GDP in 2009 and faces a long and painful return to growth as it aims to address the structural imbalances in its economy.

Both countries have much the same economic DNA. Both are large exporters, primarily to Western Europe, with around 80% of GDP coming from exports in 2007 and 2008. The lion's share of exports comes from manufacturing with a large share – greater than 20% of overall exports – coming from car manufacturing. They have therefore been hit disproportionately hard by the weakness in car demand and then benefited considerably from the German government's scrappage scheme and the sector's subsequent speedy recovery.

Both joined the European Union in May 2004 and have – to some extent – been the poster boys for European Union expansion. That said, the Czech Republic has consistently seen higher growth than Hungary. It delivered GDP growth of 6% or more from 2005 to 2007 while Hungary saw growth between 4% and 4.5% over the same period.

The pair had both, until recently, enjoyed reasonable political stability, albeit a peculiarly old-European style of stability. Governments have tended to be built on flimsy and ineffectual coalitions, but there has been broad support for democracy.

In Hungary, the Socialist Party has governed in coalition with the Liberal Free Democrats since 2002. Péter Medgyessy led the centre-left coalition as prime minister and survived in spite of revelations that he had worked as a counterintelligence officer for the secret service in the 1970s. Independent Ferenc Mádl had been elected president in 2000.

Ferenc Gyurcsány became prime minister in 2004 after Medgyessy resigned in a row with his coalition parties. The next year opposition candidate László Sólyom became president after Mádl said he did not want to run again. The Socialist candidate had been blocked by the party's coalition partners. In 2006, Gyurcsány and his government were swept back into power, but their popularity did not last long. Hungary saw violent street protests as Gyurcsány admitted he had lied to the electorate about the state of the economy during the campaign.

Nevertheless, Gyurcsány hung on until he was eventually unseated by Hungary's dire economic problems. He resigned in March 2009, only to be replaced by his economic minister Gordon Bajnai. Although some may consider the finance minister equally culpable, a change has proved as good as a rest as he has ordered public spending cuts, tax rises and public wage freezes.

However, this has not been enough to stop significant political tensions emerging – the Far Right made an impact in the 2009 European elections winning nearly 15% of the vote and gaining three seats. Rural Hungary, in particular, has been receptive to its anti-Roma message.

The Czech Republic has also seen widespread support for democracy – with a similarly ineffectual blend of coalition governments. The presidential office has been consistent – the dissident playwright and popular icon of democracy Václav Havel was elected in 1993 and remained in office until 2003, when he was succeeded by former prime minister Václav Klaus, who has ruled since. The governments on the other hand have been fragile. Between 2002 and 2010, there have been four new prime ministers and six new governments.

The real difference between the two countries has been debt – both government and consumer. The Hungarian government built up huge amounts of foreign-denominated debt to finance lavish public spending. Public debt as a percentage of GDP is the highest of any of its neighbours and will near 80% for 2009. To put that into context, Poland has the next highest debt levels at just over 50% for 2009.

Over 40% of households in Hungary pay out more than 20% of their income in debt repayments, which is a similar figure to Bulgaria or Romania. However, it is less the scale of household debt in Hungary – which, as a percentage of GDP, is in line with that of the Czech Republic – than its type. In 2008, 65% of all loans to households were denominated in foreign currencies, with only Estonia and Latvia having higher figures. The government has played its part in creating the problem as restrictive eligibility requirements for household subsidies in Hungary in 2004 led borrowers towards less expensive foreign debt.

Another problem for Hungary has been the ownership of its banking system. Approximately 80% of the banking system was owned by foreign banks, which rapidly withdrew the availability of loans as they experienced balance sheet pressures in their home markets. Equally, unlike some other emerging European countries, Hungary's banking system was diverse with many different countries' banks holding an interest.

Hungary's currency sell-off was swift. The Forint dropped 16% against the US dollar between May 2008 and January 2009 and inflated external debt. With exports dropping and no availability of funding, the markets seized up. The Hungarian banking system stood on the brink of a precipice and the country was forced to seek external help.

The IMF, the European Union and the World Bank brought together a financing package for Hungary, totalling $25.1 bn, but with strings attached to ensure adequate domestic and foreign currency liquidity as well as stronger levels of capital for the banking system going forward. Tough fiscal measures have already reduced government financing needs and the government now has one of the lowest fiscal deficits in the region.

Hungarian interest rates have remained high. In January 2009, when the rates in many developed economies were nearing zero, Hungary's main policy rate was 9.5% as the government simply couldn't risk a huge outpouring of foreign capital and further pressure on its currency if it were to bring rates lower.

For its part, the Czech Republic has witnessed a consumption boom that has proved fairly resilient in the face of global economic slow-down. Consumption remained flat or slightly ahead in late 2008 and early 2009 at the height of the global slump. Households in the Czech Republic also avoided the problem of foreign-denominated loans. Domestic interest rates were low, leaving borrowers with little need to look at euro-denominated loans. Exchange rate risk was also monitored carefully.

Equally, the Czech government has not built up anything like the external public debt of Hungary – it stands at around 30% of GDP. As a result the government had sufficient wiggle room to weather the economic storm. It has also been able to bring down interest rates, which have moved roughly in line with those of the European Central Bank.

So what of the future? Hungary has been shoehorned into significant austerity measures as a condition of its loans from the IMF and the rest. This has been swingeing – a freeze in public wages and pensions, cuts in family allowances and sick leave benefits and reduced household subsidies – while higher excise duties, VAT and corporation tax have been put in place to generate additional revenue. Couple these measures with higher unemployment and a muted recovery in exports and GDP growth is likely to be anaemic for the time being.

The Czech Republic has not been forced into any austerity measures although it has said it will reduce state employment. It has put together a stimulus package, which has included capital injections into the banks to encourage lending to exporters, infrastructure spending and subsidies for building. It will be relying on the continuing re-emergence of exports to shore up its economy.

In the long run, the measures being taken by both countries are likely to stand them in good stead. Both still have a eurozone convergence story to tell, but the Czech Republic's story looks stronger than that of Hungary, for whom its debt burden will be a headwind.

Stock market focus: the Czech Republic and Hungary

In these more sophisticated countries, the relative strength of the two economies is not necessarily reflected in their stock markets. Hungary's Budapest Stock Exchange index, the Bux, fell 68% from peak to trough during the credit crunch, from 29 790 to 9461. It has since recovered 128% to a peak of 21 560. The Czech main index, the PX 50, has had a similarly torrid time, selling off from 1918 at its peak to 628.5 at its low, a fall of 67%. However, it has failed to recover to the same extent as Hungary, rising only 90% from the bottom at most.

Company focus: Erste Bank Hungary

Austrian bank Erste entered the Hungarian market in 1997 with the purchase of the state-owned Mezobank, changing its name to Erste Bank Hungary in 1998. By the start of 2010, it had grown to be the second largest bank in the Hungarian market in terms of number of clients and the fifth largest based on assets. In addition to Hungary, the group has significant exposure to the Czech Republic and Romania.

Professional investors see banking as very underpenetrated across Eastern Europe while lending growth is gathering pace and Erste Bank Hungary has better prospects than many of the developed European banks. By 2010, Erste's short-term ambitions included increasing its market share in small and medium-sized company lending to 15% from 8% in 2009 and its retail lending market share to 20% from 12%.

7.7 THE BALTIC STATES

The three Baltic states of Lithuania, Estonia and Latvia might be termed the "Icarus economies" because they flew too close to the sun. At the very least, they ran before they could walk. Whatever cliché you prefer, they have been at the coalface of the global economic downturn. They attempted a daringly speedy convergence plan, but the credit crunch exposed the structural imbalances in their economies, particularly their debt burden. It was a salutary lesson in economic mismanagement and many of the mistakes were glaringly familiar.

For its part, Latvia spent many years looking like the big success story of emerging Europe as the economy doubled in size from 1995 to 2005 while employment rates rose and 325 000 people moved out of poverty. In 2007, the economy grew 10.31%.

Particularly strong growth was seen in the service sector, which rose at an annualized rate of 7.6% over the same period. Industry grew by 6.9%, while agriculture grew just 2.8%, reflecting the changing nature of the economy and the move to a more "Western" economic model.

But this kind of growth came at a price. Shaftan at Jupiter Asset Management says Latvia had been borrowing very aggressively from Western European and particularly Swedish banks to fuel its growth and the current account deficit hit 23% of GDP. That flow of credit dried up as these banks were forced to sort out their domestic problems, leaving Latvia unable to borrow its way out of trouble – as, for example, the UK has done – and forced to impose public spending cuts.

Unlike other countries, the Latvian government has chosen not to allow the currency to devalue and, as such, has imposed some severe austerity measures on its population. It is doing this to preserve its hopes of joining the euro in 2012 although there is, as yet, little indication as to whether this will succeed. It will be largely unprecedented if it does – no country has managed to generate a recovery without devaluing its currency.

In the meantime, the economy contracted by a staggering 19.3% in the second quarter of 2009. No recovery is in sight and the IMF is predicting a further 4% contraction in 2010. Nor does the government have the international reserves to cover its debt payments. Latvia has been forced to go cap in hand to the IMF and the World Bank and accept their rescue terms, which include restricting the budget deficit to 5% of GDP, a seemingly impossible target in its current situation. Just to make life even trickier, in August 2009 Standard & Poor's downgraded the country's debt from BB+ to BB.

The short-term picture is grim with unemployment forecast to rise to 20%, house prices down 20% to 30%, repossessions rising and benefits falling. Latvia's inflation is also the highest in the European Union at 16.7% while social unrest appears a real possibility.

One consolation is that exports appear to have held up reasonably well in spite of the higher Lat. Ultimately the success or failure of the economy may depend on the recovery of Latvia's key trading partners – Russia and Western Europe. With France and Germany returning to growth in the second quarter of 2009, there is a flicker of hope Latvia may dodge a bullet.

It may be difficult to see it at the time but, typically, when countries have been through this sort of experience, they have emerged chastened and stronger. It is precisely this type of process that has whipped Asian economies into their current success stories. It is some way ahead, but Latvia may emerge as a notable success story.

For their part, Estonia and Lithuania both saw similar problems, though on a smaller scale. They made moves to dampen economic growth and, as such, avoided the worst of Latvia's experiences. Estonia is considered the more resilient but still announced a 14% slide in GDP for 2009. Its growth had been slower, at just 6.3% in 2007, as it took steps to cool its overheating economy earlier than its two neighbours.

It also accumulated reserves during its boom years equivalent to around 10% of GDP, which has meant its austerity measures have not had to be as severe as those in Latvia. That said, it also took those austerity measures earlier and it still needs to keep its budget deficit below 3% of GDP to meet the eurozone entry criteria.

Estonia still has a target date for eurozone entry of January 2011. Andrus Ansip, Estonia's prime minister, has said the country should meet the economic entry criteria by the start of 2010. The IMF meanwhile says entry in 2011 remains possible, if tricky.

Lithuania's own entry looks shaky after it recorded an 18.5% drop in GDP in 2009 (source: IMF, estimated). Like Latvia it is clear its government does not want to devalue its currency and is retaining its peg in the hope of joining the euro.

The country has not yet had to go to the IMF for a bailout loan and said in November 2009 that it was confident of recovering without this external aid. It has managed to issue sovereign bonds worth $1.5 bn to shore up its finances but, with a chunky deficit to service, it may yet need further external funding. Like Latvia, it had previously been a developing market success story and as recently as 2007, annual GDP growth was 8.78%.

It has been an ignominious come-down for three countries that have between them seen the highest growth rates in Europe. Even after the downturn, the World Bank considered them all "upper-middle income" countries, with GDP per capital ranging from $6500 to $10 000. The big question for the Baltics is the strength with which they finally emerge from the downturn. Few expect great things, so it will be up to them to prove the consensus wrong.

7.8   THE BALKANS

Internal strife put much of the Balkans – which, for the purposes of this section, takes in Romania, Bulgaria, Croatia, Serbia, Turkey and Slovenia – off-limits for years, but with a fragile peace now in place the region is free to rebuild.

Previously, the Balkans were home to the glitterati. If not quite Monte Carlo, they certainly could lay claim to some wealth and sophistication.

Their return to their rightful place in the European hierarchy should mark an important buying opportunity, but how likely is this really?

Romania, Bulgaria, Croatia, Serbia, Turkey and Slovenia are the main investable areas in the region. Bosnia is moving up, but political instability remains a problem. Most recently this has manifested itself in black-outs after wrangling over the leadership of multi-racial power supplier Elektroprenos. Macedonia is a candidate for European Union membership, but talks have not yet started so accession will be some way off. Albania, Kosovo and Montenegro all have the right to join, but are not yet in negotiations.

European Union membership is on the table for the majority of these countries and with it a hope that they will see similarly successful convergence stories to Poland or the Czech Republic. Bulgaria and Romania were admitted in 2007, but there has been ongoing sniffiness among Western European members that they were admitted too early. Certainly, corruption and transparency remain problems for those countries.

The European Union has extended its investigation into organised crime, high-level corruption and judicial reform in Bulgaria and Romania into 2010. The investigation, which started in 2007, was due to end in 2009 but ran into problems. In December 2008, the European Union withdrew $330 m of funding from Bulgaria for failing to make speedier progress. In Boyko Borisov, the country has now elected a leader who, in public at least, has promised to tackle Bulgaria's ongoing problems.

The country's financial situation looks to be in better shape. The IMF's latest report into the region showed that although exports dipped exponentially in the first few months of 2009, imports dipped at a similar pace, leaving the public finances in surplus for the time being. Nevertheless, Bulgaria is expected to remain in recession until well into 2010.

Romania has greater problems. It has already had to go to the IMF for loans to help cover its foreign debt repayments, securing $30 bn to help it weather collapsing steel prices and a fall in demand for cars, its two main exports. The IMF has imposed conditions about cutting public spending and reducing the budget deficit, but Romania has not always abided by IMF conditions. The IMF warned in November 2009 that the country's fiscal deficit may reach as high as 9% of GDP and withheld a third installment of the country's loan until an austerity budget had been passed.

Both Bulgaria and Romania also suffer from factionalism in government, leading to weak coalitions. The past few years have seen significant growth, some of it fuelled by debt, which meant they have suffered more as the credit crunch hit. Previously, Bulgaria has enjoyed five years of 6%-plus GDP growth, while Romania's growth hit 7.1% in 2007. There is also a constant risk of both countries falling back under the influence of Russia. Even if they do manage to avoid Russia's clutches, both countries have a painful road ahead to rebuild.

Turkey has been in negotiations for admission to the European Union for decades and another deadline came and went at the end of 2009. One of a number of sticking points has been the situation in Cyprus – Turkey remains the only country to recognize the Turkish Republic of Northern Cyprus, while the European Union wants to see some measure of unification. Turkey's bid requires this to be resolved in addition to a number of human rights and judicial reforms. There are also a number of European Union members who – whether on historic enmities or for current reasons – would be happy to see the bid fail.

It is difficult to ignore some of the political difficulties in Turkey, yet, in recent years, governments have recognized the country's power as a conduit between West and East. The country has made a point of befriending its neighbours and building political alliances.

Turkey's economic situation is probably the most stable part of its bid. "Turkey is one country that has managed to turn itself from a high-inflation, economically volatile, compromise democracy place to one with a strong central bank and steady growth," says James Syme, head of emerging markets at Baring Asset Management.

"If Turkey has an Achilles' heel, it is its weak export sector, but the central bank has been quite hawkish over the years and inflation continues to fall. Interest rates have been cut and the lira has strengthened. Although, GDP has been hit hard by the global downturn, the medium-term outlook for domestic demand is very good. There is still very low penetration of consumer finance and there is potentially a strong multi-year demand boom in the making."

In the Western Balkans, accession talks have tended to stall on localized territorial disputes and political instability – for example, Croatia has been locked in a maritime border dispute with European Union member Slovenia. Equally, corruption, organized crime and ongoing ethnic tensions have made imminent membership for countries in the region unlikely.

Even so, there are moves towards greater integration. For example, under new proposals by the European Commission, citizens of Serbia, Macedonia and Montenegro should be able to travel around most of

Europe without visas from 2010. But to pretend the region had put its problems in the past would be disingenuous. In July 2009, for example, there was a bomb blast in a residential building in Serbia, which came just days after a grenade attack on a police patrol near Bujanovac.

The IMF has had to extend $4.5 bn of standby credit to the country to see it through the global downturn and the resulting withdrawal of foreign aid. Vinci Construction, a French group completing infrastructure projects for the Serbian government, pulled out after it was left with some $1.5 bn in unpaid bills.

Serbia is still the largest country in the region and had seen strong GDP growth. However, foreign direct investment into the country dipped by $1.2 bn, leaving a black hole in its finances. The IMF aid will have come with strings attached and is likely to force unwelcome cuts in government spending. Only once this indigestion is dealt with can Serbia resume its growth path.

Anyone who has been to Croatia in recent years will have seen the luxury hotels cropping up as the region makes the most of its glorious coastline to bring in the holidaymakers that left as war broke out. It has seen economic growth of 4%-plus from 2002 but the credit crunch hit relatively hard and GDP was expected to drop 5.2% in 2009. For the same year, industrial production remained almost 10% below 2008 and retail sales have seen similar falls.

Croatia is another aspirant European Union member, but needs to address corruption issues and improve its cooperation on war crimes investigations. Slovenia had put a veto on the country's entrance, but this lifted in late 2009. Croatia is one of the few countries with a genuine shot at reaching the EU's economic targets within the next few years and its government has declared itself confident of meeting the targets.

7.9 INVESTING IN THE REGION

Emerging European markets had a torrid time during the credit crunch as they gave up all their strong gains made since 2005. The MSCI EM Emerging Europe index had risen from 155 in August 2004 to a peak of 480 in December 2007 before it dipped down to 128 in October 2008. Some individual countries fared even worse – for example, the Romanian exchange was forced to close when intraday losses became too severe in the aftermath of the Lehmans crisis.

In general, the most spectacular gains made in the 2009 rebound were those countries that had lost most in 2008 but the next phase should see more discrimination among investors. Some countries had undoubtedly overreached themselves. Too much rested on the vulnerable premise that the major economies were going to join the euro. Therefore, when the credit crunch exposed the structural weaknesses in some of the economies and euro entry became unlikely, the markets were punished.

Potential investors may feel more comfortable putting money towards emerging Eastern Europe through collective funds although they should be aware that most such portfolios will also include some exposure to Russia, so – as discussed in Chapter 4 – the fortunes of the oil price will be a big issue. There is also an element of exchange-traded fund coverage for emerging Europe as a whole but, as yet, only a very limited number of such investments focus on individual markets in the region.

Still, as the markets are relatively inefficient, good active managers can add real value and may be able to protect returns on the downside by moving away from particular countries when they run into difficulties. Eastern Europe may also make up an increasing proportion of traditional continental European collective funds.

7.10 CONCLUSION

The outlook for emerging Europe has gradually come into focus. Exports have recovered on the back of the relative strength of France and Germany and stock markets have run up from some very oversold positions. While a number of countries – in particular, Hungary and the Baltics – have some painful deleveraging to do, which will hamper growth in the short term, Poland, the Czech Republic and others should recover in line with, or even ahead of, the global economy. The convergence story remains a supportive backdrop and, while the credit crisis may have shown some of the demerits of countries' euro ambitions, it remains the end goal for most of the region.

8

The Rest of Latin America

8.1 INTRODUCTION

Latin America has been home to some of the quintessential emerging markets. Certainly they have fitted many of the less flattering clichés about this type of economy – politically unstable, reliant on commodities at best (and drugs at worst), with weak currencies and dominated by the US. But Latin America now appears to have learnt from its previous booms and busts and the majority of countries in the region are trying to leave their turbulent pasts behind.

8.2 OVERVIEW

It can be tempting to see Latin America as Brazil – and certainly it is the region's largest economy by some margin, has its largest and most liquid stock market and a good share of the population. However, there are opportunities emerging elsewhere in Latin America, as countries move along the development path. Brazil aside, the principal investable markets are Mexico, Chile, Peru and Colombia.

The commodities boom and prudent management of the riches from it have enabled Latin American countries to move out of poverty and, just as important, to plan for the future. According to World Bank calculations, 52 million people came out of poverty in the region between 2002 and 2007. A nascent consumer economy has emerged across the region along with consumer banks. Income per capita has risen to levels considered the "sweet spot", where a virtuous circle begins and growth quickly accelerates. The region delivered average annual growth of 5.3% between 2003 and 2008.

In a sign of how far they had come from their chaotic past, a lot of Latin American countries banked their commodity riches. Some went into sovereign wealth funds – for example, the National Development Fund of Venezuela, the repository for the country's oil wealth, is worth approximately £20 bn.

Chile banked its copper riches in its Economic and Social Stabilization Fund, worth some $17 bn, while Brazil has sold treasury bonds to finance its new sovereign wealth fund. The Fundo Soberano do Brasil is currently "only" around $6 bn, but is intended to be a store of wealth to defend the country against further economic shocks.

Other cash went into infrastructure spending. In Brazil, for example, the government declared another $82 bn in infrastructure spending in 2009. The total for President Lula's second term is over four times that, while the country's Program to Accelerate Growth is aimed at improving Brazil's decaying infrastructure, including houses, railways and roads.

Other Latin American countries have simply built up colossal foreign exchange reserves. IMF statistics show Brazil had $53.3 bn in foreign exchange reserves in 2005. By 2008, this had reached $193.9 bn. Mexico has seen steadier growth, from $74.1 bn in 2005 to $94.6 bn in 2008.

Most importantly for the long-term economic development of the region, the wealth has filtered down to the wider population. According to the IMF, Mexican GDP per head was $6419 in 2000 and reached $10 200 in 2008. Brazil went from $3761 per head in 2000 to $8295 in 2008 while Chile went from $4943 in 2000 to $10 117 in 2008. Though many of these figures were, reasonably enough, expected to drop in 2009, they were also expected to hit new highs in 2010.

This trickling down of wealth has been reflected in consumer spending, which in turn has altered the nature of economic growth. For example, the Chile Retail report for the fourth quarter of 2009 predicted the country's retail sales would grow from about $51 bn in 2008 to more than $76 bn in 2013.

Department stores have grown to meet the growth in consumer spending while Brazil has seen real estate companies emerging – particularly new housebuilders. Many of these companies have come to the markets to raise money, making Latin American stock markets increasingly diverse and moving them away from their historic bias to commodities companies.

Also, apart from Mexico, the region has thrown off much of its historic reliance on the US. Fund flows are increasing with China and the rest of Asia. Chile now exports a similar amount to China as it does to the US while China takes 12% of Peru's exports, compared to 18% for the US. This process has been accelerated by the credit crunch. As demand from developed economies fell, China stepped up to absorb the slack.

Inflation has also been brought under control in most cases. Brazil's inflation hit 14.8% in 2003, but has been reasonably benign at between

3.6% and 6.9% ever since. Chile saw inflation heading higher in 2008, but the downturn has brought it back under control. Argentina, Costa Rica and Venezuela remain the hotbeds of inflation in the region.

Of course, the region has not been immune from the global financial crisis. The commodity exporters have been particularly hard hit as prices have slumped. The copper price, for example, slid to levels not seen since pre-boom while the fall in the oil price hurt countries with few other exports, such as Venezuela.

Foreign capital flows dried up as well – though the region had never pulled in the types of flows seen by some Asian countries. Private capital flows into the region fell from $107.4 bn in 2007 to $58.5 bn in 2008 and were forecast to be just $13 bn for 2009.

But Latin America has been neither the architect nor the biggest victim of the crisis and none of its countries – with the possible exceptions of Venezuela and Mexico – have been hit as hard as they were in the last regionally specific crisis of 2001 and 2002.

Brazil's GDP was expected to drop around 1.3% in 2009 but then resume its upward trajectory with 2.2% growth in 2010. Chile was unlikely even to register negative growth, as its reserves have allowed it to shore up its economy. Uruguay, Paraguay and Peru were all likely to see positive GDP growth in 2009 and beyond.

Mexico has been the exception as its strong trading links to the US economy have left it vulnerable to its neighbour's weakness. The trouble has been that it made too many of the US's cars, which comprised around 8% of its exports, at a time when no-one wanted cars.

Its dependence on oil has also been a problem – for many years oil was its cash cow and its reserves are now declining while the price is tumbling. Overall, the IMF expected the country to see a contraction of 7.3% in 2009, the lowest in the region, followed by anaemic growth of 1% in 2010.

But, for the most part, Latin America weathered the credit crunch well and came out the other side. In fact Nicolás Eyzaguirre, western hemisphere director of the IMF, went as far as to warn in an interview with the *Financial Times* that Latin America had coped with the crisis so well that several countries were paying the price of success with rapidly appreciating currencies and an influx of foreign capital. He suggested a bubble in the region remained a real possibility.

So what has been different this time and will the region's strength endure? Latin America has been in charge of its own destiny and has also been able to respond to the problems. High debt and inflation had reduced its options during previous crises but control over these has at last allowed it policy flexibility – for example, it has been able to lower rates to shore up domestic demand.

The region has also benefited from its ties with Asia. China and India have recovered far faster than developed markets – as has their demand for raw materials. This has meant the export decline has been muted. China has picked up the slack as demand from developed markets has faltered, particularly in commodities such as iron ore, which has been good news for companies such as Petrobras, Vale and Brazil Foods. Also, the region had little exposure to the banking crisis. Its problems have been cyclical rather than systemic.

What of the future? Augusto de la Torre, chief regional economist at the World Bank, said in July 2009 that the region has not suffered systemic damage and should recover relatively speedily. He predicted a two-tier recovery where Brazil, Argentina and Chile move up first, and Peru, Colombia and the Dominican Republic follow shortly afterwards. However, he said Mexico was likely to be a laggard, only showing a rebound in 2010.

8.3   A BRIEF ECONOMIC HISTORY OF THE REGION

During the 1980s and 1990s, Latin America was a mess of radical politics, ill-thought out economic strategy and volatility. A series of policy measures were put in place towards the end of the 1980s but, by and large, these didn't work and the region suffered a series of economic crises.

The reasons for these persistent crises were numerous. The economies were still heavily geared to the fortunes of the US. Rising interest rates and weakening investor confidence in the US as a result of the recession in the early 1990s led to a sharp reversal in capital flows. Currency pegs to the dollar left countries vulnerable to weakening currencies because they were not backed sufficiently vigorously by economic policy. Export growth did not keep pace with capital flows, which increased vulnerability. Political reform, where it happened, was piecemeal.

Cracks really began to appear in the system in 1994 with the so-called Tequila Crisis, when the Mexican government was ultimately forced to devalue the peso that December. It had operated a fixed exchange rate system but lacked sufficient foreign reserves to maintain it and, as a result, simply ran out of dollars and was forced to devalue. This dented investors' confidence across all the South American markets.

1999 marked the beginning of the Argentine economic crisis, in itself a knock-on effect of investors' mistrust of emerging markets in general in the wake of the Asian financial crisis and Russian debt crisis. Until relatively recently the region had been seen as a model of economic management, riding out the crises of its neighbours with equanimity. It had been supported by the IMF, who had directed some of the country's policy decisions, and its failure was therefore a blow to the organisation's economic strategy.

Central to this crisis was the country's public debt, which expanded in the face of a full-blown economic depression and was nearly all foreign denominated. Argentina was over-reliant on foreign lending due its small domestic banking sector and it also had real difficulties in negotiating ongoing lending.

In December 2001, Argentina defaulted on all its sovereign debt. It was the largest default in history and effectively cut off all external funding channels to the country. In January 2002, Argentina removed the peso's peg to the dollar and domestic and international confidence in the currency evaporated.

The country's collapse had a profound effect on its neighbours and, by 2002, the whole region was in a full-blown crisis. What had begun as a cyclical correction had been exacerbated by the crises in other emerging markets and then sent into meltdown by the problems in Argentina. As a whole, the region's GDP dipped by around 2% – a level not seen since the last debt crisis in 1983.

Things were bad everywhere, but some areas suffered more than others – notably Brazil, Uruguay and Paraguay, which had all been significant exporters or lenders to Argentina. Uruguay was hit particularly badly and slumped 11% in 2002. Many Argentines had held deposits in Uruguayan banks, but the country was saved from a default on its sovereign debt by an IMF loan.

Brazil also came close to a default as the imminent and eventual election of left-wing President Lula left potential international investors on edge. An outflow of foreign funds led to a currency depreciation. At the same time, a tick-up in inflation created further problems. Venezuela had its own internal problems, meanwhile, leading to a crisis of its own.

Unlike the 1994 crisis, this latest one hadn't come on the back of years of buoyant economic expansion, but had in fact followed several years of sub-trend growth in most countries. Equally, it showed many Latin American countries hadn't learnt the lessons of the previous decade and looked set to repeat, with bovine predictability, the same mistakes again and again. As a result, many investors were turned off the region.

Then, as in 2008, the global economic slowdown caused problems for commodity-dependent nations such as Brazil and Chile. Commodity prices slipped as global demand waned. Increased risk aversion reduced capital flows and foreign direct investment into the region. As risk aversion rose, emerging markets had to pay more for their debt.

It was debt that really killed individual economies, particularly foreign-denominated debt. Argentine public debt, for example, doubled between 1993 and 2001, of which around 97% was denominated in foreign currency. A lot of the debt across Latin America was denominated in dollars and, as we saw in the previous chapter, the peril of foreign-denominated debt is a lesson a number of Eastern European economies are having to learn. As the currencies devalued, these countries were left with huge debt burdens, which thwarted growth.

Of course some countries suffered less than others. The 2001 downturn in Mexico was linked to the US recession and the knock-on effects from the terrorist attacks of 11 September. However, there were fewer structural problems and the economy contracted just 0.2% that year.

Most Latin American countries were back on their feet by 2004 and enjoying robust economic growth once more. Argentina saw growth of 9%. Chile and Brazil delivered – as it turned out – a more sustainable 6% and 5.7% respectively. Mexican GDP rose 4%.

Part of this success was undoubtedly down to the countries themselves as they left behind the seat-of-the-pants policymaking that had characterized previous years. They resisted the urge to overspend in the fat years and instead aimed to build up a surplus for the bad years. Debt management policies improved, with countries reducing their foreign-denominated debt.

The regulatory reforms put in place during the crisis of 2001 and 2002 were to be important in helping Latin America weather the difficulties posed by the global credit crunch with far greater equanimity than previous downturns. Over the next five years, many Latin American countries built up large current account surpluses and an accumulation of foreign exchange reserves. Prudent monetary and fiscal policies created a buffer against the volatility of the global economy.

In Brazil, for example, as we saw in Chapter 4, President Lula proved not to be the radical socialist foreign investors had feared and in fact reined in public spending, introduced structural reforms and made the reduction of inflation a priority. He also introduced greater financial regulation in a series of policies overseen by the IMF.

Indeed, the crisis of 2001 and 2002 also ensured the region lost its appetite for radical politics and experimental policies although there have, of course, been exceptions. Hugo Chávez, the President of Venezuela, has been trying to impose a "socialist revolution" on the country during his decade in power – with the associated accusations of media manipulation and power grabbing.

His outspokenness has made an enemy out of many international politicians and he continues to be considered an "old style" Latin American leader just as President Lula has proved far more prudent than billed. The Latin American revolutionary spirit would appear to be largely a thing of the past.

While this stability has helped strong policymaking, the commodities boom has also been a key factor in generating sustainable growth in the region. The region as a whole, and particularly Brazil, is blessed with an abundance of quality natural resources. Brazil's iron ore, for example, is the highest quality in the world and the country has 30% of global supply. China imports Brazil's iron ore rather than using its own because it is purer.

The same is true for other commodities – for example, Brazil and Argentina are the world's largest producers of soy beans while Chile and Peru generate 60% of their exports through metal. Chile has 35% of the world's copper market so, as copper prices more than doubled between 2005 and 2008, Chile reaped the benefits. The entire Latin American region became a net creditor – a situation that would have seemed impossible just a few years earlier.

8.4   MEXICO – A BRIEF ECONOMIC HISTORY

The economic transformation of Mexico began in 1976 with the discovery of the Cantarell oilfield, which became the main engine of Mexican oil exports. The country took another major leap forward when its parliament ratified the North Atlantic Free Trade Agreement (NAFTA) in 1993. Trade with the US and Canada has nearly tripled since its implementation the following year.

But while these steps helped the economy in the long term, the shorter term saw bigger problems. First, political instability created tension – a guerrilla rebellion by the Zapatista National Liberation Army was brutally suppressed in 1994 and opposition to NAFTA formed part of the rebels' agenda. Then presidential candidate Luis Donaldo Colosio was murdered. The 1994 election was eventually won by Institutional Revolutionary Party candidate Ernesto Zedillo.

The new president faced an unenviable legacy. His predecessor, Carlos Salinas, had engaged in that pre-election tendency to overstimulate the economy. It has become a familiar story, but as interest rates dropped, concerns rose about the quality and quantity of the credit being extended.

In order to finance the deficit, Salinas issued the Tesobonos, a type of short-term debt instrument denominated in pesos but indexed to the dollar. This left Mexico with another age-old emerging market problem – high debt denominated or linked to foreign currency. Any weakness in the domestic currency and the debt would balloon.

The political instability raised international fears, particularly when Salinas's brother was implicated in the murder of Colosio, and international investors started putting a higher premium on Mexican assets. The country had a fixed exchange rate system that accepted pesos and paid out in dollars. This was ostensibly in place to reassure international investors but Mexico simply did not have the foreign reserves to fund the policy.

Despite his predecessor's assurance, Zedillo had no choice but to widen the trading band for the peso – an effective devaluation – when he came into office at the end of 1994. International investors were further put off and the country struggled to renegotiate its debt when the time came.

Unwilling to see its neighbour weakened and vulnerable, the US rode to the rescue. It bought pesos in the open market and then offered guarantees to international creditors. The peso slowly stabilized and growth resumed in 1996.

Mexico repaid all its loans from the US but the social impact was devastating, with millions sliding back into poverty. Political instability continued between 1996 and the turn of the century with ongoing rebellions from the Zapatistas, demanding better rights for indigenous people. But the economy proved resilient.

Since 2001, the country has grown between 3.6% and 6.4%, but some analysts – notably those at the World Bank – have suggested that, given its natural advantages, this could be seen as modest. Mexico has oil and other natural resources, plus geographical proximity to the largest economy in the world. It has a flourishing tourist industry and it has made significant progress to an open economy and government. If anything, the economists argue, Mexico should have done better.

8.4.1   The Investment Case for Mexico

Mexico's blessing and curse has been its ties to the US. In the crisis of 2001 and 2002 Mexico escaped lightly, supported by the economic strength of the US, but the global financial crisis saw the region hit hard by the weakness in its neighbour and largest export destination.

Mexico is the 11th largest country in the world, coming a significant second to Brazil in Latin America and well ahead of the next largest country in the region, Argentina, which is 22nd. But its proximity and ties to the US have given it a different economic flavour to the rest of Latin America.

It has suffered particularly badly in the recent downturn, with a confluence of factors leaving it weakened. The US is its major export partner – the destination for more than 80% of its overall exports and a huge chunk of those exports is in cars. Mexico also remains the world's seventh largest oil producer and the weaker oil price has had an impact on growth. Furthermore, its long-term health is geared to the health of the US economy and, for the time being, the US economy remains relatively weakened.

Mexico's GDP was forecast to dip 7.3% in 2009, the weakest showing in Latin America although its problems were compounded by the swine flu epidemic that started there in early 2008. Tourism is an important part of the economy and the fallout had a significant impact.

Weak productivity remains a problem too and many see it as the key factor in Mexico's slow growth – according to the World Bank, productivity in Mexico has barely grown over the last 15 years. "The region has lost much of its manufacturing to Asia and hasn't replaced it with anything more upscale," says James Syme, head of emerging markets at Baring Asset Management. "It has failed to make the transition up the productivity, value-added curve."

The World Bank suggests Mexico is "between two worlds and there are two worlds in Mexico". Less poetically, Mexico still has extremes of rich and poor – and this is likely to stall the development of a consumer economy. Mexico per capita GDP was $6419 in 2000 and reached $10 200 in 2008 and, while this ostensibly looks impressive, the country lags near-rivals such as Brazil.

There are also worries about the country's long-term future. In particular, its oil wealth looks to be in jeopardy, with 23 of its 32 biggest fields in decline. Officials have warned that the giant Canterell oilfield, which makes up around 60% of Mexico's oil revenues, is in early decline. Oil revenues historically make up around one-third of the national budget, though this has been higher in recent years. Unless it secures significant new finds, it could become a net importer of oil by 2017.

Future oil discoveries are likely to be more expensive to extract as well. Pemex, one of the country's main oil producers, is heavily in debt and needs government help to fund exploration. The oil companies are owned by the state and economists at the World Bank suggest this is hampering long-term investment. It also means that the state bears the long-term risk of fluctuating oil revenues rather than private investors. That said, the economy will be a significant beneficiary should the oil price move higher.

However, Mexico's stock market does not necessarily need a buoyant economy in order to deliver returns to investors. "There is a big difference between the equity market and the economy," says Syme. "Mexico has some cash rich, well-run, high quality companies with monopolistic or oligopolistic positions in industries such as telecoms, media, brewing, cement and retail. There are no energy or petrochemical companies."

As a result, investors have made good money in Mexico over the five years to 2009, with the index almost triple its level in 2004, and this could continue in the short term. "Earnings for companies on the Mexican stock market were forecast to rise by around 20% in 2009," says Julian Thompson, head of emerging markets at Threadneedle Investments.

"The stock market is made up of companies with plenty of foreign operations, with pricing power that should prove reasonably resilient. The export sector, which has been weak, has not been significantly represented in the stock market."

Mexico's main index is the MXSE. It hit a high of 31 975 in May 2008, but dipped to 16 978 in October of the same year. This 47% fall was high by the standards of developed markets, but lower than the falls in some emerging markets. Since then the index has recovered swiftly. It began its recovery sooner than other major markets and, by October 2009, it was back up to its 2008 high.

"Mexico is a paradox," says Urban Larson, director of emerging equities at F&C Asset Management. "It has some excellent companies that are well run, shareholder-friendly and have good corporate governance. They are used to doing business globally. But the political system is dysfunctional. The institutions were created for a fake democracy and, now they are being used in a real democracy, they don't work. There are some structural growth problems the country can't get over.

"So the top-down is very unappealing, but there are lots of good investment options. You can do well if you invest in the right companies. The fashion in emerging markets has been for a top-down, country-specific approach, but that just doesn't work in Mexico."

Company Focus: America Movil

By 2010, Mexican group America Movil was the largest listed company in Latin America while, by subscribers, it was also the third largest wireless provider in the world. The company provides coverage for a combined population of more than 800 million and operates across Central America, South America and the Caribbean. It was spun off from Telmex in 2000 and has since built a subscriber base of more than 180 million.

America Movil, which by 2010 had a market share of around 40%, has profited from – and contributed to – the vast expansion in mobile phone penetration since 2000. The company estimates this has gone from 13% at its inception to around 80%. It made a fortune for Mexican billionaire entrepreneur Carlos Slim Helú. A little like Vodafone in the UK, it is so large that, love it or hate it, all professional emerging markets investors need to have a view on it.

8.5   ARGENTINA – A BRIEF ECONOMIC HISTORY

When Argentina launched its strike on the British-governed Falkland Islands in the early 1980s, it was under military leadership led by General Leopoldo Galtieri. As in the UK, the war served a political end – Galtieri aimed to galvanize support for his regime.

The loss of the war led to the resumption of civilian rule under Raúl Alfonsin in 1983, but the economy had been fractured before the war and was well and truly broken afterwards. The country suffered hyper-inflation with prices changing daily. Ultimately, the IMF was brought in to resolve the problems.

It wasn't until the election of Carlos Menem of the Peronist party as president in 1989 that the country began to resolve its problems. His hand forced by international financiers and the IMF, Menem brought in an economic austerity programme. Industries were privatized and government spending saw huge cutbacks. Socially, it was painful, but it improved the economy and the next few years saw significant economic expansion.

But it was in resolving this disaster that the seeds of the next crisis were sown. In order to ensure the government was never again allowed to devalue its currency by printing more money, the international moneymen had two main conditions to protect their interests: they demanded that, going forward, the peso would be worth as much as the dollar and that the total currency in circulation would be strictly indexed to the number of dollars held by the central banks. In doing this, Argentina inextricably linked its monetary policy to that of the US.

While things were going well, this did not matter much. Between 1993 and 1998, the economy grew at a rate of at least 5% every year. Inflation fell to single digits and capital inflows began to surge. The country dealt swiftly with the Mexican peso crisis that afflicted its Latin American neighbours and people even talked of its "economic miracle". Its economic programmes were overseen by the IMF and the country was generally considered to be "on track".

Argentina's structural weaknesses were exposed in the late 1990s as the country endured three years of recession. Exports were growing steadily, but did not keep pace with imports while the government was increasingly relying on private sector capital to fund its borrowing needs.

Although not unduly profligate, it was hampered in this by court-ordered compensation payments after social security reforms in the early 1990s. A small domestic financial system meant both public and private sectors looked externally for funding and, by the time Fernando de la Rúa of the centre-left Alianza opposition coalition won the presidency in 1999, he had to deal with a $114 bn public debt.

This was significant in the context of the country's exchange rate regime and, by the end of the decade it was simply running out of dollars to support the currency. The regime to which it had committed itself robbed it of policy levers.

There was also social upheaval, including a general strike, which raised Argentina's risk premium in the global financial markets. The IMF came in with another rescue package but it proved to be insufficient to avoid meltdown. Draconian measures by the government to try to stop an exodus of cash from the country's banks only created even greater turmoil.

In December 2001, the Argentine leader, President Adolfo Rodriguez Saá, announced his intention to default on all sovereign debt. It was the largest default in history and effectively cut off all external funding channels to the country.

Then, in January 2002, Argentina removed the peso's peg to the dollar and domestic and international confidence in the currency evaporated. The fallout was painful – Argentina's economy contracted by 4.4% in 2001 and by 10.9% in 2002. The IMF's intervention had been proved a failure, prompting plenty of hand-wringing.

President Eduardo Duhalde had managed to rule for just long enough to steer Argentina out of crisis, but the manner in which he did so created its own problems. He converted dollar accounts and loans to pesos at different rates. He froze utility bills. History has generally viewed his efforts as overly complex and misguided.

From that point on, it has been a painful recovery for the country, but with unemployment soaring and more than half of Argentines below the poverty line, growth could really only go one way. Néstor Kirchner, a leftist Peronist, came into power in 2003 and his presidency has been viewed as largely successful.

At the very least, he avoided the corruption that had dogged his predecessors. The next few years saw international negotiations for debt restructuring and the government finally reached agreement with some of Argentina's international creditors in 2005 and paid off its IMF obligations.

Kirchner's wife, Christina Fernandez, became President in 2007, but there is a sense that he still holds some of the reins of power. He famously said Argentina would never go back to the IMF after it finished paying off its debt in 2006, which did not endear him to foreign investors.

And the poor economic decisions just seem to keep repeating themselves, from the snap nationalization of private pension funds to crude attempts to curb the power of critical media groups. The government has latterly attempted to build a rapprochement with the international finance community but it has a mountain to climb.

8.5.1 The Investment Case for Argentina

We say "investment case for" but when index provider FTSE downgraded Argentina from an emerging market to a frontier economy in its September 2009 review, it was a symbol of how the mighty are fallen. The country provides a salutary lesson in how not to manage an economy. Among its natural advantages are its abundant natural resources, its educated workforce and its sheer size, yet it has lurched from one financial crisis to another due to reckless economic mismanagement.

"It is a sad story of wasted potential and it is not the first time they've done it," says Larson at F&C Asset Management, summing up the view of many investors towards Argentina. "Will they ever figure it out? In Argentina, there is a view that the wealth is there to be shared, whereas in Brazil, they believe wealth should be created."

Argentina has many of the abundant natural resources that have propelled Brazil to global prominence but, for Larson, the difference is one of attitude. "Brazil understood that in order for people to invest, they need to be treated reasonably," he says. "Brazil is simply a much more predictable, shareholder-friendly place to invest. Argentina has lost its competitive advantage because Brazil is a more welcoming place."

The question now for investors is whether Argentina can regain the trust of international investors, or whether it will go the way of Venezuela, which is now largely closed to external investment. Winning back trust will be a long process.

After its currency and debt crisis at the turn of the century, the country finally managed to issue government debt again in 2006, but international capital markets remain uninterested in the region and any buyers have generally been Venezuelan.

Argentina is currently in negotiations to repay $6.7 bn of debt to the "Paris Club", a 19-strong rich nations' club, whose members include the US and Germany, but the country reneged on a commitment to repay its debts in 2008. It is still embroiled in law suits with some bond holders, who refused its 2005 settlement offer.

Its unpopularity among international investors means the Argentine equity market is consistently among the first to be sold off at times of heightened risk aversion. In the recent rout, the benchmark Argentine Merval index fell from 2351 in October 2007 to 994 in November 2008. This 58% fall was high even by emerging markets standards, although the market had seen some significant gains from the height of the country's crisis in 2002, rising consistently from levels of around 200.

Argentina has weathered the global credit crunch better than some of its emerging market peers. GDP was expected to drop by around 1.5% in 2009 and to be marginally ahead in 2010. That said, per capita income levels had only just recovered to pre-crisis levels, so Argentina is still looking at a lost decade of growth.

The commodities boom had strengthened its financial position, as increasing agricultural prices and demand brought cash rolling back into the government coffers. As business and consumer confidence returned, domestic spending rose and supported GDP growth, which consistently registered above 8% until 2008. However, there remain significant structural problems.

Inflation, for example, has been a constant. Although the global economic downturn has tempered inflation, in 2007 and 2008 consumer price inflation registered 8.8% and 8.6% respectively. Foreign investment, understandably, remains elusive. Argentina's somewhat cavalier attitude to the international investment community has kept people away.

Argentina looks unlikely to regain the ground it has lost to Brazil. It would be tempting to suggest a change of government might turn things round in the region, but successive governments have made the same economic mistakes and mismanagement is starting to look entrenched. There may be money to be made for the brave, depending on whether Argentina has gone as low as it can go. Equally, there is a chance that the current government's negotiations may win round international investors once again, but it is a slim one.

8.6   CHILE – A BRIEF ECONOMIC HISTORY

In common with many of its Latin American neighbours, Chile has had a turbulent economic history. The early 1970s saw a familiar blend of political instability, rampant inflation and stagnant growth, culminating in the bloody dictatorship of General Auguste Pinochet, who ruled from 1973 to 1989.

Still – and controversial though it may be to say it – important economic reforms were implemented in the Pinochet era. Few would argue these reforms were worth the social upheaval that went with them – not only was Pinochet's regime violent, it also prompted high unemployment, increasing poverty and a widening gap between rich and poor – but they ultimately formed the basis for the later strength of the Chilean economy.

The period saw the establishment of an open economy. Import tariffs were lowered and extraneous trade controls removed. Inflation was brought under control and government debt was reduced. It was not without its problems – notably the peso crisis in 1982, which was linked to the fixed exchange rate – but the military dictatorship negotiated economic turmoil successfully to the extent that, when democracy finally came in 1989, international investors wondered whether the economic momentum could be sustained.

As it was, Chile was the big Latin American success story of the 1990s. Between 1991 and 2000, it averaged 6.5% GDP growth a year – the highest in the region and well ahead of Brazil, which could only manage an anaemic 2.5% average growth at the time.

This success was largely fuelled by a rapid growth in exports. They were well diversified geographically though commodity focused – particularly on copper. Chile largely escaped the Latin crisis of 1999 to 2002 although it did suffer a moderate recession in 1999, which was exacerbated by a severe drought.

The copper price began its impressive ascent in early 2003. Comex high-grade copper futures were trading at around 72 in March of that year but the next five years saw the price rise to a peak of 390 in April 2008. The slump from June to December 2008 was dramatic with the price dipping to levels not seen since October 2004, but the price has recovered substantially since then.

8.6.1   The Investment Case for Chile

If Argentina demonstrates how poor policymaking can mess up some natural advantages, then Chile shows the opposite. Barring the aberration of Pinochet, Chilean politics has been relatively benign by Latin American standards while its economic management has been second to none. Its problem, if anything, has been its very dependability. It lacks excitement for investors.

The strength of copper has been both Chile's strength and weakness. From 2002 to the start of the credit crunch, the high copper price allowed it to maintain its strong GDP growth. Between 2002 and 2008, this GDP growth ranged from 3.2% to 6%, which was lower than some of its neighbours but neither had Chile been brought low by previous crises. The wealth effect was seen throughout the economy. According to the World Bank, income per head rose from $5265 in 2000 to $8613 in 2008 and a consumer economy developed.

But in spite of this strength, Chile could not avoid the effects of the global credit crunch. It is still primarily a commodity exporter and, as such, was hit hard by tumbling commodity prices and declining global demand. The country was also at risk as its open economy left it vulnerable to problems in the global banking system.

Prudent economic policies have helped it weather the storm – for example, the government's Economic and Social Stabilisation sovereign wealth fund has been busy squirreling away the country's excess copper revenues in recent years. The fund is now worth $17 bn and has allowed Chile to cut rates, boost infrastructure spending and generally stimulate the economy to see it through the downturn.

Chile also benefited from its relatively diverse export base. Although Europe remains its largest export partner – making up just over 20% of overall exports – 18% of exports go to China and 20% to the US. The remainder is split reasonably evenly between Japan, Asia and other Latin American countries.

Interest rates dipped more than 7% over the course of 2009 – falling 2.5% in February alone – to reach 0.5%, and the government has also been spending a lot to get growth going. As a result, GDP growth in Chile was expected to be positive in 2009 and jump up to 3% in 2010. In the region, only Panama, Peru and Guyana were expected to be higher. Brazil's predicted growth of 2.2% seems relatively dull in comparison.

The Heritage Index of Economic Freedom, which compares the relative economic freedom of different economies based on trade freedom, business freedom, investment freedom and property rights, now has Chile in 11th place in the world, just one notch behind the UK and ahead of almost all major European countries.

Its profile says: "Chile's record of economic reform includes transparent and stable public finance management and strong protection of property rights. Macroeconomic stability and openness to global trade and investment have encouraged stable long-term growth. Chile has pursued free trade agreements with various countries around the world. Its financial system is diversified and stable compared to those of other regional economies, with a sound regulatory and supervisory framework."

Equally, the Chilean economy has plenty going for it in the longer term. The Chileans are good at saving money for a rainy day – the country has a high savings ratio and a large personal finance industry – and there is little burdensome debt on a personal, corporate or government level. The country has high literacy rates – around 96%, according to the World Bank – and stability of government. According to the Central Bank of Chile, its exports rose from $41 267 m in 2005 to $66 456 m in 2008 and its foreign exchange reserves from $16 960 m to $23 156 m over the same period.

One of Chile's big problems is its lack of diversity. The economy is still copper-focused – making up around 41% of exports – and while that bias has been well managed, it remains a long-term risk. It is also little changed in 25 years, according to the Central Bank of Chile. The sector has suffered problems with inflation in the past, but weakening commodity prices have seen off that particular risk in the short term.

The other problem is that it's just not very exciting. "Chile is the third biggest market in Latin America and everything works perfectly," says Larson at F&C Asset Management. "There is a strong domestic pension fund industry, which supports the stock market, making it less volatile and more expensive.

"The country is generally well run – in 2009, it managed to ramp up government spending very quickly as the global economy turned. It had been running a surplus of 5% to 6% of GDP and the government apparatus is relatively efficient. It is a very global, very open country. The stock market can be frustrating, however – all the companies are pretty good but it's hard to get excited about any of them."

Certainly the Chilean stock market has not replicated the steady growth of the wider economy in the short term. It soared from lows in 2002, with the DJ Chile index moving from 101 to a peak of 536 in October 2007. Nor could the country's healthier economic outlook stop it seeing drastic falls during the fallout from the global credit crisis. The market dropped around 50% to lows of 246 in October 2008. Nevertheless in a mark of its relatively defensive nature, it has recovered sharply to close in on its all-time highs.

It may be that Chile doesn't remain an emerging market for much longer. In 2009, the OECD graciously extended an invitation for Chile to join its ranks on the basis that Chile's economic and social policies have become a "landmark for the region". This could finally provide the missing excitement for investors, drawing in substantial fund flows to the region and pushing up valuations.

8.7 PERU AND COLOMBIA

Peru and Colombia make up a fraction of the Latin American index but are still considered to contain some of the more exciting investment opportunities in the region. "These countries are a lot smaller, but have lots of great stocks," says Larson.

"They both had difficult times in the 1990s and have come back very strongly. At the moment there is a lot of unmet consumer demand. The governments are both quite market-friendly and the domestic pension funds provide plenty of liquidity. These two markets are underrated."

In Peru, real GDP has accelerated in recent years, rising from 6.8% in 2005, to 7.7% in 2006, 8.9% in 2007 and 9.8% in 2008. The country did not go into recession at all during the credit crunch and is expected to show growth over 2009 – the only major Latin American country to do so.

"Peru is relatively small in stock market terms and is largely commodity-driven," says Thompson at Threadneedle Investments. "There are some financial companies, but investors can't buy anything in any great size. Some of the companies operating in Peru are listed elsewhere and that can be a way to gain exposure."

Colombia's growth has been less spectacular, but GDP was still expected to drop just 0.3% in 2009. The story in Colombia is more that of its remarkable turnaround. From a no-go zone for tourists and foreign investors, the country has pulled itself back from the brink in the past few years.

Tourist numbers are up – partly on the back of a government-sponsored advertising campaign with the slogan "The only risk is wanting to stay" – foreign investment is coming in slowly and investors report a shift in approach among Colombian companies. Instead of thinking one or two years ahead, they are thinking globally and long term. The relative peace of the past few years had enabled a longer-term mindset.

These countries both fall into the "ones to watch" category but, with sizeable populations and strong natural advantages, they may yet prove to be profitable for investors.

8.8   INVESTING IN THE REGION

There are four major investment regions in Latin America, of which Brazil is by far the largest, comprising nearly three-fifths of the benchmark S&P Latin America 40 index at the end of 2009. Mexico had around 30% of the index, compared to 9% for Chile and the remainder in Argentina. As we have just seen, some smaller countries have flourishing stock markets, such as Peru, but they have yet to achieve the capitalization to feature in the major Latin American indices.

Some investors still view the whole of Latin America as a pure commodities player and undoubtedly commodities companies do feature heavily in the stock markets of the region. However, it is no longer the only game in town. In fact, the largest company in Latin America is a telecoms company – Mexico's America Movil – and, while materials and energy make up around 40% of the S&P index, the remainder comes from utilities, telecoms and financials companies.

There are also signs that the stock markets are diversifying further, particularly in Brazil and particularly in consumer-focused stocks. For example, Wal-Mart de Mexico and Brazil's brewing group AmBev both feature among the S&P index's 10 largest stocks, a reflection of the emerging consumer economy in the region. However, consumer discretionary stocks still only make up some 3% of the index.

For the individual markets, the main indices are the BOVESPA in Brazil, the IPC (Indice de Precios y Cotizaciones) in Mexico, the IGPA Gen in Chile, the SCE in Colombia, LimaGen in Peru and the Merval (meaning stock market) in Argentina.

As we have seen elsewhere, those looking towards a fund for their money have two main choices – actively managed or passive. The number of passive funds, such as exchange-traded funds, available for Latin American markets has increased significantly as liquidity in the region has improved. Passive funds have seen significant inflows of money in recent years as institutional investors have sought to participate cheaply in their extraordinary growth.

Although the cost of Latin American exchange-traded funds and other passive vehicles will be higher than for one, say, linked to the S&P500 in the US, it will still be considerably lower than for an active fund. The downside is that the fund will be concentrated on a few large sectors, such as financials, commodities and telecommunications, and may not offer adequate access to new trends, such as the emerging consumer.

For its part, active investing has the potential to add considerable value in Latin American funds. In general, these markets are less efficient and less analysed and so greater valuation anomalies can exist. However, with increasing global investor interest in the region, those anomalies may dry up quickly.

Risk management should also be inherent within active investment. In the past, Latin America and other emerging markets have seen a lack of quality corporate governance and earnings data and active managers may be expected to factor this into their investment strategy.

Active investing in Latin America has changed, as it has in most emerging markets. Active managers used to take a macroeconomic view – allocating to individual countries based on their economic outlook and strength – but that has shifted to a more stock-specific approach.

This is partly a reflection of the fact that Latin American companies do not simply depend solely on the domestic market, but also the strength of their export partners. It is also because there are some stock markets that have performed well even as the wider economy has struggled – Argentina being the most obvious example.

Latin America attracts plenty of boutique fund managers and specialists as an awareness of the cultural differences, the ability to negotiate the different legal structures and an experience of the internal workings of the region's companies can give fund managers a significant edge.

It is frequently asked of some Latin American markets why investors would not just invest in the underlying commodities. This is particularly true of the likes of Chile, where so much of the performance depends on the copper price. So why not just buy copper?

Certainly there are some easy and liquid ways to do this but, because there are other risks and variables – for example, the economy, corporate governance, liquidity, quality of management and extraction costs – the share prices of copper companies will not move exactly in line with the copper price. Of course, this may be an advantage or a disadvantage, but it is why investors make the distinction.

8.9   CONCLUSION

Latin America has many aspects in its favour. It is commodity rich at a time when the world looks set to continue to need commodities. It still has the potential to generate a robust consumer economy and early signs have been promising.

Crucially, the region has – for the most part – stable governments that look to have well and truly learnt their lessons from past crises. Any real problems centre on productivity – to match the growth of its Asian rivals Latin America needs to improve its productivity levels, which should help generate long-term economic momentum.

9
Emerging Markets – The Final Frontiers

9.1 INTRODUCTION

The so-called "frontier" economies – with all their Wild West con-
notations – probably chime more closely with most people's idea of
emerging markets. These markets tend to be concentrated in the Middle
East and Africa and will have all the political and economic risk that has
historically been associated with emerging economies – and then some.

9.2 OVERVIEW

Whereas "emerging" markets have become so disparate that packaging
them together as one homogeneous group is starting to seem illogical,
"frontier" markets are somewhat easier to define – at least from an
investment point of view. In this context, frontier markets are areas with
underdeveloped capital markets, which means the capitalization of a
frontier stock market as a percentage of GDP will be low – typically
between 20% and 40%.

Not that there isn't debate at the margins as to what constitutes a
frontier market, with Africa and the Middle East considered such for
different reasons. Countries such as the United Arab Emirates or Qatar
have GDP per capita that in some cases is higher than developed markets.
The CIA World Fact Book lists the GDP per capita for Qatar at more
than $110 000, the second highest in the world, while the United Arab
Emirates posts a more than respectable $44 600 – higher than Hong
Kong.

However, exact data is hard to come by – the World Bank does not hold
economic statistics for many Middle Eastern countries – and therein lies
the problem. These countries are considered "frontier" because of corporate governance issues or onerous restrictions on foreign ownership
of shares, rather than their net wealth.

At the other end of the scale, African markets are considered "frontier"
because they have only just opened up to new investment and lie at the

bottom of the global economic tables. GDP per capita will tend to be low and stock markets will have just a handful of companies listed. In general, liquidity will be weak, as will corporate governance and transparency.

In each case the risks will be different although it is possible to isolate certain characteristics about frontier markets. For a start, the companies on the stock markets tend to be tiny relative to global peers. The Merrill Lynch Frontier index, for example, is made up of the most liquid stocks in the frontier markets. The companies must have a market capitalization of at least $500 m, a three-month average daily turnover of at least $750 000 and a foreign ownership limit above 15%. Approximately 50 stocks across all frontier markets fulfil these criteria.

Meanwhile a report by Acadian Asset Management in 2007 suggested there were 540 "frontier" stocks across 22 markets with a total market capitalization of $165 bn. While this represents a significant increase on just two years previously, by way of comparison, China Telecom by itself has a market capitalization of more than $36 bn.

The companies also tend to be domestically rather than internationally focused, which means they are more geared into the macroeconomic health of the countries themselves. UK-listed Unilever, for example, derives its earnings globally and therefore the weakness of the UK economy will have less impact, but the majority of companies listed in frontier markets will derive their earnings domestically and therefore cannot transcend any weakness in the local economy.

So why invest? The raison d'être for frontier markets is much the same as that for emerging markets generally – the growth rates tend to be higher. As mentioned, the countries will often be more insulated from the global economy and therefore the growth is not as vulnerable to swings in global demand. Of course, there are times when this will be a good thing and times when it won't.

"A lot of what we see now in frontier markets we saw in emerging markets 20 years ago," says Scott Crawshaw, emerging markets portfolio manager at Russell Investments. "These are countries in the very early stages of development – either from an economic or capital markets perspective. A number of them tend to be rich in resources. Africa, for example, is benefiting from the flow of Chinese money to get hold of commodities.

"In the longer term, consumer economies will develop and the aggregate population is very large. Even if these countries move from

extreme poverty to poverty, it means they can start to afford basic consumer goods. This is one catalyst for ongoing growth."

The GDP growth also translates more rapidly into corporate earnings.
"The companies that list initially tend to be 'BBC' companies – banking,
brewing and cement," says Michael Power, global strategist at Investec
Asset Management. "Telecoms are also increasingly being added to that
list. So a stock market may have, say, three banks, two cement companies
and one brewer. These companies that have oligopolistic controls are in
a position to have higher profit growth than the wider economy. There
is a real 'whoosh' in the early stages."

Diversification is also an important lure for some investors to frontier
markets. This held particularly true after the credit crunch, when correlations of many equity and bond markets increased dramatically and as
such pushed investors to look for new sources of diversification.

However, with the commendable exception of Tunisia, frontier markets were hit as hard as – and in many cases harder than – developed
markets. Although many of the economies were insulated from the credit
problems that hit larger economies, the markets were pushed down by
widespread risk aversion, global investors' "flight to quality" and a
weakness in their currencies.

This doesn't mean the diversification argument does not apply as,
over the long term, the correlation between, for example, the S&P500
and the S&P/IFC Frontier Markets index is weaker. As Crawshaw points
out, correlations are a moveable feast.

"Initially correlations with developed markets and even other emerging markets were very low – at 0.2% to 0.25%," he says. "During the
credit crunch, correlations rose across all risky assets and frontier markets did not escape that. But correlations started to lower again as the
global economy and markets recovered."

As a general rule, as we have seen, countries with a high commodities
weighting will be more geared to the health of the global economy as
economic prosperity tends to generate demand for steel, oil and other
commodities involved in industrial production.

Clearly frontier markets will have their drawbacks, with liquidity a
key concern. Power labels it "Hotel California syndrome" – you can
never leave. Daily trading volumes in frontier markets are tiny – the
turnover on the Nairobi stock exchange for the whole of January 2010
was equivalent to $83 m and that is one of the largest exchanges. Only
the Middle Eastern states have significant volumes – the highest being
the United Arab Emirates.

As such, getting money into and out of a frontier market takes patience. Other market participants may respond to large orders and raise prices, particularly for foreign investors, and frequently domestic brokers have to disclose they are acting on behalf of a foreign buyer. It will take time to build a position, so these are not markets that can easily be traded, and bid/offer spreads tend to be large. The buying and selling of investments becomes a key skill in a way that doesn't happen in other markets.

"The problem with frontier markets is that they are a bull-market phenomenon," says Richard Titherington, chief investment officer and head of the emerging markets equity team at J.P. Morgan Asset Management. "People get more and more enthusiastic and they want to take on more risk.

"For example, at the top of the bull market in 1994, one fund management group launched a Vietnam fund. The Vietnamese Stock Exchange didn't come into being until 2000 so it launched six years before there was even a stock market. The group ended up winding up the fund shortly before the Vietnamese market went up five times. Fund managers typically launch these funds at the wrong time. Consequently, markets are expensive. The idea of investing in frontiers is not a bad one – it's just that people typically do it at the wrong time."

Frontier markets will also tend to have more of the political risks traditionally associated with emerging markets. In reality, areas such as India or China now have relatively limited political risk, but some parts of Africa and the Middle East clearly have ongoing problems. Transparency International's 2009 Corruption Perception index saw many frontier markets at the bottom of the tables. Out of 180 countries, for example, Nigeria was ranked 140th, Kenya 146th and the Central African Republic 158th.

Corporate governance and transparency are also weak. In Nigeria, for example, a company's end of year accounts statement barely runs to an A4 page and gives very few details. A lack of data or visibility on earnings or dividends should be enough to deter the prudent corporate analyst.

Even macroeconomic data is relatively scarce. The World Bank has minimal data for the majority of frontier markets and some fail to provide any data at all. There is also a question mark over the reliability of any data from frontier countries with a weak or unstable government.

This leads naturally to another issue – government interference remains a problem, with stock exchanges routinely manipulated for political ends. One of the key problems for New Star Asset Management's Heart of Africa fund, which was suspended in December 2008, was that cash from selling securities in Nigeria was held up by newly implemented foreign exchange restrictions.

However, Larry Speidell, founding partner and chief investment officer at Frontier Market Asset Management, argues these risks should not be overestimated. In his white paper "Investing in the unknown and the unknowable – behavioural finance in emerging markets", he points out that many frontier markets score higher on the Heritage Scale of Economic Freedom than other emerging or developed markets.

For example, 17 frontier market economies, including those of Bahrain, Cyprus, Jamaica and Mauritius, score higher than France on this scale. A further seven score higher than Italy. With that in mind, it then comes down to a question of picking the right country.

The domestic focus of the frontier markets is both a risk and an opportunity. Over the course of the financial crisis, it was those countries that were reliant on exports and/or external capital that suffered most – notably in Eastern Europe. But all markets have suffered and only Tunisia, Qatar and Mauritius were ahead over the three years to 2009.

Although a strong domestic focus can have its advantages, it also means macroeconomic events have a disproportionate effect on corporate earnings. For example, the prolonged drought in Kenya from 2006 had a deleterious effect on the stock market. "To be a pure stockpicker in frontier markets is a luxury investors cannot afford," says Power.

9.3 THE MIDDLE EAST

Middle East countries don't naturally appear to fit the model of frontier markets as they boast considerable wealth by emerging market – and even global – standards. Gross national income per head in Kuwait, for example, was $38 420 in 2007, just a fraction behind that of the UK's $40 660. Life expectancy in the region is good too, ranging between 76 and 79, while plentiful oil reserves shore up wealth across all the countries and there is a domestic consumer market with high mobile phone and internet penetration.

So why exactly are the major markets of the Middle East – Bahrain, Kuwait, Oman, Qatar, Saudi Arabia and the United Arab Emirates – seen as frontier? The key reason is access. The majority of these countries have been effectively closed to external investors – either that, or investors have had to negotiate a complex minefield of tax laws and ownership rights that have made investment a still more risky business. These markets are also leveraged to the oil price, which is fine when the oil price is soaring, as in late 2007, but that is not always the case.

That said, opportunities do exist. These countries built up plentiful reserves during the oil price boom, which have been stored in sovereign wealth funds and put to work in international markets – for example, it was Middle Eastern money that came in to prop up Barclays Bank during the credit crisis. These sovereign wealth funds invested not only for a good risk-adjusted return, but also to gain access to technology, ideas and skills and to improve productivity.

While many of these funds were hurt during the downturn, they are still huge players on the international investment stage and therefore wield considerable power. Exact assets are not always publicly available, but it was estimated at the end of 2009 that the Abu Dhabi Investment Authority held assets in excess of $625 bn, making it the largest sovereign wealth fund in the world.

These petrodollars are not just being stored away either but are being reinvested domestically in areas such as infrastructure, telecommunications and banking. Over 2007 and 2008, according to the World Bank, annual GDP gains were robust – averaging between 6% and 8% across the region with the United Arab Emirates higher and Saudi Arabia lower. Overall, GDP growth for the region was 6.3% in 2007 and 5.2% in 2008.

Ultimately, however, the region is dependent on oil, which in turn is dependent on the health of the global economy. The sliding oil price forced OPEC to cut output, which hurt many Middle East members. For example, at the peak, Saudi Arabia was holding approximately 4 million barrels a day off the market at a cost of around $100 bn a year – or 25% of its GDP.

The IMF was predicting that GDP growth in the Middle East would slow to 2% for 2009 and rise again to 4.2% in 2010. Saudi Arabia, the United Arab Emirates and Kuwait were all likely to see a contraction in growth for the period. In addition, many of these countries were using their reserves to prop up domestic demand and so may find their healthy surpluses eroded by the downturn.

Still, the Middle Eastern equity markets have become more accessible to international investors. Saudi Arabia, the Middle East's biggest stock market, gave access to foreign investors in August 2008 while research on the region by large institutional investors, such as Merrill Lynch and J.P. Morgan, has also expanded, with some groups setting up offices there.

The Middle East undoubtedly has wealth, but benefiting from its growth as an external investor is a different matter altogether. Much of the region's strength comes from oil and there are easier ways to invest in oil. Any investment in the Middle East is really a play on it opening up to external investors rather than on its economic growth.

Country focus: Kuwait

Kuwait teeters on emerging market status but, despite the wealth of its citizens and its resources, it remains "frontier" by dint of its weak government and poor access for foreign investors. In all other respects, it is a developed market economy. In 2007 its gross national income per citizen hovered around $38 000 while its stock market capitalization was 167.7% of GDP. It has more than one mobile phone for every citizen and internet penetration is high.

It has preserved plenty of its oil wealth too, with the Kuwait Investment Authority sovereign wealth fund estimated to hold more than $200 bn, which is largely generated from oil. GDP growth was a healthy 6.4% in 2008 and there were clear signs the economy was becoming more diversified as non-oil GDP grew 7.3%, according to the IMF.

But the fall in oil prices and production hit the region hard and GDP was forecast to dip 1.5% for 2009. This was still relatively benign on a global scale, but it inevitably hit domestic consumption growth, which as a result was expected to grow just 1% in 2009.

Kuwait is also hampered by political problems. Ratings agency Moody's put Kuwait on a possible ratings downgrade in March 2009, following the resignation of its cabinet for the second time in two years. The catalyst was a motion filed against the prime minister.

While the stock markets are broad and relatively liquid, few companies are open to foreign investment. The country's stock exchange has a "non-Kuwaitis" sector, which houses some 15 stocks that are largely cement companies and banks. It rose from 7951 on 18 August 2006 to a peak of 14 240 in late 2007 but then slumped to lag other frontier markets. Kuwait's fortunes still very much depend on the oil price, which in turn depends on global growth.

Dubai: When things go wrong

The run-up to the credit crunch saw plenty of examples of hubris, but perhaps nowhere were these more concentrated than in Dubai. With hindsight the signs were clear – the vanity building projects, the extravagant parties and the reckless build-up of debt – but when Dubai World asked for its debt to be rescheduled at the end of 2009 it sent global stock markets into a panic. In the end, Dubai's finances were – at least temporarily – shored up with a multi-billion dollar loan from Abu Dhabi, its neighbour in the United Arab Emirates.

In addition to excessive debt, Dubai's climate of secrecy contributed to this particular crisis. There were few official statistics about economic growth and development and crude public relations aimed to disguise the real extent of the debt problem. International markets drew their own conclusions and withdrew investment savagely. Rating agencies cut the region's debt rating.

Most professional investors operating in the region believe the problems have been contained and that, with some stability in the oil price, many Middle Eastern countries should make a robust return to growth. However, the crisis hurt investors in the short term – the MSCI United Arab Emirates index fell 16.9% in the final three months of 2009 (but remained 33% up for the full year).

It will take time for the real legacy of the Dubai crisis to unfold and to uncover which companies and countries are exposed to losses. In the meantime the country is having to deal with the fallout, including the widespread job losses and falling property prices. Dubai's glitzy excesses provide a neat parable for what can go wrong in emerging and frontier markets in a very short space of time.

9.4 AFRICA

From an investment point of view, Africa still conjures up images of wild plains and lawlessness, of military rule and famine and, as such, it is difficult to reconcile this with a potential investment opportunity. But at a time when industrializing nations are crying out for commodities, Africa is suddenly finding a lot of new friends. The real question therefore becomes whether the wealth generated will filter down into the wider population and so create sustainable GDP growth on the continent.

There are three main areas of investment in Africa. North Africa comprises the larger markets of Morocco, Egypt and Algeria while

South Africa is the biggest single market in the continent with a stock market capitalization of almost $800 bn.

Along with the three major markets of North Africa, South Africa is easily robust enough to be considered "emerging" – although it is geographically convenient to consider it within this chapter – so it is only Kenya, Mauritius, Nigeria and Tunisia that are considered frontier markets

Africa's strengths lie in its mineral and agricultural resources, which have drawn global investors to the continent. The Chinese in particular have been investing in the hope of shoring up their supply of much-needed commodities to support their industrialization. More than 35 African countries are now engaging with China on infrastructure finance deals.

Bilateral trade and Chinese foreign direct investment in Africa grew fourfold between 2001 and 2005 and was accompanied by an influx of Chinese migrants to the region. 2007 saw around $4.5 bn in Chinese funds flow into Africa for infrastructure projects.

African governments have been quick to welcome this money as it doesn't come with strings attached – at least, not of the kind that, for example, IMF funding demands. Hydropower and roads have been the main beneficiaries and the money has flowed disproportionately into Nigeria, Angola, Sudan and Ethiopia.

Since Africa still has huge infrastructure needs estimated at around $20 bn per year, not even Chinese investment can provide the whole answer. Weak, expensive and unreliable infrastructure still stymies growth across Africa and will need to be addressed before growth can properly accelerate.

As any investor would expect, China's investment is not entirely without self-interest. It imported $22 bn of commodities from Africa in 2006 and wants to ensure it retains friends in the region. The majority of this is oil and China now obtains around 30% of its oil from Africa.

China is not alone in its interest in the continent with, for example, Russian President Dmitry Medvedev visiting Africa in August 2009 to build ties. Dwindling domestic reserves have left Russia with a greater reliance on the rich resources available in Africa. In turn, Medvedev was seeking to strike deals to sell Russia's technical knowledge on energy to Africa. Russian gas giant Gazprom has also linked up with the Nigerian National Petroleum Corporation to help build the trans-Sahara gas pipeline, which will channel gas from Nigeria to Southern Europe.

Of course, many Western companies have been investing and developing projects in Africa for years – particularly the global oil majors.

Country focus: South Africa

South Africa is difficult to pigeonhole as an emerging market – as readers can probably surmise from our placing one of the more important players in the space within the chapter on frontier markets. In investment terms, there are a number of ways the country transcends Africa but there are also a number of ways in which it is still very much on a par with the rest of the continent.

South Africa has some claims to be considered alongside the BRIC economies – and at the very least it has some notable natural advantages. It is resource rich at a time when the world wants resources; it has stronger corporate governance standards than many of its emerging market peers; its capital markets are broad and robust; and it offers a gateway to the largely untapped riches of the African continent. But its political situation remains something of a ball and chain as – even 20 years on – it struggles to shake off its grim history.

International investors certainly still get twitchy about South African politics. It is generally left-leaning and there are still powerful radical elements at work. In particular, calls from trade unions to nationalize mining assets have been worrying the financial community, which hates government interference in privately held assets. The government has thus far resisted any temptation to meddle but some market watchers fear this restraint may depend on how loud the clamour grows.

The country has other problems too. Almost a quarter of the workforce is unemployed and although the governing ANC keeps promising job creation, little has materialized. Inflation has been an issue, running as high as 11.5% in 2008. By the start of 2010, it had fallen to 6.2%, but it remains a lurking menace. Debt is also high as the government has spent its way out of the recent economic problems. The country's commodity focus also means it is geared more than most to the fortunes of the global economy.

South Africa's hosting of the football World Cup in 2010 has been viewed as offering an opportunity to address some of the structural problems within the economy. The authorities have been clear about what they think the tournament should be able to bring to South Africa – not least that it should go some way towards remedying the country's creaky infrastructure and help foster broadcasting, telecommunications and technology expertise. It should also help bring about an image makeover for the country, selling it as a destination for tourism and business. The authorities also hope it will create jobs.

South Africa enjoyed steady growth for most of the first decade of this century, largely on the back of its commodities wealth. It averaged 1.8% growth per year between 1991 and 2000, but this picked up to more than 5% between 2005 and 2007. However, it could not escape the commodities slump and fell into recession in 2009 with output falling 2.2%. Industrial production began to pick up in the third quarter of 2009 while exports rose strongly from the second quarter of 2009. The country was expected to post unexciting GDP growth of 1.7% in 2010.

Much of the country's attraction for investors lies in its position as a conduit to the rest of the continent with more pan-African companies listed on its stock exchange than in any other country in Africa. It also tends to have better transparency and standards of corporate governance than elsewhere.

South Africa's stock markets have followed the rise and fall and rise of commodities. The JSE index fell from 32 700 in May 2008 to a low of 18 066 just six months later – its lowest level since 2005. By March 2010, it had recovered to 28 262.

While it undoubtedly has some world-beating and long-established commodities companies, such as Anglo American, South Africa can also lay claim to significant global players in finance, retailing, telecommunications and consumer goods and services. Financial services giant Investec, for example, has long transcended its South African roots.

Country focus: Nigeria

Nigeria is an obvious target for investors new to African markets. Its plentiful oil reserves allowed it to build up cash during the boom years and it has a long-established and well-diversified stock market with an overall market capitalization of some $40 bn. Liquidity meanwhile is adequate – the total value of trades done on 10 March 2010, for example, was $26.9 m – and the economy has also expanded with GDP growth of 5.9% in 2007.

However, politics continues to prevent the country from properly exploiting its oil wealth. Ongoing instability at the heart of government and vested interests have kept wealth firmly in the hands of the few. Gross national income per head was just $1160 in 2007 while mobile phone penetration, a key sign of economic development, is low, even for Africa. A tiny middle class is emerging, driven by telecommunications, banking and services, but the country remains largely one of a few very wealthy people and a lot of very poor ones.

President Umaru Yar'Adua has promised to tackle the special interest groups and corruption that have been so deleterious for widespread prosperity in Nigeria, but two years into his rule, little had progressed. Worse still, while his predecessor conserved much of the wealth amassed from oil and ran a budget surplus, Yar'Adua is now running with a deficit, despite some unprecedented highs in the oil price during his term of office. The country has also suffered from the weakness of the US, which remains its biggest trading partner, taking 45% of all exports, according to the United Nations.

The performance of the stock market has tended to reflect the volatility of the underlying economy and political situation. The MSCI Nigeria index dropped by a fifth in 2009 and, as a result, was significantly in negative territory over one and three years. With the exception of Estonia, it was the worst-performing frontier market over five years.

Some two-fifths of Africa's oil still goes to the US and, as such, it is not immune from global economic forces.

So how else can Africa build up its infrastructure? A controversial new trend has involved leasing its land to Middle Eastern and other investors, who use it to grow wheat, barley and rice and then export it back home. These foreign investors are given incentives to do this and the idea is that the programmes bring agricultural skills to the continent.

However, the controversy has come about because the deals have not necessarily been done on the best of terms for Africa. Furthermore, point out the critics, many of the countries leasing their land are receiving food aid from the World Food Programme.

Although Africa is attracting investment and GDP rates are rising, albeit from a low base, there remains a significant question over whether the wealth generated will trickle down to the wider population. In Nigeria, for example, the huge wealth generated by its oil reserves has remained stubbornly in the hands of a very few and the majority of the population lives barely at subsistence level.

In order to see a sustained pick-up in GDP growth, Africa needs to show real signs of domestic economic expansion, rather than the rather more familiar story of a lucky few people getting rich from the commodities boom, among other things. It would be a mistake to extrapolate the problems of a few rogue states into those of an entire continent, but much of Africa still has a long way to go and the ride will be rocky.

9.5 INVESTING IN FRONTIER MARKETS

Even if investors decide they are willing to take the risk on frontier markets, they are soon confronted with a second dilemma – how best to access them. Index-tracking funds are one possible solution and these are increasingly presenting themselves. Exchange-traded funds based on individual frontier markets, or a basket of countries, have been launched as appetite has grown. For example, db x-trackers launched the S&P Select Frontiers Index in February 2008.

Invesco PowerShares offers exchange-traded funds on the Middle East and North Africa, plus an overall Frontier Countries Portfolio, which is listed on the Nasdaq in the US. Other options include the Claymore/BNY Mellon Frontier Markets and the Market Vectors Gulf States and Africa exchange-traded funds. Lyxor, part of Société Générale, launched an exchange-traded fund on the Kuwaiti market in August 2008 on the basis it was the most liquid market in the region.

Costs will be higher than for conventional exchange-traded funds and, as discussed elsewhere, index investment does have its limitations. "The index provides a good idea of the free-flow adjusted opportunity set in frontier markets, but it is not very indicative of portfolio manager-constructed portfolios," says Russell Investments' Crawshaw, who specializes in selecting active managers in the region. "The problem is less a concentration in the large commodity stocks, as you might expect, but in exposure to financials, which will often make up around 60% of frontier market indices."

Global frontier market managers – the preferred route for Russell Investments – can judge the risk in individual countries and get out if it is increasing. Even so, investors need a manager who knows his stuff and has established relationships in the markets in question.

"Investing in frontier markets can be expensive," says Crawshaw. "Setting up local custody arrangements is expensive, for example, and fixed investment costs are high – maybe as much as 3%, compared to

0.2% or 0.3% in Brazil or South Korea. The bid/offer spreads can be larger too, so investors need to have a longer time horizon for putting money to work. Fund managers tend to turn over their funds much more slowly."

Achieving the exposure you want in frontier markets can also be difficult. Crawshaw says markets can often adjust relatively slowly to changing economic conditions. "The listed markets tend to comprise commodity companies, banks, telcos and drinks companies at the start," he says. "While many countries are improving the ability of companies to come to market, this is still driven by broader global liquidity."

Many professional investors simply do not want to take the risk of stocks listed in such volatile markets and instead prefer to gain access via companies listed in developed markets that generate a considerable amount of their earnings in frontier markets.

Lonrho would be a typical example of this. It generates the majority of its earnings from infrastructure, agribusiness and support services in Africa, but it is listed in London, with all the corporate governance and disclosure advantages that entails. Meanwhile many African companies aim to give themselves greater credibility by listing in South Africa, but will derive a share of their earnings from the wider continent. Old Mutual, for example, is listed in South Africa and generates around 70% of its profits across the continent.

An update from Standard & Poor's in August 2009 suggested a number of active managers had underperformed passive or index-tracking funds since the start of that year, largely because they had been too cautious and had held too high a level of cash. In theory, however, active managers should be able to move in and out of weaker markets to good effect and, ideally, protect on the downside too.

Microfinance funds offer another route into frontier markets. This is the provision of financial services and loans to help entrepreneurs in developing nations to grow small businesses. It came to public attention in 2006 when Dr Muhummad Yunnus won the Nobel Peace Prize for his pioneering work in Bangladesh in this field. His Grameen Foundation is estimated to have reached approximately 80% of Bangladesh's poor families.

The borrowers are mostly women and default rates are low, with the norm being around 2%. These low default rates are maintained through strong vetting procedures, including detailed site visits. Collections tend to be weekly or every other week.

There are funds that offer a way in, and these are generally diversified across regions and borrowers. However, minimum investment levels are usually high and it is not a practical route for the smaller investor. That said, microfinance does appeal to socially motivated investors, who prefer to be helping people on the ground, rather than corporations.

9.6 CONCLUSION

Frontier markets come emblazoned with a significant health warning but, of course, if they were less risky, the opportunities they present would diminish accordingly. As with any investment, people need to ensure, first, that they don't underestimate the associated risks and, second, those risks are adequately factored into the price paid. These markets are not for the faint-hearted and there will be winners and losers, but the rewards are rich for the winners.

For investors who prefer a little less excitement in their lives, we refer back to the words of Bob Yerbury, chief investment officer at Invesco Perpetual, in Chapter 2. "As an investor, you don't have to be the pioneer," he says. "You can wait until things have developed a little more in terms of accounting and governance. Some investors have a compulsion to find 'the latest market' but you are always better off operating where you have more confidence."

10

2020 Vision – The New Economic Order?

Former US Secretary of Defence Donald Rumsfeld famously once said: "There are known knowns. These are things we know that we know. There are known unknowns. That is to say, there are things that we know we don't know. But there are also unknown unknowns. There are things we don't know we don't know."

Possibly if he been part of a more popular administration and probably if the idea had been put forward by someone like Plato or Descartes, it may not have received so much ridicule. In fact it might even have been considered an insightful piece of philosophy. Is that too strong a description? Perhaps we should just say the statement provides a useful framework for summing up emerging markets investing.

Thus the known knowns may be seen as the opportunities we know exist, and have outlined, for the emerging markets and those who invest in them – for example, demographics, growing middle classes and consumer societies, infrastructure spending, outsourcing and valuations plus whichever ones you choose to prefer from our menu of arguments in Chapter 3.

Equally, the known unknowns are all the things we know could derail those various opportunities – and then again they might not. We have aimed to cover risk fairly extensively throughout this book, primarily in Chapter 2, and then where appropriate in the geographical chapters – for example, demographic time-bombs, civil unrest, poor choices on infrastructure spending, rogue regimes, questions of corporate governance and other trust-related issues and so forth.

With the thread of increased consumer spending running through the whole of this book, one of the most crucial known unknowns for the emerging markets is the degree to which the prevailing mood of austerity, environmentalism and sustainability in parts of the developed world could impact on corporate ambitions across the emerging markets.

Still maintaining our position on the fence, we again merely note that it will be an interesting match-up between the environmental lobby and the millions of newly middle-class consumers in the emerging markets if and when they are informed they should not enjoy the standard of living and associated luxuries the developed nations have taken for granted for decades.

Mind you, that does raise the question of what might replace the West's so-called "growth model" of overconsumption and zero savings, which in turn leads us to the unknown unknowns and the added wrinkle that, once you have raised the possibility of their being unknown, unknown unknowns automatically become known unknowns, leaving their former friends still lurking there just out of reach in the darkness. Still unknown. Who knew Rumsfeld could really be so profound?

Speculating along those lines throughout this book has raised the spectre of possibilities such as water shortages in China, advances in technology derailing demand for certain commodities, the BRIC economies attracting attention and, more crucially, investment away from other emerging markets, the full intentions of certain countries in their dealings with Africa and China's slow journey towards democracy – or not.

Edward Bonham Carter, chief executive and chief investment officer of Jupiter Asset Management, has a list of his own. "What happens when interest rates start to rise?" he says. "How is the 'Axis of overspending' going to finance their projected deficits? Is China the saviour of the global economy or its Achilles' heel? Which 'shatter zone' – for example, terrorism or a pandemic – will cause the next crisis? What would $200 for a barrel of oil do to the green shoots of recovery? And is the US dollar's reserve currency status threatened?"

It is as well, perhaps, that Bonham Carter isn't setting economics exam papers as attempts to answer some of those questions could each fill their own book – and please feel free to have a go yourself. Touching on that last point, however, the position of the US in any future economic order is a fascinating point for debate.

We have already made reference once or twice in this book to the Goldman Sachs expectation that China will overtake the US as the world's biggest economy in 2027 and, by 2050, will boast GDP of $70 bn. The US would then be second on $40 bn, followed by India, Brazil, Russia, the UK and Japan.

"Goldman Sachs had originally suggested China would surpass the US in 2035," says Michael Konstantinov, head of global emerging markets equities at Allianz Global Investors' RCM. "However, they have brought forward the timeframe because they have just seen the growth momentum becoming more sustainable and faster in recent years."

But is that only one half of the equation? Surely the US itself has a say in all this – so the question becomes how much does it want to get involved? Certainly the world's – still – largest economy appears happy enough to let China and, to a lesser extent, the other BRIC economies build up quite a head of steam in The Great African Resources Race and this looks symptomatic of the US's attitude to the evolving global economic picture.

Whether this is down to nonchalance, complacency or ignorance isn't really the point anymore – the danger is of the US realizing in 10 years' time that it has missed the boat. "A fundamental concern is the US and the fact it has not yet woken up to the new reality – and then how it eventually does react to it," says one senior fund manager. "Americans can be quite ignorant in global affairs – and that's being polite.

"You saw it with the Bush administration and its attitude to the Middle East and Latin America and so on – and that's not helpful. That sort of attitude coming from the US creates a reaction – in Russia, in China and so on. So, for example, when the Americans complain about currency manipulation in China, the Chinese reply, OK, what are you going to do about it? That's when the US wakes up and realizes it needs other countries.

"President Obama may be more mature than the previous administration but he is still instinctively protectionist – US self-interest will always come first. So this is more about the US's willingness to engage with these countries. Yes, there are extremist elements around the globe but, generally speaking, the emerging market countries want to engage more – you see it with the Middle East, you see it with Latin America, you see it with China – and their populations want to be more a part of the world."

So how keen are the US and the rest of the developed economies on engaging back? And, presuming they are at all interested, what will be the nature of the relationship? In terms of give and take, the emerging markets story of the last three decades can be seen as mainly taking by the developed world, with overseas investors piling into Asia and Latin America with a view to making hay while the sun shines – and then making their excuses and heading for the door at the first sign of trouble.

This time around, the emerging markets are likely to want something a bit more permanent and a bit more two-way – and the global financial crisis may be just the catalyst to help bring this about. Certainly, perceptions must have changed, both for the investors and those they invest in.

In the latter case, the emerging markets cannot help but gain confidence from the knowledge that, this time, the blame for a major financial crisis cannot be laid at their door and, what's more, the measures they undertook after previous experiences meant their economic, financial and banking systems coped better than those of the developed world.

At the same time, most investors would have to accept that the risks associated with the emerging markets have lessened or that there is a lot more risk in the developed world today than there was before the crisis – or possibly both. Either way, the gap between the two has narrowed.

"The contrast between the developed world and the emerging markets in the wake of the financial crisis is literally a mirror image," says Slim Feriani, chief executive officer of Advance Emerging Capital. "For the developed world, the financial crisis was brought about by fundamental structural problems while in the emerging markets it was more of a cyclical setback prompted by global risk aversion.

"There are some serious structural problems in the developed world and you have to worry about what the outlook is like. You see the politicians in the US and Western Europe scratching their heads and struggling to work out how they are going to get their countries out of this mess. On the other hand, you have emerging markets that are starting out from a very comfortable position, with piles of cash, and they can just start to invest in their infrastructure, in their health care, in their education systems and so on, so they are in a much better position."

Throughout this book we have tried to be scrupulously neutral, balancing the varied attractions of emerging markets investing with an equally varied number of reasons to show due care and attention. However, as we enter the final pages of the final chapter, a short list of points that compare the emerging and developed worlds in the wake of the global financial crisis makes for stirring reading.

- Developed markets could expect limited or, in some cases, declining growth for 2009 and 2010 while the emerging markets were still growing – albeit at slower rates in the short term.
- Developed markets look set to account for a diminishing portion of world GDP, while the emerging markets should take a greater share.
- Developed markets are suffering from massive indebtedness at government, corporate and household levels while the emerging markets have low corporate borrowings, nascent mortgage and credit markets and, in some cases, the backing of sovereign wealth funds.

- Developed markets have vulnerable financial systems while those of the emerging markets are in a healthier position.
- The low real interest rates of developed markets leave little room for further monetary stimulus while the higher real interest rates of the emerging markets do leave plenty of scope for such measures.
- Developed markets have ageing populations and infrastructure whereas emerging markets enjoy more favourable demographics and more capacity to spend on infrastructure.

Heady stuff indeed, so time perhaps for one more risk warning – or at least a risk reminder. The world's emerging markets do represent an exciting investment opportunity but the associated risks mean that opportunity is not one to be taken lightly. Investors should always be aware that there are times when the value of their investment will fluctuate dramatically and so, ideally, they should try to take a long-term view of at least 10 years.

They should also look to invest in emerging markets as part of a balanced portfolio and, within that emerging markets allocation, consider a range of different regions and asset classes in order to spread risk. Collective investments can be a practical way of achieving this goal and also introduce the option to "drip-feed" money through regular savings. Finally, investors should never lose sight of the fact that emerging markets remain a higher-risk investment, so they should not invest money they cannot afford to lose.

We began this book by wondering if, for the emerging markets, it really could be different this time. Not wanting to risk the wrath of the investment gods, we will settle for suggesting the opportunity now exists for this to be so.

As discussed earlier, that opportunity has come about partly as a result of the emerging markets' own positive actions in the wake of their catalogue of economic crises suffered in the past and partly from the damage done to the Western financial system – both reputationally and arithmetically – by a crisis that was very much of the West's own making. The credibility gap has narrowed and the playing field has been levelled.

"Perhaps, thanks to the credit crisis, it is happening too early," says Bonham Carter, "but that noise you hear is a rather nasty crunching of the gears as the developed world hands over the baton to the emerging markets."

Index

Index compiled by Terry Halliday